ALSO BY JAMES SULLIVAN

Over the Moat

U N S I N K

FIVE MEN AND THE INDOMITABLE
RUN OF THE USS *PLUNKETT*

The Navy built 66 Gleaves-class destroyers between 1938 and 1942. Though launched with five 5-inch guns, *Plunkett* removed one of its 5-inchers as a weight-saving measure (the middle one in this schematic) and put a 1.1-inch gun in its place.

ABLE

JAMES SULLIVAN

SCRIBNER

NEW YORK   LONDON   TORONTO   SYDNEY   NEW DELHI

SCRIBNER

An Imprint of Simon & Schuster, Inc.
1230 Avenue of the Americas
New York, NY 10020

First Scribner hardcover edition December 2020

SCRIBNER and design are registered trademarks of The Gale Group, Inc., used under license by Simon & Schuster, Inc., the publisher of this work.

For information about special discounts for bulk purchases, please contact Simon & Schuster Special Sales at 1-866-506-1949 or business@simonandschuster.com.

The Simon & Schuster Speakers Bureau can bring authors to your live event. For more information or to book an event, contact the Simon & Schuster Speakers Bureau at 1-866-248-3049 or visit our website at www.simonspeakers.com.

INTERIOR DESIGN BY ALEXIS MINIERI

Manufactured in the United States of America

1   3   5   7   9   10   8   6   4   2

Library of Congress Cataloging-in-Publication Data has been applied for.

ISBN 978-1-9821-4763-1
ISBN 978-1-9821-4783-9 (ebook)

Photograph Credits

Frontispiece: US National Archives via Researcher At Large
p. 1: Courtesy of the Gallagher family
p. 111: Courtesy of the Simpson family
p. 211: *U.S. Navy Magazine*, courtesy of Christine Mott

Insert Photograph Credits

1. Courtesy of the Burke family
2. Courtesy of the author
3. Courtesy of the Brown family
4. Courtesy of the Brown family
5. Courtesy of the author
6. U.S. Naval Academy Lucky Bag
7. Courtesy of the Simpson family
8. Courtesy of the Simpson family
9. Courtesy of Jim Feltz
10. Courtesy of the Gallagher family
11. U.S. Navy
12. Courtesy of the author
13. Courtesy of the author
14. Courtesy of Jim Feltz
15. Courtesy of Mark Gallagher
16. Courtesy of James Gebhart
17. Courtesy of the Gallagher family
18. Courtesy of Pat Garner Morrone
19. Courtesy of Neil McManus
20. Courtesy of the author
21. U.S. Navy
22. Courtesy of the Gallagher family
23. Courtesy of Jim Feltz
24. Courtesy of Jim Feltz
25. Courtesy of the author
26. Courtesy of the author

This book is dedicated to the five men, Jim Feltz, Ken Brown, Ed Burke, Jack Simpson, and John Gallagher, and to their shipmates on the USS *Plunkett* (DD-431).

CONTENTS

LIST OF CREW MEMBERS

ABOARD *PLUNKETT*

Edward J. Burke, commander, captain of *Plunkett*, January
1943–February 1944

Kenneth B. Brown, lieutenant and gunnery officer

James D. Feltz, water tender third class (on repair party and later in
fire room at general quarters)

John J. Gallagher, water tender third class (on 20mm gun at general
quarters)

John P. Simpson, first lieutenant, led ship's damage control parties

ENLISTED MEN

Thomas A. Garner, water tender third class

Irvin J. Gebhart, machinist's mate third class

Hugh F. Geraghty, machinist's mate second class

Kenneth P. "Dutch" Heissler, chief commissary steward

James P. McManus, gunner's mate first class

John D. Oakley, gunner's mate third class

James H. Shipp, shipfitter third class

Edward A. Webber, machinist's mate second class

Vitold B. Zakrzewski, machinist's mate second class

OFFICERS

David H. Bates, lieutenant, ship's doctor, until late September 1943

Sherman R. Clark, squadron commander, 1942

James P. Clay, squadron commander, from November 1, 1943

John F. Collingwood, lieutenant and executive officer, 1943–1944

John C. Jolly, lieutenant and executive officer, 1943

Wesley E. Knaup, lieutenant (jg), succeeded Bates as ship's doctor

Lewis R. Miller, captain of *Plunkett*, September 1942–January 1943

John B. Oliver, lieutenant (jg)

Russell S. Wright, ensign

FAMILY AND FRIENDS, AT HOME AND AT WAR

Mickey Betts, Betty Kneemiller's aunt

Adele Burke, Captain Burke's wife

Joseph A. Donahue, a neighbor of Gallagher's in Dorchester who served as a gunner's mate on the USS *Niblack*

Irene Feltz, Jim Feltz's mother

Bernice Meehan Gallagher, Charlie Gallagher's wife

Charlie Gallagher, John Gallagher's brother

Frank Gallagher, Fifth Army medic, John Gallagher's brother

Martha Gallagher, John Gallagher's mother

Betty Kneemiller, Jim Feltz's girlfriend

DESTROYERS WITH *PLUNKETT* IN THE MEDITERRANEAN

USS *Rowan* (DD-405)

USS *Buck* (DD-420)

USS *Benson* (DD-421)

USS *Mayo* (DD-422)

USS *Gleaves* (DD-423)

USS *Niblack* (DD-424)

USS *Ludlow* (DD-438)

USS *Edison* (DD-439)

USS *Maddox* (DD-622)

USS *Shubrick* (DD-639)

THE DAWN

PART I

CASABLANCA. 11·26·42

By the time *Plunkett* went into Casablanca in the second wave of Operation Torch, Gallagher (lower right) and Feltz (between the dark-skinned French sailor and Irvin Gebhart) had joined the ship's engineering crew. Vitold "Ski" Zakrzewski is squatting beside Gallagher.

1: THE GODDAMNED HARBOR

JANUARY 1944

Every year on the Fourth of July through the early 1970s, my extended family gathered in the backyard of our house in Quincy, Massachusetts. They came with dented metal coolers, crockpots, and foil-covered casserole dishes, in Bermuda shorts and headscarfs, with webbed lawn chairs and Polaroid cameras, from jobs as union pipe coverers, tool-and-die mechanics, and subway car drivers (the men) and housework and child-rearing (the women). They'd bang the earwigs out of the aluminum tubes of their lawn chairs, set them in a great circle, and call for the younger kids to fetch cans of Schlitz and Narragansett. My great-uncle Frank Gallagher used to call for his whiskey with two thick fingers waved overhead, as if giving the signal to move out, and some obliging niece or nephew would pour him a neat one from the gang of bottles on our porch. Most of the great-uncles, like Frank, had gone away to World War II, which was a circumstance of personal history so ordinary in that backyard on those languorous afternoons that the details hardly qualified as something to talk about. Little was said, for example, about the shell that blew my grandmother's youngest brother, Eddie Martin, out of a foxhole after he'd waded ashore at Omaha Beach and fought his way into Normandy. (They recovered Eddie upside down in a tree, good to go for another thirty years, albeit with one leg missing.) As a boy, I'd have liked to have heard that story, or what it was like for my great-uncle Billy Lydon to burst into Bastogne on a tank during the Battle of the Bulge. Billy saw more combat than any of us, my great-uncle Leo Meehan told me after Billy died, shaking his head over what he knew. Instead in those days, rather than remember the horror and the anguish of what they'd seen and experienced, they talked about what was funny or improbable. One great-uncle's most frequently told story involved an ice cream machine he'd dropped in the Pacific when he was trying to transfer it by haul line from his supply ship to another Navy vessel. Another great-uncle liked to tell about how he'd tapped an electrical circuit in a colonel's bunker so his crew in the neighboring bunker, on a godforsaken beachhead, could also have light. And then there was the time Frank Gallagher slipped from camp and made his way into Naples, Italy, one day in January of 1944 . . .

It was before sunset, and a U.S. Navy destroyer, the USS *Plunkett*, lay at anchor in 32 fathoms (180 feet) of water. From the bridge, the officer of the deck had recorded the ship's position in the deck logs with respect to several local landmarks. Fort Dell'Ovo, a modular fifteenth-century edifice known in English as Egg Castle, rose sheer from the water's edge about a half mile distant. Clockwise through twenty-five degrees of arc that included the storied seaside neighborhood of Santa Lucia was Nuovo Castle, a more archetypal citadel with rounded, crenellated towers. And farther still to the right was the mile-long reach of the harbor's principal pier, or mole as they called them along the Mediterranean seaboard. Seven other U.S. Navy destroyers were moored nearby, embedded in a larger contingent of the Allied fleet, preparing for the greatest invasion of the war thus far.

After the Allies had come ashore at Salerno four months earlier, the march on Rome had ground to a halt at the Germans' Gustav Line near Monte Cassino, halfway between Salerno and Rome. The Germans commanded the high ground here above two valleys the Allies had not been able to punch through, and needed to, if they were to take Rome. Ever the man for military micromanagement, Winston Churchill concocted a scheme to do an end run around Cassino with an amphibious landing. In Naples, which the Allies had taken three weeks after the Salerno landings in September and whose port was funneling the American Fifth Army into the war on the Italian mainland, everyone knew an invasion was imminent—just how imminent no one could say. Every day more vessels crowded the harbor. They were on the verge of *something*.

Late that Sunday afternoon, Private Frank Gallagher stole away from his camp, without a pass, and made his way into Naples, half-filling a jerry can with Italian red wine along the way. They'd been telling everyone to stay out of Naples, the typhus was running rampant, but Frank figured "that was the shit." At the harbor's edge, he walked along the mole, scanning a panorama of ships for hull number 431.

A medic in the 36th Infantry Division of the Fifth Army, Frank had come into Italy from North Africa at Salerno, on a beach so hot German Panzer tanks had rumbled right down onto the sand in the midst of the American assault. The beachhead was tenuous for a week after the initial landing, prompting the Fifth Army's commander, General Mark Clark, to think about evacuating back out to sea. If this next invasion was to be anything like Salerno, Frank wanted to see his brother John one more time.

On shore, no one Frank asked could tell him whether *Plunkett* was among the anchored vessels. At the Navy task force's flagship—the "admiral's ship," Frank called it—he addressed one of the topside sailors, asking whether *Plunkett* was out there. It was in the area, he was told. There wasn't any way out among the ships from the mole, so Frank walked the edge of the harbor until he came into the neighborhood of Santa Lucia, which inspired a song that Neapolitan immigrants carried to America in the late nineteenth century. The lyrics of the song invite a boatman to shove off in his boat to enjoy the cool of the evening. "Come into my nimble little boat," the song goes. "Oh, how beautiful to be on the ship!" The boatman Frank encountered was offering no such palliative.

Instead, after coming down a stairway from the Santa Lucia promenade onto an ample stone terrace jutting into the water, Frank hopped into a little boat, a bumboat, tied to one of the terrace's cleats, and told the boatman to row him out. The man protested, arguing back in Italian that was Greek to Frank.

"No," Frank said, cutting him short. "Row out in the goddamned harbor."

At a glance, Frank didn't appear physically intimidating. He was of average height and build, his face square and no-nonsense. He was naturally abrupt, and skeptical, but ever alert for the possibility of a little fun. He'd been hauling off that can now and then, and he was already a little glorious with the wine this afternoon.

The Italian worked his oars, and the boat jerked from behind a crescent of breakwater stones and headed out among the moored

Navy vessels. Frank directed the boatman to steer for the telltale profiles of two-stacked destroyers, casting about for the hull number that would identify the ship as the one he wanted. "And don't you think I saw the *Plunkett*," he said.

The destroyer was as long as a football field plus most of its end zones, big but by no means titanic. It had four boilers, two propellers, thirteen ship's officers, plus seven additional squadron officers, and 265 sailors, including a twenty-seven-year-old water tender from Boston's Dorchester neighborhood whose day job on the ship was in the aft fire room, but whose battle station at general quarters was on a 20mm machine gun, one of six on *Plunkett*.

The shanghaied Italian mariner brought his boat up to *Plunkett*'s accessibly low fantail, the deck just four-and-a-half feet above the waterline, and Frank hauled himself and his can up and aboard. "I should have been shot dead," he said. "I had a can. It could have been a mine or anything."

One of *Plunkett*'s sailors was onto him straightaway. "Where'd you come from?"

"That little guinea just rowed me out here," Frank said, referencing the Italian as the Irish disparaged them back in Boston.

The sailor summoned *Plunkett*'s skipper, Eddie Burke, a thirty-six-year-old graduate of the U.S. Naval Academy, who'd grown up in a small town outside Wilkes-Barre, Pennsylvania, and who'd won acclaim as an All-American football player, and as a light heavyweight boxer. Six feet tall, and built like a linebacker still, with a broad, fleshy face and a gap between his front teeth, Burke looked like the kind of guy James Cagney would send for to do the heavy work.

As Burke laid into Frank on the fantail, a boatswain's mate in the ship's bridge piped a shrill whistle into the intercom, as he did every afternoon before sunset and before dawn, when German bombing attacks were most likely. In the wake of the whistle came the boatswain's call: "General quarters, general quarters, all hands man your battle stations." Then he activated a klaxon, and a harsh, electric whang throbbed from the ship's speakers like the pulse of a magnificent metal beast.

No one on *Plunkett* dallied. No one played sluggish. They vaulted the eighteen-inch-high thresholds of the bulkheads between compartments below deck and scrambled up and down ladders with a facility honed over six months in combat. Men heading to forward positions streamed up the wider, starboard side of the ship; men heading aft moved portside. As the crew hustled to station that afternoon, Mount Vesuvius loomed over the bay, coughing up clouds of ash. A week earlier, lava had begun channeling down one of the volcano's outflows for the first time in decades.

"They were all there, about two hundred and fifty sailors on the destroyer," Frank said. "They were all up on the bridge and down. And I'm standing, little khakis, and my five-gallon can of wine, and [the skipper's] blasting the shit out of me."

This was always the moment in Frank's story, the one that reverberates across the decades in shimmery sepia light, flickering through the imagination like a scene from one of those Movietone newsreels that played in cinemas before the coming of television, backed by trumpets and trombones and narration by journalist and broadcaster Lowell Thomas. The camera pans the armada of Navy ships, and the sailors at their battle stations, to pause on one soldier in khaki getting chewed out by the skipper. And then finally settles on another sailor, leaning over the skirt of his gun tub on the starboard side of the ship by the no. 2 stack, together with two of the men who worked on his gun, looking toward this scene playing out on the fantail. John J. Gallagher stared at this spectacle, as amused as any of his shipmates, and then all of a sudden he's way more interested than any of them. "That looks like my brother. Jesus!"

He hopped out of the gun tub and approached Burke to confirm that, in fact, this wayward infantryman was his brother. Burke looked at the vaguely familiar water tender, whom he recognized as one of his machine gunners, and he did something he never did if we're to read from how Burke handled men at captain's mast when he revoked liberties and brought down court-martials. He went easy on Frank.

"Go down and bunk with your brother [until] we find out what we're going to do with you."

I might have been seven or eight when I first heard this story, and after that first time, I heard it repeatedly. In time, each of us, the children and grandchildren of all the Gallagher brothers and sisters, was capable of painting the broad brushstrokes of Frank's story as eloquently as someone sat down before one of Ken Burns's cameras. It was always lying to on the near horizon of any Gallagher family get-together, from the Fourth of July to Christmas when we all gathered in the stately Victorian the Gallaghers had moved into in 1919 and where an oil portrait of John in his dress blues hung from the parlor wall. In this anecdote, there was serendipity and pathos, and for each of us personally an inextricable link to the most cataclysmic event of the twentieth century. Each of us knew in a general way how the story ended, though none of us knew what had transpired through two years of the war or exactly what had happened at the end.

On the verge of a family holiday to Italy in 2016, I googled *Plunkett* and found a citation for Edward J. Burke, who'd received the Navy Cross for action on January 24, 1944. Another page on the web archived a handful of old photos of the *Plunkett* and listed a man's name at the bottom for crew contact and reunion information. It hadn't occurred to me that anyone from the *Plunkett* might still be living. In my family we'd printed the legend and failed to consider the existence of facts—facts that would prove to be the substance of a story more wrenching and imbued with more drama and sorrow than any of us could have imagined. That was all to be found out. In the meantime, I phoned Ted Mueller off that website. He was ninety-two years old and had organized the last several reunions of *Plunkett* sailors. They'd "disbanded" three or four years earlier, he told me, for the "World War Two guys are getting old."

Ted sent me a roster from the last *Plunkett* reunion, in 2011, and I began to phone, somewhat frantically, cognizant of the clock. First, I checked the name of the man against the possibility of an obituary, more often than not finding one. Occasionally I'd get a voice on the other end of the line. I'd ask to speak to the name of the man on the roster, and my question would be as quickly countered by the flattened voice of a woman who wanted to know who was calling, having been down this road many times before with telemarketers. I'd tell her my name, and that I was a journalist, and that I was calling about the USS *Plunkett*. Everything changed with the invocation of that word, *Plunkett*, as I touched a chord that vibrated back decades and resonated with the signal experience of a life. There would be joy in her voice as she passed off the phone.

One *Plunkett* sailor didn't let me get past the part about my being a journalist before he blurted, "And I'm on welfare!" There would be no money coming my way from him if that was why I was calling.

I rushed the rest of my introduction. "I'm calling about the USS *Plunkett*."

Waves of silence rippled over my deployment of that word. "Oh," he said, suddenly muffled. And then the words, almost sotto voce. "Yes, I was on the *Plunkett*."

This was a thing that was holy within him, within them, and should never be associated with people who just wanted a few minutes of his time. We talked for twenty minutes, and he told me that when *Plunkett* was under attack they'd go at the enemy with the five-inch guns first, and then as the planes came closer, with the 40mm gun, and then if they got closer with 20mm guns, and then if they got closer with potatoes. "Potatoes?" I asked, and the old sailor just laughed.

I began to scrub histories of the war in Europe, looking for the destroyer, and found the ship all over the place, intersecting with the greatest events and personages of the war, like Forrest Gump. One of *Plunkett*'s crew put it to me this way: "We was everyplace, all the time." I found the ship at Casablanca, at Gela in Sicily, at Salerno and Anzio in Italy, and then on Omaha Beach, so close to shore at the landings that she about scraped her hull in the sand. The ship had been in on every invasion in Europe. What happened to the ship at Anzio, where the Germans met the Allied invasion with twenty-five thousand men and hundreds of aircraft, was so "savage," so harrowing, and so relentless the Navy wasn't sure any other destroyer in Europe had been through what *Plunkett* had.

Somewhere else online, I found reference to the ship's gunnery officer, Ken Brown, who'd been living in La Jolla as recently as 2009. I clicked into an obituary for a Ken Brown and read that this Ken Brown was the son of the Ken Brown I was looking for. His survivors included a sister named Karen Fratantaro of Costa Mesa, California, and there was only going to be one of her in Costa Mesa. A few clicks later, I had a phone number, and a few moments later, I was leaving a voice mail. The next morning, my phone rang, and I picked up on a woman who said, "Hello, Jim, I'm Karen Brown, and it so happens I'm with my father right now."

It had taken my great-uncle Frank all of three-and-a-half minutes to tell the Naples reunion story in 1998 when I sat down with him and a tape recorder after my grandfather died and it had occurred to me that once a voice was silenced, it was liable to stay that way for good. Frank didn't put any pressure on the set piece of his Naples story for any larger meaning about family or war, or why we remember things. And he never talked in any great detail about what happened afterward. His story rose to that one incredulous moment when he found himself on a Navy destroyer in the midst of the war, when "ornery" Captain Burke was "blasting the shit" out of him, and John recognized him. "That looks like my brother," Frank would always say, quoting John. It was the darnedest thing.

Hours after boarding, while he and John and other men in the engineering department played cards on a bunk in their quarters below the fantail, the ship resounded with what Frank remembered as a red alert. The crew hurried into preparations to get underway, and it was now imperative to get this wayward soldier of the Fifth Army back to shore.

They all knew where they were going. They'd been talking about the destination at dinner parties in Naples. The Italian vendors on the shore were hawking postcards of the destination. And there was talk about what Nero had done there back in the day when Rome was burning.

Anzio. They were going to Anzio.

2: BOSTON

JANUARY 1942

Off Chelsea Street in Charlestown, Ken Brown passed through the gate of the Boston Navy Yard carrying an olive-drab sea-pack suitcase and high expectations. It was January 23, 1942, mid-afternoon, and warming temperatures had slushed the snow and made a mess of the shine on his Florsheims. Inside the gate, he passed the old Commandant's House with its ample first-floor terrace and bulbous corners. Looming just beyond was the Bunker Hill Monument, a 221-foot obelisk of light gray granite, looking as much like a fixture from the future as a design out of old Egypt. Boston, this cradle of liberty, was an auspicious place to get underway.

Ken was twenty-one years old. His build was slim, the hair light and swept up off the forehead left to right. If you'd put him in knickers, he could have passed for a boy just up from adolescence, except for two contradictory details about the mouth—lips that were protuberant and somewhat soft, but a voice that seemed to issue from vocal cords lined with granite and suggested a man of twice the girth. In college, where they'd grouped his class in companies by height and where he rated placement among the shortest, they'd noted that his "stentorian bellows" could startle underclassmen who thought they might otherwise "ignore a harmless sandblower."

The yard this Friday morning was as expectant as Ken, humming with a vigor as aggressive as the lead headline on that morning's *Boston Daily Globe*—"M'Arthur Fights Horde." The subhead was just as dramatic—"British in Malaya Smash at Japs as R.A.F. Rides Skies." More than thirty-six thousand welders, shipfitters, pipefitters, machinists, electricians, shipwrights, and sundry helpers and laborers worked in the yard and its area annexes now, churning out destroyers at a pace that suggested tomorrow depended on getting it done today. In the shipyard's dry dock, the USS *Kearny* idled in a clutch of wooden scaffolding, waiting on a boiler to replace the one they'd lost when a U-boat torpedoed them off Iceland, killing eleven crew—the first American troops killed by Germans in the war.

Past the joiner's shop, Ken's route led toward piers where soldiers manned anti-aircraft nests on the roofs of waterfront buildings. The seaside facades of the shops and foundries looked smart in a fresh coat of camouflage paint.

Ken had been in Boston a week already, working a staff job until his ship came in. Waiting for *Plunkett* to return from another convoy run to Iceland, the Navy had put him to work decoding transmissions with an aluminum strip. It was mind-numbing work, substituting an "a" for an "f" if that's what the protocol wanted that day. He'd tried to shirk the duty with proposals to more effectively deploy his time, but his superior officer greeted Ken's energetic appeals with more strips. The reprieve had come in that morning. He'd reported for duty and learned that *Plunkett* had arrived late the previous evening.

At Pier 6, he found the hull number he was looking for, 431, the ship tied up to the starboard side of another destroyer that looked just like it, the USS *Knight*. Ken walked across the *Knight* and over the short gangplank onto *Plunkett* at midship, as disappointed all of a sudden as a man on a blind date who cringes at the first glimpse of his prospect. Lines for water, steam, electricity, and telephone ran all over the ship like Gulliver under the Lilliputians. Yard workers combed the decks, each preoccupied by some urgent task that was either bound to right the vessel or scuttle it, he couldn't say which. Hammers sounded all over, and the air was offensive with the smell of cutting torches as yard workers welded new equipment onto the ship. White-hatted sailors emerged from the vessel's bowels, each shouldering crates of five-inch shells and powder, which they were transferring to a lighter that had tied up at *Plunkett*'s starboard. They'd have to reload all of this ammunition again when they got underway; in the meantime, the ship had to idle in the yard free of explosives. At a nearby pier, the wooden-hulled USS *Constitution* strained at its cleats, drawn back into active service the previous year after its first commissioning in 1797, this time not for battle but to serve as a brig for naval officers awaiting court-martial.

Stepping aboard *Plunkett*, Ken saluted the officer of the deck, who stood just opposite the gangway, and then headed for the wardroom, where the carpet was still soaked with seawater from the ship's transatlantic crossing. There'd been cause for anticipation since he'd learned four days before graduation that he was bound for DD-431. Unlike older World War I–era destroyers, which creaked across the seas like antiques with their four stacks and unbroken "flush" decks, *Plunkett* was a recently minted marvel, with a raised forecastle to keep the forward guns dry in heavy seas, and modern appointments throughout, from its five-inch, .38-caliber gun battery to its commodious staterooms. It was named for a Navy man, as nearly all destroyers were, who'd chiseled himself into history during the First World War and then worked as gunnery officer on a cruiser and three different battleships. To the extent that destroyers acquire the characteristics of their namesake, as many believed, the fledgling *Charley P.* was bound to groom itself as brusque, unyielding, and unafraid to voice an unpopular opinion as Charles P. Plunkett. Ken appraised the miserable spectacle of the wardroom a moment, the magazine racks drooping with moist titles, the floors heaped with sodden boxes and other detritus. My God, he thought, did anyone ever think to clean this place?

On board, he met a classmate, Dale Reed, whose original assignment was for a ship now sunk in Pearl Harbor, and John Chapman Jolly, *Plunkett*'s gunnery officer, who'd come out of the Naval Academy—the trade school, as graduates frequently called it—in '39. Jolly was from Philadelphia, and bore a nickname, Hap, that was inevitable but ironic, too, since his countenance trended in the other direction. His brow hunkered over his eyes in a way that made him look slightly worried about something trivial, a problem of addition or subtraction that might be easily resolved, except it never was so far as Hap was concerned.

They got down to business while unaccountable poundings and whirrings sounded all around them. *Plunkett* was a top-heavy vessel, and so had jettisoned one of its original five-inch gun mounts and replaced the metal top on one of the others with a lighter canvas awning, a ragtop. Making weight for a destroyer was a constant struggle, like a welterweight trying to stay on the good side of that 140-pound threshold. Hap assigned Reed to work as an assistant gunnery officer, and Ken to work as torpedo officer, deepening the twenty-one-year-old's disappointment. First, there was this shambles of a ship, and now this second-rate job assignment. Even then, it was clear that torpedoes were a secondary priority on a destroyer, that most of the action was to emanate from the ship's four five-inch guns, its 1.1-inch gun, and its six 20mm machine guns. Ken hadn't grown up with guns, didn't hunt as a kid or distinguish himself as a marksman in any way, but on the one training cruise he'd had at the Academy—the others canceled due to mobilization—he'd warmed up to the work he'd been assigned on the battleship *Texas*, manning a three-inch gun. It was thrilling and was where he wanted to be. Reed was only sojourning here, and yet he'd pulled the plum, while Ken would manage impotent tubes between the ship's stacks. To add insult to injury, the ship's executive officer also appointed him commissary officer and gave him a clipboard for checking off fifty-pound bags of potatoes as they were emptied into the spud locker. The gunnery officer sensed his disappointment and told him they needed their torpedo officer to be permanent. They wouldn't want to train someone and then lose that person too soon.

The tidings weren't all dismal that first day. As an officer, Ken merited relatively deluxe accommodation, though he'd have to share the space with a roommate, a reserve officer named Jack Simpson. Jack stood about Ken's height and was born the same year, 1920, but he'd acquired the bearing of a more seasoned man. The early-onset baldness might have had something to do with Jack's aura of maturity. His piercing blue eyes, as if in compensation, deflected attention from the balding, and he carried himself with a posture that was erect but more the prerogative of a young man on the make than military indoctrination. Still, the smile in his welcome was wholehearted, not at all like the groomed displays of trade school boys who were as apt to fix a picture-taker with a look as grim as their guns. Jack introduced himself with a grip as crushing as a CO's. He was a Southerner, soft-spoken and well-spoken, and Ken liked him immediately.

Jack had grown up on a farm not far from Atlanta. After high school, he followed his father into the meat business, driving trucks by day and aspiring to something more with night classes. He'd enlisted in the Naval Reserves and did a pair of two-week summer cruises on a destroyer as a deckhand. As war loomed, the Navy invited young men with three years of college into a new officer's training program, and Jack went for it, throttling a motorcycle from Atlanta to Chicago for training at Northwestern University. It was a grueling program. Thirteen candidates bunked in his room, and the inevitable bad luck preyed on six of them. Seven emerged as officers. Jack then went to communications school for three months before requesting assignment on a destroyer in the Pacific. Instead, they sent him to Boston, where he was on the day Pearl Harbor was bombed, watching the first hockey game he'd ever seen played as he waited for *Plunkett* to come in from its convoy. Now he was just back from his first trip across the North Atlantic, which was anything but pacific in January. The seas had been heavy and punishing; they hadn't so much steamed home as bounced home.

In their stateroom, they bunked on thin mattresses, supported by springs and draped with a sheet and gray blanket. A wide expanse of lockers claimed all of the wall between the head of their bunks and the curve of the hull, with tiers of drawers and larger compartments above. The contents of Ken's suitcase might claim half of one drawer. The rest of the storage was for the steady stream of paperwork produced by the ship's yeomen. A desk wide enough for two men promised bureaucratic obligations, as did another tier of file cabinets. There was a stainless-steel sink in its own little alcove, with a mirrored medicine chest above. The toilet would be outside, and shared. They called the entirety of this space a stateroom, which sounded like a joke until you had a look at where the enlisted men bunked. A stateroom it was.

Ken learned a few things in the days right after he'd come aboard *Plunkett.* That his roommate exercised incessantly with wooden-handled contraptions that must have been responsible for that extraordinary grip. That they'd "pinged" a lot of fish with their sonar and no wolf packs of German U-boats on this most recent convoy across the Atlantic. That *Plunkett*'s junior officers called the ship's executive officer "Goo Goo" behind his back and loathed the man's approach. When men on liberty came back hung over, Goo Goo would direct them to the sick bay for a purgative of cascara and some other mineral, a laxative concoction they called a "black-and-white" and that sent men running for the head. Another time after they'd come into port following a particularly rough convoy, Goo Goo wouldn't release the crew to liberty until they'd been buzzed by the ship's barber. The pent-up crew's frustration had almost tipped the ship into mutiny.

Of course, Goo Goo was acting on orders from the ship's commanding officer, William Standley, a man of some stature, and not only because he was *Plunkett*'s CO. His father was an admiral who'd stepped up as chief of naval operations in the 1930s and was just then, in early 1942, in Moscow serving as U.S. ambassador. Standley was a fine ship handler. They'd learned that much about him over convoy runs that winter, but the crew didn't sense he cared all that much about their welfare. He cared about advancement and playing it by the book. One evening soon after he'd come aboard, Standley called Ken to his quarters, and together they went through the torpedo manual page by page. Ken managed to keep a lid on his smart-aleck tendencies, and asked questions that Standley thought were solid. At least, that's what one of the ship's officers told Ken later: Standley had said he thought the Academy was doing a great job, getting these kids ready.

"He screwed up on that one," Ken said.

As the ship was provisioning for its next run into the North Atlantic, Standley insisted that Ken, in his capacity as commissary officer, provide a complete accounting of all the ship's stores. "I want you to inventory every can of peas down there," he said.

In *Plunkett*'s storeroom, Ken started work on the assignment with his chief commissary man from the enlisted ranks, Pat Flanagan, who offered some early-on advice on how to handle peas.

"This is a case of peas," Pat said, "and there are twenty-four cans in a case. There's no point in taking each can out."

Ken counted the cases, factored by twenty-four, for peas and everything else that came in bulk. Then he reported to Standley.

"Did you count every can?" Standley asked his new commissary officer.

Ken told him about the math.

"Go back, as I said, and count them," Standley said.

This is stupid, Ken thought. He complied, came up with the same number of cans but learned, moreover, that junior officers could exercise only so much of their own initiative. This was a lesson he would have to relearn again and again.

Standley's subordinates didn't think much of another one of the CO's prerogatives: the correspondence course. He had all of them taking a class by mail, and if they didn't get their homework in on time, he'd restrict them to the ship. Shortly after he came aboard, Ken signed up for a lesson.

It was a correspondence course that was point A on a continuum that put Ken Brown on *Plunkett* at point Z. The summer before his senior year in high school, his father had coupled himself to the notion that his son ought to attend the U.S. Naval Academy at Annapolis. William G. Brown was a typewriter salesman with accounts all over Chicago, and if he thought you needed a typewriter, by golly, you were going to own a typewriter because he was going to stay on you till you purchased one. He cultivated business from the stockyards to Wilson Sporting Goods to Army and Navy offices, and Ken suspected it was there, among the uniformed men who bought his Royal typewriters, that the idea had hatched. The elder Brown enrolled his son in a correspondence course to prepare for an entrance exam, and then began working political connections in Chicago to lobby for an appointment. "I don't know what really started him on it, or what got him into this feverish state. But I knew my dad's ambition, he was a nut for it, and I was going along for the ride."

Through the late winter and early spring of 1938, they waited on word from Annapolis, a decision that would have profound consequences for Ken's life and seemed at the same time to be the end of all his father's striving, indeed the very purpose to which his father had been put on Earth. When the word came, Ken had been out to the horse races in Elgin, Illinois, in defiance of his father's prohibition against the racetrack. A cop stopped him as he motored back to Glen Ellyn, and told him to get home, his father was looking for him. Then, when he stopped at Wally Catlin's service station for gas, Wally told him to get home, his father was looking for him. And then, when he got home, his mother and father were standing in the driveway, back by the great stone chimney. He'd never forget the image of the pair of them standing there, his mother in a simple housedress, her deep-set eyes, his father as irrepressible as ever: The man had actually broadcast an alarm across Glen Ellyn that day for Ken to come home. He could not be put down. They were clearly not upset about Elgin—he read that in a glance as he braked the '36 Ford convertible coupe his father had got for him—but they were there as if chased from the inside of the house by something, and there was nothing for them to do but stand there, side by side, a nineteenth-century couple on the verge of sixty. His dad was holding something, pinched between a thumb and curled forefingers. It was then that he knew. This was the letter, this was why the urgency, this was why the call into the police station, the calls all around town. The need to know. His dad wouldn't be kept waiting, not on this. It was unopened when they handed it to him, and a fleeting thought ran through his mind: Should he upend expectation, thank them for the letter, and walk into the house? But no, this was his dad, and she was his mom, and sometimes it seemed their entire lives had boiled down to the contents of this envelope. It was a warm spring day. Daladier had just become prime minister of France and appointed a man who favored appeasement. Britain had just signed an agreement that recognized Italy's control of Ethiopia. And Gary Cooper was in a new one down at the Glen's cinema, *The Adventures of Marco Polo*. What an ordeal this had been, and now it would be over, one way or the other. He opened the letter from Annapolis, and read the text, careful to let nothing show in his face. He was still a kid. He could still shrug up his shoulders for a picture. He could still twist a joke out of thin air if need be. You grew up gradually, not suddenly. But a chapter was coming to a close as he stood there on a cinder driveway in Glen Ellyn on a warm spring day in April of 1938. He looked up at his mom and then his dad. "Well, I got a two-point-five on both of my substantiating exams and I am in," he told them.

Ken set up at the U.S. Naval Academy in Annapolis as a man on the lookout for a good meal and a midshipman who knew how to joke. He had a "capacity for being happy" and people liked him for it. He played some baseball, and wrestled, too, not varsity but at the intramural level. He worked on the school's magazine, *Trident*, for two years and was on the Stunt Committee that fall. He'd had a terrifically fun run at the Academy, harvesting as much as could be had in the regiment, though he couldn't quite understand, when he took the time to think about it, why he flirted so frequently with disaster, with the drinking especially.

Ken was in the middle of a burger in downtown Annapolis when he got word that Pearl Harbor had been bombed. The news exerted a magnetic compulsion on midshipmen all over town, each of them returning to the grounds of the Academy to sort the ramifications and confront still more changes to the run of their year. At the Academy, over the building's loudspeakers, the executive officer of Bancroft Hall, where the midshipmen lived, briefed the nascent naval officers on the attack. The consequences set in at once. For starters, the dance that was to be held that evening in Bancroft, with a slew of dates or "drags" coming in from Baltimore, was canceled. The Academy assumed a more vigilant atmosphere. Midshipmen would stand watch with pistols all over the campus, and the enlisted men at the gates would grill everyone seeking access to the grounds. Graduation, which had already been moved up from June of 1942 to February, crept closer, the ceremony now scheduled for December 19.

Of the 547 midshipmen who filed into Dahlgren Hall for graduation that day, nearly 500 of them would be commissioned as ensigns in the Navy and 24 would step up as second lieutenants in the Marine Corps. Twenty-five of the new officers would stay on at the Academy for four months to train men coming into the Navy Reserves. Others were headed to engineering school, and into naval aviation programs, and many more were headed for ships. Several had been scheduled for duty on the USS *Arizona*, now sunk in Pearl Harbor, and had to be reassigned.

As Ken took his seat in the vastness of Dahlgren Hall, resplendent in his dress blues and embraced on all sides by a crowd that included his father and brother, he understood now that much of the action in the war would flare first in the Pacific, not the Atlantic. When he'd identified his preference for a ship and a sea six months earlier, he'd put in for a destroyer in the Atlantic because wolf packs were decimating merchant shipping in a period of pickings so easy that German U-boat commanders referred to their success as the "Happy Time." He'd wanted on a destroyer because he figured assignment on a tin can might be less fraught with pomp, circumstance, and regulation. The latter might be true, but the former, it now seemed, most definitely was not.

Secretary of the Navy Frank Knox stood before the ranks of serried midshipmen, fresh from a trip to assess the damage at Pearl Harbor. Eight days earlier, Adolf Hitler had referenced the secretary by name in Germany's declaration of war against the

United States, noting that Knox himself had confirmed that three American destroyers, the *Greer*, the *Kearny*, and the *Reuben James*, had attacked German submarines. Knox was in his mid-sixties, a onetime Rough Rider with Teddy Roosevelt, a former newspaperman, and a Republican candidate for the vice presidency in 1936. As he'd confirmed a few matters of fact for Hitler, he now confirmed for Ken that he was nevertheless at the red-hot center of the world's attention. "Millions of young men would like to be in your place. . . . You enter on this greatest war the world has ever seen—trained," Knox said.

He talked about Japanese treachery at Pearl Harbor, how we ought to have been on guard against it, and how there was at least one great lesson to be learned from the assault—"that one of the greatest and most effective factors in war is the element of surprise." Knox was heartened by the allies at America's side, from the British Commonwealth to Russia, by the might of America's technology and industry, and by the "gallant courage and a complete disregard of personal danger" exhibited by the men at Pearl Harbor.

The midshipmen trooped up to the stage, one by one by company, to receive their commissions from Knox. When midshipman Issac Kidd stepped up to the stage, the entire regiment stiffened. Ken watched as an aide whispered something to Secretary Knox. The photographers leapt for a better vantage and their bulbs flashed as Ken joined the regiment in a thunderous cheer for Kidd, whose father, Admiral Kidd, had been killed on the *Arizona* at Pearl Harbor. When it was over, Ken drove back to Glen Ellyn with his father and brother, his commission in hand and orders for Boston after the holidays for duty aboard the USS *Plunkett*.

Shortly after the news about Pearl Harbor broke across Boston, John Gallagher and his friends huddled at Costello & Kelly's, a barroom in Field's Corner that admitted mixed company and was, for Gallagher, a complement to Callahan's, a men's only tavern closer to home on Adams Street. He met Franny Driscoll, George Hurley, Welchie, Hack, and a few others from the "corner," as they referred to the stomping ground that bound them. At Costello's, they could eat rotisserie chicken and barbecue, and drink the likes of Pickwick Ale and Schaefer Beer, which, according to the advertising jingle, was the one to have when you were having more than one. By the time that afternoon was over, at least three of them had decided to enlist in the Navy. At midnight, they trooped into the Federal Building at Post Office Square downtown, which opened early to accommodate the deluge of young men who wanted a "crack at the Japs," as the papers put it. John, Franny, and George told the Navy they could be ready to go by six-thirty that morning, but the Navy said they could take a few days at home.

That Monday morning, shortly after six-thirty, a photographer showed up on the same floor of the Federal Building and snapped the most famous recruitment picture to make the rounds after Pearl Harbor. In it, a dozen would-be sailors form a line before a man in a suit holding a sheaf of papers in his left hand. A U.S Navy sign hangs from a bracket mounted to a doorframe. Four of the recruits look like boys. Several wear leather jackets, with hair clearly held in place by something like Brylcreem. One man clutches his fedora, and three still wear them. They're listening intently to instructions, sensitive to the need for gravitas on this day, while a photographer readies an image. You have to wonder how the whole thing played out for these men in particular—the kid with the inflated chest, another who might have been Armenian, and one who bears more than a passing resemblance to the actor John Cusack. The caption doesn't identify them, and the picture, like so many of these poignant images from our past, seems more an imagination of history than an actual assemblage of men who went on to serve in the war, some of whom may not have survived, some of whom probably did and went on to have families that may or may not know that their father or uncle is part of how we today visualize the fervor that gripped the nation the day after Pearl Harbor.

Until Pearl Harbor, John had been working as a presser in the Baker Chocolate Factory in Lower Mills, earning $20 per week, which was somewhat better than his brother Charlie's work as a clerk at wholesale clothier R. H. White's, than Tom's work as a clerk on a steamship line, and only slightly better than his sister Gert's work as a telephone operator. Martha Gallagher still had all her kids at home, from Helen at thirty-one years of age and Tom at twenty-nine, all the way down to Joe at twenty. It was as if losing her husband, Tom, to tuberculosis in 1924 had endowed her with even greater gravity, her children reluctant to break from that orbit. Indeed, neither of her two oldest children would ever leave the house on Oakton Avenue, and it was assumed their reluctance to leave was a matter of fidelity to a woman who'd "taken a shock," as it was always said of her stroke, and who needed them at home.

Three days after his first trip to the Federal Building, John was back at the recruiting station, enlisting, filling out an application in which he revealed he'd quit school after finishing the eighth grade; that he did not drink intoxicating liquors (a lie); and that he'd been arrested once for fighting and served two years' probation. He answered no to myriad general health questions they wanted answered, among others whether he'd urinated in bed in the last five years, whether he'd ever worn arch supporters, and whether there was any insanity in his family. He hadn't, and there wasn't. He signed his own name John James Gallagher, all three words, and then signed his mother's name, though he didn't have to—he was twenty-four years old—and crossed it out.

In the physical exam that followed, the Navy learned he was 5' 7" and 145 pounds. He had dark brown hair, a ruddy complexion, blue eyes, 20/20 vision, and a scar on the left side of his forehead from when his brother Charlie encouraged him to coast down the kitchen stairway on a tin baking sheet when he was five years old.

Six days after that exam, the Navy signed off on his two-year enlistment in the Reserves as an apprentice seaman at $21 per month. He swore an oath before a retired lieutenant commander, and they sent him to a training station in Newport, Rhode Island, sixty-five miles south of his home on Oakton Avenue. In Newport, they gave him a short haircut and issued him a uniform, dungarees, sea bags, and a thin mattress. "All of a sudden, we all looked alike—with crew cuts and dressed in ill-fitting uniforms," wrote a neighbor from Dorchester, Joseph A. Donahue, who was at Newport with John. They told the recruits they'd have no need of personal clothes and sent those clothes home.

They drilled outside, *hup, two, three, four,* and fumbled with rifles in cloth gloves. They learned how to pack clothes in a white sea bag, and how to bundle up mattress and hammock. It was winter, but this was the Navy, and they had to pass a swimming test that sent them two lengths of a large indoor pool.

There were more physical exams in Newport, where they found that John was missing eight teeth, all molars and "non-vital." They inoculated him against cowpox, typhoid, yellow fever, and tetanus, and found that he had a deviated septum. The Navy awarded him a $118.95 uniform gratuity, and on January 7, after three weeks in Newport, he got his orders for *Plunkett*. Nearly all the seamen from Newport were dispatched into the Atlantic Fleet.

First, though, he got to go home to the modest Victorian house they'd moved into shortly before his father contracted tuberculosis. It had been twenty years since Tom Gallagher had returned home from a yearlong sojourn in Saranac, where he'd hoped the open-air "cure porches" of the famed treatment center might invigorate his lungs and undo the disease. They did not. Tom struggled another year against the disease, and then it took him at the age of forty-two when he was in the prime of his family life and his professional life as a broker for Charles Storrow & Company. Such was the esteem they felt for Tom at the cotton and wool brokerage on State Street, that Storrow continued to funnel money to Martha Gallagher so she could keep that home. That, and the odd property tax abatement from Mayor James Michael Curley, allowed the Gallaghers to live in a home burnished with ornate interior woodwork, chandeliers, and oriental carpets.

Home from training, John stood for a photograph in the dining room, puffed up before the oak mantelpiece in his dress blue uniform with one stripe around the cuffs. In the picture his hair is buzzed short in a boot haircut, shorter than it is in any other photograph taken during the war. His right arm is propped on the mantel, and he's looking at the photographer with his chin slightly uplifted and with a grin that might have mirrored the photographer's, each of them somewhat abashed by the artifice of this uniform. Who's he to be wearing *that*! There are thin, unlit birch logs stacked in the fireplace, and a picture hangs on the wall, of a teenage John in a tie and a sweater, standing astride his beloved German shepherd Rex. The prominence of the photo suggests that it went up after he went to Newport, for this was mostly how the Gallaghers would see him over the next two years.

The morning after Ken Brown reported for duty, forty-three apprentice seamen bussed into the Navy Yard from the receiving station in downtown Boston. It was a warm afternoon for January, with temperatures cresting fifty degrees. A headline on that day's edition of the *Boston Daily Globe* blared "Japs Close on Australia," while the type just below reported the "US Holds in Philippines." Ernie Pyle had filed a column from Tacoma, Washington, that ran in that morning's edition. Ernie hadn't put on his steel helmet yet. The soon-to-be-legendary war correspondent was reporting from the home front, complaining about how much it now cost to eat bacon and eggs for breakfast. What had been 35 cents was now $1.40. "If they don't get me in the February draft, I think I shall go into the bacon and egg business for the duration," he complained.

At noon on the ship's bridge, Jack Simpson relieved Ensign Jack Collingwood from Washington State as officer of the deck and met the recruits with a yeoman and his clipboard. On they came, the ship moored as before that afternoon, a roll call of names scooped from a cross section of America's ethnic porridge—Jews, Irish, Italians, Germans, Poles, and English, the yeoman scribbling them all down before he'd type them up for the ship's deck logs later. There was Bill Alverson from Little Rock and Tom Garner from Camden, New Jersey, and Irvin Gebhart from Hockessin, Delaware, though his first name was mistyped as Twing. Not that it mattered; everyone would come to know Irvin as Dutch. There was Vitold Zakrzewski from South Boston, whose name had also been misspelled. No one ever worked at trying to get Zakrzewski spelled right or pronounced properly; they just called him Ski. On they came, forty-three men in all, including Gallagher. It was January 24, 1942, as they came aboard, two years to the day and almost to the minute before the klaxon would yank them to battle stations for the sixth time that day off the Italian coast at Anzio—Dutchie to the after engine room, Ski to the ship's forward engine room, and Alverson, Garner, and Gallagher to gun tubs on the starboard side of the ship.

All of these names and eighty others were signed on the back of a ship's picture that hung in the house on Oakton Avenue for decades after the war was over. They were listed, too, in that roster Ted Mueller sent me, though most of the men, he'd told me, had passed on. Still, there was one man Ted knew, who'd been on the ship at Anzio. That man lived in Missouri. He'd lost his wife recently, but he was still sharp. His name was Jim Feltz. "He might talk to you," Ted told me.

I phoned Jim Feltz on his cell phone the next day, a Saturday, and caught him at a "home show," which was just great, this ninety-one-year-old man out shopping for material, as if being in his tenth decade was no deterrent to yet another renovation of his kitchen. His voice was old man rickety, yet steady, and he habitually concluded his sentences with a sound like "mmm" that seemed to provide a more decisive end to what he'd just said than mere stoppage of talk. After talking several minutes about my interest in his ship, I told him I'd had a relative on the *Plunkett*. Though it had been years since I'd worked as a journalist, I told him I was looking into this story about the *Plunkett* from a professional point of view. He was happy to hear that somebody was interested in the *Plunkett*, and he did want to talk to me, but could I call him back tomorrow on his home phone? I told him I would, and then thought to give him one more piece of information.

"Just so you know, my great-uncle's name, it was John Gallagher," I said.

There was silence on the other end of the phone, and I was hoping against hope he'd remember John as one of the 265 enlisted men on the ship. I sensed he was casting about in his memory, or perhaps summoning an explanation so as not to disappoint. The silence went on and on, and I thought for a moment the call had dropped, but it hadn't dropped, and Jim Feltz came back to me then with a smile in his voice as big as the moon. "Johnny Gallagher was a very good buddy of mine," he said.

3: UNDERWAY

MARCH 1940

Eleanora Plunkett expected more from that first swing, however tentative, but the bottle of champagne in her hand wouldn't give. She
glanced at the assembled dignitaries and swung the bottle once more
against the steel hull of a new Gleaves-class destroyer that was being
named for her late husband. She wore a fur stole against the March
chill, a feathered hat, and a tight-fitting jacket that showed off a figure
that might still be described as hourglass, no matter her seventy-five
years. But the bottle still wouldn't break, and now there was a question
about whether she had it in her. What would her husband make of
this? Charles P. Plunkett, had he not succumbed to heart disease nine
years earlier, would have been seventy-six years old this day. He'd
been appointed to the Naval Academy as a fifteen-year-old, and
later commanded destroyers, an armored cruiser, and a battleship.
In the summer of 1918, with war grinding away in the trenches,
Plunkett realized his finest hour when he commanded a battery of
five fourteen-inch naval guns on railroad carriages at Saint-Nazaire
in France. With those naval guns raining fourteen-hundred-pound

projectiles down on the German trenches, there was nothing for the Kaiser to do but surrender or sign an armistice, according to General John J. Pershing, who was the commander of American troops in Europe during World War I. It would be a stretch to argue that Charles Plunkett ended the Great War, but he'd played a critical hand, and for this he was getting a destroyer. They'd gathered this March 9, 1940, on the edge of the Hackensack River in New Jersey, at the Federal Shipbuilding and Dry Dock Company in Kearny. Two destroyers were to be launched, *Plunkett* (DD-431) and the coincidentally named *Kearny* (DD-432). Eleanora relished the honor. She was Plunkett's third wife—he'd been previously married to a pair of sisters, one after the other's death—and he was her second husband, but such was the esteem she felt for Charles that she would decide two years later to be buried with him at Arlington.

A heady breeze blew the pennants off *Plunkett*'s bridge, and people stood on the bow of the ship, forty feet above, leaning over for a look at the hapless widow's third attempt, which was successful. The bottle burst, the crowd cheered, and *Plunkett* slid down the ways into the river. The government had spent $5 million building this ship, which was about five thousand times as much as the typical American family earned in a year. By contrast, an Arleigh Burke–class destroyer built in the twenty-first century cost fifty thousand times as much as the typical twenty-first-century American family earned in a year. *Plunkett* carried 431 as its hull number, which meant this was the 431st destroyer commissioned by the Navy since they'd started building this type of ship at the turn of the century. It was 348 feet from bow to stern, and 36 feet wide at the beam. Without its crew and provisions, *Plunkett*'s hull displaced 1,650 tons of seawater, and measured a draft of 11 feet from the waterline to the bottom of the keel, leaving as little as possible to the ambitions of a torpedo. Propelled by six steam turbine engines that turned two propellers, or screws, the ship was capable of thirty-seven knots at maximum speed, what the Navy called flank speed. In a speed trial the previous year, another destroyer of the same class had throttled off flank speed and was brought to a complete standstill in fifty-eight seconds. *Popular Science* magazine gushed about the possibilities of this new class of destroyers, calling them "the light cavalry of the sea," and would feature a cartoon rendition of *Plunkett* on its March 1941 cover, the colorfully tricked out ship plowing a V through the sea at the vanguard of a destroyer squadron.

Over the next four months, *Plunkett*'s maiden crew ran the ship through a series of sea trials, testing its speed and maneuverability to ensure the ship performed the way it was supposed to. In the middle of July, *Plunkett* steamed out of the Kearny yard for the last time and moved to a berth in the Brooklyn Navy Yard. The following morning, 170 members of the crew, who would become known as plank owners since they were with the ship when it was put into active service, and five officers stood in formation on the ship's fantail for the commissioning. The ship's first commander, a Butte, Montana, native named Peter G. Hale, had come up from Annapolis and read orders from the Navy Department, directing him to take command. And then, at last, the commandant of the yard congratulated the crew, "urged them to maintain the traditions of the Navy," and put *Plunkett* in service.

The destroyer is the quintessential ship of the American imagination. In the lore of the U.S. Navy, and as a manifestation of America's appreciation for the scrappy Revolutionary underdog, no ship embodies the founding ethos of the country the way the destroyer does. There are more imposing ships, more effectively lethal ships, and ships that require greater courage to get underway, but none are quite as romantic or compelling. The destroyer is the minuteman behind the stone wall, the grunt on point in the jungle, that one otherwise unassuming kid who's going to upset expectation and charge into harm's way because someone has to do it. John Paul Jones, father of the U.S. Navy, anticipated the destroyer in the 1770s when it was said he boomed a phrase that echoes still today: Give me a fast ship for I intend to go in harm's way. Jones's phrase wasn't quite that pithy, nor a thing uttered, but a desire he spelled out in a letter while shopping for a frigate in France where he "wished to have no connections with any ships that do not sail fast, as I intend to go in harm's way." The Second World War's most colorful naval hero, Fleet Admiral William "Bull" Halsey, considered himself a "destroyer-man" at heart. No other ship endeared itself to its crew in quite the same way. Nobody fancied himself a cruiser-man or battleship-man. At the end of the war with Japan, when Halsey sent his ships into Tokyo Bay to accept the surrender, he put three destroyers at the head of his column, a gesture not unlike the one General U. S. Grant afforded Joshua Lawrence Chamberlain, the hero of Little Round Top, in the stillness at Appomattox.

World War II destroyers didn't do one thing, they seemed to do everything. They went after battleships with torpedoes, at submarines with depth charges, at aircraft and coastal targets with an array of guns that fired projectiles as small as 20mm and as heavy as 52 pounds. "They came on tall and thin, like the cutting edge of a knife seen from ahead," wrote Wirt Williams, a destroyer officer

during the war. They rushed "into battle like terriers attacking Great
Danes," according to Theodore Roscoe, who in the early 1950s compiled an exhilarating survey of destroyer operations during World
War II. The spirited herd dog is frequently invoked when talking
about destroyers, especially when picturing the ship on convoy duty,
"running breathlessly and tongue-lolling around her flock, shoo-
ing stragglers into line." They were sometimes called "small boys"
for their relatively diminutive size (a battleship's displacement was
fifteen to twenty times greater than a destroyer's), but mostly they
were called cans, tin cans, for the three-eighths-of-an-inch thickness
of their steel hull. They were built light to go fast. The hull of a
battleship was more than a foot thick and designed to weather a
toe-to-toe slugfest in surface combat. Destroyers didn't brawl that
way. They screened bigger ships like the Secret Service, constantly
on the lookout for hidden hazards, poised to spring. They patrolled
the edges of convoys as the first line of defense against enemy submarines. And though they'd first come into the fleet at the turn
of the century as a delivery platform for torpedoes, the advent of
aerial warfare during the First World War reoriented their mission.
Plunkett wouldn't fire a single torpedo during World War II but was
relentlessly under enemy assault from the air.

On the day Japan officially surrendered, September 2, 1945, there
were thirteen times as many destroyers in service as aircraft carriers,
sixteen destroyers for every battleship, and three destroyers for every
two submarines. Five hundred fourteen destroyers steamed into the
Second World War, and seventy-one were lost. No family of ship
suffered as many casualties. They gave as good as they got. Better.
They sunk more than one hundred Axis subs and as many surface
ships; they brought down an untallied number of planes, and who

knows how many auxiliary craft, trucks, troops, and transports on shore. The enemy dreaded them, enemy submariners especially, for it was the destroyer and its somewhat slighter sibling, the destroyer escort, that hunted submarines. The last thing a submariner wanted to see in the viewfinder of his periscope was a destroyer, plowing a great wide white V straight at him. The name of the ship made no bones concerning what it was about. A destroyer was built to wreck things.

Historians trace the genesis of the destroyer to action on the Roanoke River in 1864, and to a desire by Union and Confederate navies to punch their opponents below the waterline. In the fall of that year, a twenty-one-year-old lieutenant with the Union Navy guided a shallow-draft, steam-powered picket boat upriver with a torpedo rigged to a long spar or boom protruding from the bow. Under the cover of dark and rain, the lieutenant, six fellow officers, and a crew of eight lowered the boom and drove their torpedo into the *Albemarle*, wrecking the new Confederate ironclad. Around the same time, the Confederates dispatched another new kind of craft, this one hand-cranked and submersible but rigged with the same menace, a thirty-foot spar tipped with explosives. This one rammed a Union frigate, sinking her, as well as itself. From this primary purpose, each evolved, like Neanderthals and Homo sapiens, each to its own look and feel, the destroyer and the submarine.

What the Navy learned in the wreck of the *Albemarle* was that David could be very effective against Goliath. For twenty-five years after the Civil War, the so-called torpedo boat came to the fore bigger and faster but with that same awkward proboscis for ramming enemy craft. The Austrians and the British developed self-guiding, mobile torpedoes that could be launched from tubes in the 1870s, but it wasn't until 1890 that congressional allocations allowed the Navy to field ships equipped with the same technology. The United States would commission thirty-five of these destroyers between 1890 and 1898, mostly for coastal defense. As a hedge against the torpedo boat, navies around the world started fielding torpedo boat *destroyers* in the 1890s. These boats carried torpedoes, as well as a battery of guns that might take out a torpedo boat from a distance. As defenders of the fleet, these destroyers, as they were soon to become known, were built bigger and faster and capable of passage on high seas. Congress called for sixteen destroyers in this first class of 1898. The following year, with the keel laid for the first of its kind, the destroyer type was officially born with Torpedo-Boat Destroyer No. 1, the USS *Bainbridge*.

These turn-of-the-century destroyers displaced 420 tons. Their top speed was 29 knots, and they could travel 2,700 nautical miles at 8 knots. They burned coal, not oil, which meant they couldn't refuel at sea. They could be built for less than a million dollars each, and mostly they hugged the coast as a defensive shield. But their function was evolving, from ships that defended the coast to ships that defended the fleet. A 1910 Navy memorandum made it official: "Destroyers exist to protect the armored fleet from attack."

With this redevelopment of purpose came the need for a change in design. At first, the Navy wanted a single destroyer for every battleship. Now the Navy was looking for four destroyers for every battleship. These ships had to be able to travel four thousand nautical miles, which prompted the switch from coal to oil. They built up the bow to keep the ship dryer and put some flare in the bow to increase the deck space and berthing below. Until the First World War, the Navy launched these ships in modest numbers, a handful here of this class, a handful there of another. The War College said in 1912 that the torpedo was "the only useful destroyer weapon." World War I would change that.

In 1914, a German U-boat sunk a British naval ship with a so-called automotive torpedo, the first time that ever happened. Surface ships combatted this submarine threat with hydrophones that could listen for underwater movement, and depth charges, which were rolled off racks at the stern of a ship and would in time be "thrown" by Y guns or K guns in proximity of a sub. That same year, pilots started dropping bombs over the sides of their cockpits, and the era of the bomber was born. Strategic bombing evolved quickly during the war, and in response, the Navy started installing anti-aircraft gunnery to counter threats from above. In just a few short years, the destroyer's mission evolved from a combatant in a single dimension to one that was fighting antagonists on the sea, below the sea, and above the sea. The destroyer tripled in size, and Congress authorized the construction of more than two hundred ships known as "four-pipers" for their four smokestacks and "flush deckers" for their unbroken decks running from stem to stern.

Until 1920, the Navy spelled out a ship's type designation all the way—Destroyer Tender No. 1, for example—but then they shortened the designation with a classification symbol, DD, the first D for destroyer and the second D a repeat of the first because the ship didn't have a subclassification. Prior to this abbreviation, the Navy had begun in 1909 to identify all commissioned ships as USS for United States Ship. A ship didn't earn that badge until its commissioning and lost that designation as soon as it went out of commission.

The United States went on a shipbuilding spree during the First World War, putting 242 ships in harm's way by the cessation of hostilities. With the Armistice, and hopes that the war to end all wars had just been fought, the Navy discharged 83 percent of its personnel, and put much of its destroyer fleet in mothballs. A treaty between the major world powers in 1922 put limits on the size and composition of their navies. Another treaty in 1930 capped the size of a destroyer at 1,850 tons. Throughout the 1930s, the archetypal U.S. destroyer took shape. The Navy designed one class with eight torpedo tubes, some with as many as sixteen. They mounted four or five five-inch guns on the centerline. In 1938 at Bath Iron Works in Bath, Maine, they built four destroyers of a new class, the Gleaves class, which was named for the first ship of the class to be launched. A curious thing happened along the way to Bath. The destroyer had become, quite simply and perhaps accidentally, a beautiful vessel— long, lithe, and exquisitely proportioned, as if nautical architecture had realized its apogee in this type of ship. After Bath built the first four, the next two ships of the Gleaves class were *Plunkett* and *Kearny*.

Now, about the men. In June of 1940, President Roosevelt characterized America's young men as "mollycoddled," despite the Depression and what that may have forged in the mettle of the country's youth. Around the same time, an Army general told a reporter that he became depressed when he thought of the men stepping up to fight. "I'm afraid the Americans of this generation are not the same kind of Americans who fought the last war." Such reservations were nothing new. Since the time of the *Iliad*, when Nestor berated Achilles and Agamemnon as less worthy fighters than those of the previous generation, the grass was always greener back in the day. While some American leaders didn't think they had the kind of men necessary to fight the war, many Americans across the country didn't want any part of any war any way. The America First Committee agitated against involvement all the way to Pearl Harbor, no matter the Japanese depredations in the Pacific, no matter the myriad invasions by Nazi Germany. Roosevelt's antagonists considered him a warmonger and sought to thwart executive steps toward the country's entry in another European war.

England, meanwhile, was sinking. They'd salvaged their army from Dunkirk in June of 1940. The Battle of Britain erupted the following month. And then in September came the Blitz, a series of nighttime bombing raids that, many believed, was the prelude to an invasion. The Germans had wrecked half of Britain's destroyer fleet at Dunkirk, and damaged eleven more destroyers in July. The Brits had asked Roosevelt for fifty U.S. destroyers in May, and Roosevelt was rummaging about for a legal way to satisfy the request. The vigilant isolationists would be up in arms by any extension of arms to Britain, necessitating a game plan for Roosevelt that would preclude the inevitable protest. Meanwhile, Germany was preparing for an assault on England by mustering tens of thousands of troops on the coast of Northern France. Their convoys moved with impunity through the English Channel. Authorizing the transfer of those fifty destroyers, Churchill wrote to the president, was "a thing to do now." Roosevelt found rationale for the transfer in an executive order that would swap the destroyers for British bases in Newfoundland and the Caribbean—bases that, ostensibly, would serve as a greater resource to America's defense than fifty old four-pipers. And so, on September 9, 1940, Roosevelt did that thing, and the destroyers headed for Britain.

A week later Congress voted to enact the first peacetime conscription in American history. The snowball was underway. In November, Roosevelt was elected to an unprecedented third term as president, and Britain was at the end of its financial rope. "Even if we divested ourselves of all our gold and foreign assets, we could not pay for half we had ordered, and the extension of the war made it necessary for us to have ten times as much," Churchill wrote, describing Britain's predicament that fall. In the same way that a neighbor would lend his garden hose to help put out a fire at the property next door, Roosevelt proposed helping Britain by lending and leasing materiel that would, at the same time, help the Brits win the war and forestall the need for America to send troops. Debate on the matter raged for weeks. Senator Robert Taft said Lend-Lease would lead to "a kind of undeclared war all over the world." Charles Lindbergh said it was "another step closer to war." But Roosevelt's Republican opponent in the recent election, Wendell Wilkie, argued for Lend-Lease. Churchill declared that with Lend-Lease, Britain would not "need the gallant armies which are forming throughout the American Union." And Congress was won. The bill passed with overwhelming margins in both the House and the Senate, and Roosevelt signed the measure into law on March 11, 1941.

In *The Winds of War*, Herman Wouk's magisterial fictional treatment of World War II, published in 1971, a naval officer frustrated by one dry-land bureaucratic assignment after another is finally released by Roosevelt for sea duty on the first Lend-Lease convoy to England in March of 1941. Though Lend-Lease was now law, and the United States might legally supply Britain with war materiel, the isolationists still objected to participation by the Navy in any convoy. "Convoys mean war—a shooting, bloody war," cried America First in one of its pamphlets. This first Lend-Lease convoy wasn't officially a so-called convoy. Wouk's admiral tells the frustrated naval officer Pug Henry that he and his squadron of destroyers are to form up "screens on cooperative merchant vessels which you may encounter." It just so happens that Henry and his destroyers encounter such a screen of merchant vessels off Newfoundland. Pug Henry is keen to be back on the water. "Even in the North Atlantic in March, even in a destroyer, even on such risky and peculiar business, going back to sea was a tonic. Pug paced the bridge of the U.S.S. *Plunkett* all day, a happy man, and slept in the sea cabin by the chart house."

Pug Henry spent most of his time on this fictionalized *Plunkett* monitoring the performance of fifteen destroyers screening seventy-one merchant ships as they zigzagged toward a rendezvous with the Brits, who came out to meet them in the four-pipers the Americans had sent the previous year. He didn't like how "ragged" the columns were. There were "minor collisions and near-misses in the zig-zags." He became enraged by the slapdash way in which the screen conducted its combat drills. He didn't trust *Plunkett*'s navigator. And when he got back to Norfolk, he noted the poor performance of the destroyers to Admiral Ernest King, the real-life chief of naval operations during the war.

What Jim McManus remembered most from that actual convoy to Iceland, *Plunkett*'s first foray into the sizzling North Atlantic, in the spring of 1941, was the china and the toilet paper. McManus was a twenty-one-year-old apprentice seaman from Fall River, a mill town fifty miles south of Boston on the upper reaches of Narragansett Bay. He'd had designs on the Navy since graduating from

Durfee High School in 1936. His father had driven him to the Navy recruiting station in Boston the day after graduation, but the Navy had rejected him for high blood pressure and an irregular pulse. He'd tried to enlist again in 1937, and then again in 1938, but his blood was a little too aggressive for the Navy and they shut him down each time. In 1940, though, McManus succeeded. His sign-painter boss didn't want to lose him and boosted his salary to $15 per week. When that didn't work, he discouraged Mac with a reference to his disposition, assuring him he wouldn't make it in the Navy with his temper.

In November of 1940, Mac went anyway. At the Newport Naval Training Station, the Navy introduced him to chili con carne over rice, a new dish for Mac and one he rather liked. They collapsed his training program from three months to six weeks and put him in company with seventy-two recruits, most of them aged seventeen or eighteen, whom Mac remembered, when he wrote his memoirs as an old man, as "crybabies and wimps. They complained about the food, the work, drills and living conditions." After training, they put him on an overnight boat to New York, and he found his ship in dry dock, looking more like a canoe in a bathtub. "Lord 'o Lord what have I got myself into," Mac thought, looking at what would be his home for the next five years.

Mac was five-foot-eight and 138 pounds. He had an ample nose, and a wide, thin crack of a smile. He always had a lot to say, an opinion to offer and a story to stretch. Shortly after he'd come aboard *Plunkett* after Christmas in 1940, he watched a boatswain's mate manage two deckhands trying to rig the booms used to lower and raise the ship's motor whaleboats. He saw problems all over the place with their approach.

"They'll never do that in a hundred years," Mac said to one of his buddies, remembering the booms he'd used to raise signs in Fall River.

The boatswain's mate overheard him. "You're so goddamned smart, how would you do it?"

After McManus rigged the booms properly, the boatswain's mate decided to steer the new seaman into his crew. "The hell you will," McManus said.

Later, one of the ship's officers told him he'd been selected to go to sonar school in Key West for three months.

"I don't want to be a ping jockey," Mac said.

"Key West's better than convoy duty," the officer said.

"No thanks," Mac said.

He had designs on *Plunkett*'s five-inch guns, in particular the ship's no. 3 gun that had retained its metal shield but had its top replaced with canvas as a weight-saving measure. Mac got what he wanted, and in the summer of 1941 they sent him to gunnery school.

He hadn't known what he wanted on that first convoy run, though. He hadn't known anything about being at sea, and neither, it seemed, did many on *Plunkett*. "The North Atlantic wasn't a good place for chinaware. It was like a three-ring circus trying to hold on to your plate and eat."

Likewise on this maiden run, they learned a thing or two about provisioning the ship for long runs. After thirty days out, underway so long they'd decided that USS actually stood for Underway Saturday and Sunday, they'd run out of toilet paper. Coming back into Brooklyn, "there wasn't a newspaper or magazine left on that ship."

After the ship's first feint toward war, *Plunkett* steamed through simmering North Atlantic waters on escort and convoy duty through spring and into the fall of 1941. Roosevelt knew the United States would have to weigh in on the European conflict eventually but was engaged in a minuet with public opinion. Americans weren't inclined to "fight England's battles." In April of 1941, 50 percent of the country opposed convoys; only 41 percent approved. But then the USS *Greer*, a four-piper en route from the seaport of Argentia in Newfoundland to Reykjavík, Iceland, encountered a British patrol plane that signaled news about a German U-boat in the vicinity. It was daybreak on September 4, and *Greer* zeroed in on the submarine's position 10 miles away and hurried at twenty knots, and then ten knots as its sonar pinged for a precise location. *Greer* grabbed hold of the sub with its sonar 150 miles south of Iceland, and held on, the next move a crapshoot. For two hours, *Greer* tracked the sub's course and reported its situation to planes and ships within earshot. The Germans wouldn't have it and dispatched a torpedo that missed its mark by one hundred yards. *Greer* bore down on the sub and attacked with a pattern of eight depth charges. The sub dispatched another torpedo, missing by three hundred yards this time. Roosevelt now had license to take one more step into the fray. A week after the action, he freed the Navy to shoot on sight in hostile waters.

The following month, *Plunkett* and *Kearny* rushed from Reykjavík to the aid of a convoy set upon by U-Boats. The Germans attacked and struck *Kearny* with a torpedo that killed eleven men. Later that month, a U-Boat in waters six hundred miles west of Ireland put a torpedo into the destroyer *Reuben James*, killing 115 officers and men. *Greer* had been the first American vessel targeted by the Germans,

Kearny the first ship struck by the Germans, and *Reuben James* the first ship sunk by the Germans. And the war hadn't yet officially begun for the Americans.

At 3:45 p.m. on December 7, 1941, one of the lead engineers on *Plunkett*, a man known as the "oil king," opened the level control valves on two of the ship's fuel tanks and let seawater flow into the depleted compartments as ballast. The sun was close to setting, and *Plunkett* was trying for twenty-five knots in heavy North Atlantic waters, detached since that morning from yet another convoy run. They were headed to Newfoundland now, to Placentia Bay and the port of Argentia, where President Roosevelt and Prime Minister Churchill had met several months earlier.

As the oil king closed the valves on twenty-four hundred gallons of ballast, a Japanese dive bomber nosed down out of the clouds above the Hawaiian island of Oahu, nearly six thousand miles west of the destroyer's position. Some 360 Japanese warplanes trailed this dive bomber in two great waves that would, over the next two hours, sink five of eight battleships in Pearl Harbor, maul three destroyers, destroy more than two hundred aircraft, kill twenty-four hundred Americans, and extinguish once and for all America's ambivalence about the war. Meanwhile, oblivious as the rest of North America to the sweep of planes over Hawaii, *Plunkett* slowed its speed to twenty knots and then fifteen knots.

Jim McManus was that afternoon thinking about Christmas. After a pit stop at "god-forsaken" Placentia Bay, *Plunkett* would steam south to Boston for the holidays. Half the crew would get leave over New Year's, and half would get leave over Christmas. Mac was to be part of the crew that would be off *Plunkett* at Christmas, and he was headed home to Fall River.

But then *Plunkett*'s radioman tuned in to a message coming in by Morse code, and sprang from his station with the news, hurrying about the ship like the town crier. "This is not a drill," he was shouting. "Pearl Harbor is being attacked."

Pearl Harbor, McManus thought, rooting around for reference to a place that had never once lit on his radar screen. For him, like so many of the men on *Plunkett*, everything about the looming war had to do with the Germans and action on the Atlantic. Where the hell was Pearl Harbor?

4: OVERLAND

DECEMBER 1941

That Sunday, Jim Feltz parked his black '34 Plymouth in front of the dollar store on the Woodson Road in Overland, Missouri, and stepped outside to wait for his manager, Ed, to return from lunch. The three great storefront windows of the dollar store, where Jim worked six days a week and where Ed managed the staff as a floor-walker, brimmed with dependable merchandise, with new lines of porcelain dolls and men's ties, a small Philco phonograph, boxed sets of cutlery, a blizzard of Christmas cards pinned to a wooden hutch they used as a prop, most of the would-be presents artfully poised on shelves you could barely see for all the product. Over all, on a ledge above the building's center entrance, was a life-size mannequin of Santa Claus, arms akimbo, as if to say *Isn't it about time you bought something?* These windows, like many of the storefront windows of the shops up and down Woodson, were Ed's doing. He had a knack for decorating, and he'd recruited Jim as a gofer that day.

Monday through Saturday, Jim worked as a stock boy at the dollar store, or the dime store as they also called it, or Siegal's for the name of the proprietor. He earned $9 per week and gave half that to his mother, Irene. Much of the rest, he'd poured into a '27 Nash that his brother Charlie had picked up and that had been nothing but trouble. Jim had junked that clunker for $7.25 after removing the new battery he'd purchased, and then bought the Plymouth for $120, which left little enough for that Philco, and the likes of "Elmer's Tune" and "Chattanooga Choo Choo." Still, that he acquire a phonograph was now imperative.

Two months shy of seventeen, Jim was slightly below middling height, eager and industrious for a kid, fresh-faced and good-natured. He had a crooked smile, which was something of a trademark in the family, and hair that he swept back off the forehead with only the slightest consideration of a part. He made friends easily, and fast, and was still tempted on occasion to indulge the shooting games they played up at the town dump with .22 rifles and a tin can.

Through that early afternoon, Ed orchestrated one winter wonderland after another. It was the usual holiday fare—a Christmas tree with a toy train circling the base, more mannequins of Santa Claus and elves, gifts wrapped and hung from the ceiling by fishing line. While Ed wedged himself into the window fronts and worked off his hands and knees, Jim hovered nearby, cutting colored paper and garlands to length, and retrieving props as Ed called for them.

Mid-afternoon, they started on a ladies' dress shop, this one with a dousing of cotton that was far deeper than the snow ever seemed to get in Overland. There'd been less than an inch so far that month, and the temperatures this afternoon had climbed above freezing. While Ed manipulated his props inside the window, a horn started sounding at the far end of Woodson, paused, and then came closer. In between bursts of the horn, Jim heard someone shouting. It was a disconcerting thing to have happen in Overland on a Sunday afternoon, on any afternoon, and he went to the door as a man in a truck came down the street with his head thrust through the window. "The Japs!" he was shouting. "They've bombed Pearl Harbor!"

That winter the war pulled a plug on Overland, draining the town of its young men, imperceptibly at first but then with a swirling, ineluctable force and a sucking sound that was hard to ignore. Three kids from town and a nearby parish had been killed in Hawaii that morning of December 7, two of them on the *Arizona* at Pearl Harbor. A short time later, two of the town's Baker boys lost their lives, one with General MacArthur in the Philippines and another off an aircraft carrier in the Coral Sea. Their father was so distraught he gave up a $500-per-month job as a locomotive engineer and enlisted in the Navy, while his wife went to work in an aircraft factory and poured her money into war bonds. The Japanese dimension to the war was as surprising to Jim as the attack itself: In grade school, he'd met refugee children who'd come into his school to talk about how hard life had been under the Nazis in Germany.

Though still more than a year from draft age, Jim was in no rush to go anywhere, not since he'd seen what he'd seen at the dollar store one day. Mickey Betts, a saleslady who'd already come up into her twenties, was chatting with a girl who had wavy brown hair marcelled off her forehead and then down to the shoulders in a cascade of tresses. She had massive brown doe eyes and a skeptical way of smiling, as if alert to the possibility someone was trying to give her the business. He'd caught all this in a glance, and he wondered whether to hazard another but didn't. He'd seen enough.

Over the next week, Jim moderated his work habits, paying less attention to what he managed in the storerooms and more to what he was putting up on the shelves. The appearance of the brown-haired girl could have been a fluke. Overland was bigger than neighboring towns, and Siegal's did draw customers from those places, though Jim figured he'd have recognized most of the people who shopped the store from the likes of nearby St. Ann and St. John: She might have just been passing through. But then it happened again. She came into the store. She talked to Mickey. She didn't buy anything. Now he knew this was no mere customer. Mickey knew her, somehow, and there was a very good bet she was going to return and strike up yet another conversation with the saleslady.

Indeed, the girl was Mickey's niece, and a refugee from St. Charles County, where the government had recently seized twenty thousand acres by eminent domain, including the towns of Howell and Hamburg, for the development of a $15 million munitions plant. Jim had heard about all of this activity downriver, but like so much of the doings of the wider world, none of this had mattered as much to him as what was happening in the orbit of the dollar store, and his home on Tudor Avenue: the crystal set he fiddled with so he could listen to pilots talking to the control tower at the nearby airport; the shooting games he played with Charlie Page; the adventures he still tuned in to on the radio, of *Fibber McGee and Molly* and *The Green Hornet*. But all of those priorities were on the verge of reorientation, gradually, in the days leading away from that first glimpse of Betty Kneemiller, and then dramatically after he and Ed finished dressing their last storefront on Woodson.

Overland in 1941 was a fair-size town of not quite three thousand people, named for the emigrant trail that routed northwest out of St. Louis, bound for a Missouri River crossing. Local lore said Daniel Boone constructed a single-room cabin here in the early 1800s. Downtown wasn't much longer than five blocks, with most of the merchants lining Woodson and Ashby. Kroger's and A&P supplied groceries. There was a bakery, a funeral parlor, a movie house, and clothing stores—more clothing stores (ladies' dress shops), it seemed, than anything else. Only one little diner was open at the time, a greasy spoon, serving hamburgers it would continue to serve for the next seventy-five years and then some.

The Feltzes lived in a small, four-room stucco house, across from Ritenour High School. They had plumbing, and a radio, but no phone. Jim's mother and father had repurposed a dining room as their bedroom. His sister Juanetta and her husband, Charles, kept another room as their bedroom. His brother Charlie and Charlie's wife, Cora, slept on a fold-out sofa in the living room. Jim slept in the living room, too, on a cot. Jim's father was the son of a German immigrant, who'd enlisted in the Union Army in the waning days of the Civil War—a fact Jim didn't know until he was in his nineties, neither the part about his grandfather being from Germany nor his service during the Civil War. Around the time of Jim's birth, his father had quit work as a farmer and was working as a laborer. One day, he and a coworker were driving an old Mack truck when some railroad cars carrying coal uncoupled from their train and smashed into their vehicle. John Feltz's partner was killed, and he himself "was dinged up pretty good" and lived on from there as a "crippled-up man," who sometimes worked at a filling station at the corner of Red Rock and Woodson.

Jim had worked there, too, the summer of 1940, pumping gas into a ten-gallon reservoir on top and letting it out for sale a gallon at a time. He sold papers at the same station, earning 3 cents for every five papers sold. After his freshman year in high school, he decided he wanted to make work, any work, a regular thing. His mother, who worked as a janitress at the high school, agreed to let him quit school on one condition: that he got a job first. Not a temp job selling papers, or pumping gas, but something established, something that might serve as a building block for whatever else Jim might do with his life. And so one day, Jim lied to Mr. Siegal about his age and got a job at the dollar store.

He worked twelve hours a day six days a week, keeping the store's inventory in his head, and his eyes on the makeup counter. He didn't have any plan for what to do when he saw her again. Asking Betty Kneemiller out required an ambition that hadn't yet fully formed within him, but Mickey had her own ideas about what she wanted to happen. One day she suggested that Jim go to the movies on a Sunday night. "And I'll get Betty to go, too," she told him.

They met at the dollar store and walked up Woodson to the movie house, Betty and Mickey talking all the way, more like sisters than an aunt and a niece. Jim wasn't sure she'd known he was coming along with them, and throughout the evening, whenever he perked up with a comment, he noticed a slight, birdlike jerk of her head in his direction, as if he was continually surprising her by still being there. He was a kid and still looked like a kid, but she'd already graduated from the gawky throes of adolescence to the mature elegance cultivated by her aunt. He understood that first date to be their last date, but then Mickey suggested he go to the show again, and then to join them for a trip to a ballroom in St. Louis.

The dance floor at Tunetown was as vast as a roller-skating rink, and low-ceilinged alcoves stretched along its length for tables. That was where Jim parked himself. Betty and Mickey took to the floor immediately, with Mickey's friend, an Italian fellow who'd anglicized his name to Joe Jaye, doing double duty as a partner, first with Mickey, then Betty, then all three of them in a clump. An orchestra commanded an elevated stage, with saxophones, trumpets, trombones, and a rhythm section, and broke from a series of medium-tempo tunes to a fast-tempo number that sparked the dancers into all kinds of new manipulations. Men rolled women over their backs or shot them sliding between their legs. Jim couldn't make sense of it. He looked for patterns and similarities and saw nothing of the sort, but instead: men with their arms forming two sides of a triangle overhead while their heads pecked in and out like a hen from its house. Women twirled everywhere, some with skirts that seemed purpose-built to flare in a circle rippling horizontal to the floor, their legs and hips sheathed in modest undergarments. Though his eyes zoomed about as couples erupted in all sorts of sudden flights, he was tethered to Betty and what he was coming to see as her distinctive flourishes, the rock back on her heels and the swivel of her toes, and best of all, the quick stop, when she'd freeze in one pose or another, as if caught suddenly by a photographer's lens. She never held the same pose twice; it was always something new, something dramatic, and something that filled him with a desire so strong he couldn't help but remember each of those images in turn, like a collection of photographs of a girl so wondrously beautiful he couldn't quite believe he was there with her.

Jim couldn't dance and what's more couldn't imagine himself

dancing. It was a constitutional thing. You had it or you didn't have it, like an aptitude for spelling. It was a world beyond his world, with a language all its own, where people talked about the Shorty George, and the Lindy Hop, and how to be a "hepcat." Cats were what people seemed to become when they came onto the dance floor. And Jim felt disqualified from that world, from the things they did, and the things they said. "When the jitterbug bites," they said, "it bites deep." But it wouldn't bite Jim.

His time with Betty was over, he thought, after that first night out to Tunetown. Accompanying an uncommunicative date to the movies—well, that was her problem, not his—but to show off a timidity so overwhelming he could not bring himself to budge from an alcove at the ballroom, that was his problem. He wasn't timid in every department, but he couldn't reveal as much to Betty. Telling her about the time he and Charlie Page had shot biscuits out of each other's mouth with their .22s, and Jim's reputation as an excellent shot, was not going to impress this girl. Hopping onto that dance floor might, and he'd resolved to do as much when Mickey, unaccountably, invited him again to Tunetown, where he leaned against an arch of the alcove—all night long—and watched her. It was over, he kept thinking, but Mickey kept inviting him out, and then one day, again unaccountably, Betty invited him to her house for dinner.

Archibald Kneemiller worked at the TNT munitions plant in Weldon Springs, salvaging that much opportunity at least from the home he'd lost when the government cleared the county of its residents for the new munitions plant. He made money other ways, too. He sold Chevrolets, and then he purchased another farm and worked that land when he could and had men work it for him when he couldn't. Meanwhile, he was cultivating a growing reputation as an auctioneer on the weekend. He had a firm command of vigorous language, and a bearing reminiscent of those Civil War colonels who used to auction off plunder, and so he, too, became known as the colonel.

Betty had grown up attending school in a one-room schoolhouse, going back and forth by horse, but when the Kneemillers moved to the western fringe of St. Louis proper, close by Overland, she transitioned into the Stanford Brown business school. The colonel believed his oldest child was on the road to a bright future, not merely as a secretary but into a career and a vibrant life that might be hobbled if she latched herself to a stock boy whose father pumped gas down on the Rock Road.

The dread that overcame Jim after that first time out to the movies, and then Tunetown, depressed him further after this first dinner at Betty's. The dancing, that might come in time, but Betty's father's bias against what his work today as a stock boy said about his prospects tomorrow, and moreover what his father's work revealed as a precedent, was a hurdle altogether higher. Fortunately, Jim didn't get the sense that Mr. Kneemiller was actively campaigning against them. He didn't prevent them from dating. The Kneemillers set a place for Jim at dinner occasionally, but every time that phrase sounded—"the dime store"—at dinner or in reference to their plans, Jim heard a clock ticking. Mr. Kneemiller would wait him out. That, or the war would do the trick.

=====

That spring, no matter how consumed he was by the need to be with her as much as he could—on the phone from the drugstore, at the movies, out to Babler State Park, where he'd rig an old phonograph he'd finally acquired in the backseat of the car to play records, and even to Tunetown again and again—and no matter that he'd only just turned seventeen in February and wouldn't be subject to the draft until February of 1943, the undercurrent of war streaming through Overland was more than Jim could resist. It was better, they were telling him, that he go to it before it came to him. The Navy, they said, was the way to go. The food was hot, and you had a dry bunk for a bed.

"I want to join the Navy," he told his mother one day.

"You don't want to join," Irene Feltz told him. ·

"They're going to draft me anyway. I want to join the Navy, and I'll need your signature," he said.

In the same way she signed off on his decision to drop out of school, she signed off on his decision to enlist.

When Jim arrived at the Great Lakes Naval Training Center outside Chicago on the evening of June 10, 1942, the Navy issued him a bonanza of clothing that enabled "a change a day," something new. There were three white uniforms, two blue uniforms, a dress jacket, a pea jacket, a pair of boots, two white hats, a dress blue hat, a work uniform, a pair of galoshes, low-top white tennis shoes, a mattress, pillow, two blankets, a pair of gloves, six pairs of socks, and "lots more," he catalogued in a letter to Betty.

It was a luxury, all that clothing, but a bunk for a berth was a fiction, at least it was in basic training. The Navy berthed new recruits in hammocks, and there were a lot of them. When the Japanese attacked Pearl Harbor, there'd been just six thousand recruits on the five-hundred-acre base. With the country's dec-laration of war, the base almost tripled in size, and by the time Jim arrived, there were eighty thousand recruits segregated into companies of one hundred men. In the morning, they'd rise at 5:30, make up their hammocks, air out their pillows and blankets, then fall out for exercise. Only afterward did they get chow. There would be drilling or a lecture before lunch at 12:30 and then they'd clean their barracks. In the evening, there would be an opportunity for a show or a ballgame, and time to write.

"Write every night so I'll get one a day," Jim wrote Betty, telling her he'd feel sick and lonesome if the mail came and there wasn't a letter from her. Betty did her level best over the next couple of months. Though she had access to a typewriter at school, Jim asked her to refrain from typing. "I'd rather have you write for they seem more from you," he wrote. The penmanship "isn't bad at all."

That first week apart was all the more wrenching because they'd spent most of Jim's last evening in Overland together, pushing their affection for one another as far as they dared. Betty hadn't known how hard their parting of the ways was going to be. She couldn't tell sometimes whether she was "eating or sleeping," and once while taking a speed test on dictation at school, she inadvertently wrote his name twice. Jim wasn't faring much better. One day at drill, he was so preoccupied by the memory of their last night together that he missed an order to turn and "walked straight." He brought her into his prayers every evening, and one evening after everyone went out to a show that he wouldn't go to because it would remind him of the shows they went to together, he lay on the floor of his barracks and penciled out a poem.

There are many men around me
But still I'm all alone
My heart is aching inside me
There is an ache in every bone
My mind is homeward wondering
Of the girl I left behind
Wondering if she'll be waiting
For a sailor who is 4 years signed

Though Betty shied away from Tunetown after Jim left, the compulsion to dance exerted a force too powerful. Soon, she and Mickey were back at the ballroom, and out to the *Admiral*, too, a boat on the Missouri that shoved off evenings with an orchestra. Jim had heard about the *Admiral*, and about the "smooching" that sometimes took place on the top deck. "I hope I won't have to worry about that," he wrote.

Betty preferred Tunetown. Tony Pastor started leading the band after Jim left, and "Brother, has he got the jive," Betty wrote. She started wearing new high heels to the dances, and she'd had her hair permed, finally. One evening, she'd let an Italian fellow take her out. His dancing impressed her, but his ethnicity didn't impress her mother. "Mother is against me going with any Italian fellow," Betty wrote. But "they are good dancers and since that is all I go for I can't understand what is wrong with them." Jim didn't know much about Italians, but he allowed to Betty that "mothers are right most of the time." Betty's father, and his feelings for his daughter's company, were another matter.

At the end of July, Jim got his orders and told Betty there wasn't any chance he'd be coming home before he shipped out. On July 31, he arrived in New York and was put up at Pier 92 in Brooklyn while the Navy decided what to do with him. The Navy referred to the pier as a ship, but it wasn't, no matter the piping boatswain and the captain who made the sailors stand at attention even when his wife was passing. Pier 92 was an old, two-story industrial warehouse, jutting one thousand feet into the East River, nothing but steel girders and brick, and tiers of bunks that stacked would-be sailors eight high. It was a dingy place, and though it might have been redeemed by the food somewhat, because the Navy was renowned for its good food, the Army was dishing out the grub here, resorting to such dishes as beans and catsup on a regular basis. The famous radio announcer Walter Winchell called Pier 92 a "concentration camp," and Jim confirmed it in a letter to Betty. The accommodation was "awful." If he wasn't doing calisthenics in a parking lot, he was standing on a neighboring pier, guarding the *Normandie*, a luxurious French ocean liner that had caught fire and rolled belly-up months earlier.

Two days after Jim showed up, the *Queen Mary* set sail, unescorted, from a neighboring pier, carrying all fifteen thousand troops of the 1st Infantry Division. Every thought about what Jim wanted from his next assignment in the Navy, including the possibility of submarine school, was now subsumed by a desire to get off Pier 92. He and a fellow sailor named Petry cornered the master of the pier, asking for advice on how to expedite their departure. Get up early in the morning, the pier master told them, and check the calls for volunteers on the bulletin board. Jim and Petry checked the next morning, but there was nothing. Guarding the rolled hull of the *Normandie* the next day, they confronted the pier master again. He wanted to know what time they got up and then told them to get up earlier than that. At 3 a.m. the next morning, Jim and Petry found a call for volunteers from a destroyer then tied up at the Brooklyn Navy Yard. They put in for the duty, and they both got orders later that day to cross town for assignment on the USS *Plunkett*.

That summer of 1942, they'd painted *Plunkett* in a new camouflage scheme that was heavy on the pink, so much so that after another destroyer came into its mooring nearby, its skipper sent a message to the ship's wheelhouse: "Send over three quarts of tootie-fruitie." That was how Jim found the ship, in razzle-dazzle and ready, literally, for its close-up. A Navy photographer snapped pictures of the ship the day after Jim came aboard, and *Plunkett* readied for departure. It was August 5, 1942. This had been the summer of the Battle of Midway, and Guadalcanal, the summer of Anne Frank's first diary entry, and the end of the U-boat's second Happy Time along the U.S. East Coast. It was the summer Walt Disney's *Bambi* made its debut in London. Bandleader Kay Kyser's version of "Jingle Jangle Jingle" was everywhere that summer, but rival Glenn Miller was going to master that year's soundtrack. He'd commanded the airwaves with "Chattanooga Choo Choo" in the No. 1 spot for all of January, and then "Moonlight Cocktail" through April and May. And he was going to see off *Plunkett* that afternoon. Jim was standing by the depth charge racks as *Plunkett* shoved off and the Navy Yard's speakers crackled with a song about a freckle-faced kid. The song kicked off with drums, and then a trumpet plunged for wah-wah and a chorus of trombones before a vocal group known as the Modernaires queried saxophonist Tex Beneke on his new romance.

The temperatures were perfect, in the mid-seventies and climbing toward the mid-eighties that day, but with little of the awful humidity they'd be dealing with back in Overland this time of year. All around the Navy Yard black iron cranes stood off the piers like salutes, and the sky was smudged with dissipating clouds of industry spewed from the smokestacks around the bay. In a few weeks, Eleanor Roosevelt was going to launch the battleship *Iowa* from the yard, a ship that displaced more than twenty-five times what *Plunkett* did, and they'd already begun work on another of the big battle wagons, the *Missouri*. Listening to the yard's speaker, Jim knew the song at once and could all but see the long slides of the trombones pumping like pistons for "Kalamazoo." Brother, has he got the jive, Jim thought, and then thought once again of days that spring when he and Betty would drive with Mickey and Jay out to the park, where he'd rig his Victrola in the back of his Plymouth and play it as if he drove a car that actually had a radio—a fiction that lasted only as long as a song because he had to keep running back to change the record with every play.

That morning in August, he'd dropped a letter to Betty, telling her he'd been assigned to a ship that was about to get underway, and who knew when he'd be able to post another letter. He knew now he couldn't expect Betty to wait on him for the duration. He loved her, and though he dutifully signed off his letters "With love," he couldn't really declare as much. "I like you lots," he told her over and over again in his letters that spring and summer, and Betty returned the favor: "P.S. I still like you." They were sixteen and seventeen years old, and all that affection was a thing Jim knew he could not bank on, not with other local boys prowling about, and the Italian fellows, with Tunetown like a siren sounding and her father's reservations. He was "4 years signed," and he wanted to be prepared for the worst. In that last letter to Betty before he shipped out, he acknowledged that he knew she'd be out on dates. He didn't ask her not to go, and he wouldn't ask her to tell him all about the other fellows, but he did ask her to tell him some, "so I'll know what to expect when I come home." As the ship made to clear Wallabout Bay for the East River and Gravesend in New York Harbor, where they'd take on ammunition for a convoy of troopships ferrying soldiers to Scotland, Jim clung to the song receding from him, the music in his ears as light and fetching as Betty's fingertips on his arm. He strained to keep the song going—"Years have gone by, my my how she grew," Tex was singing. When *Plunkett* left port, the only thing that mattered to Jim was getting back to Kalamazoo.

5: CASABLANCA

NOVEMBER 1942

In 1942, the Americans hoped to make quick work of the war in Europe with an invasion across the English Channel. The Soviets, who were bleeding lives by the tens of thousands as the Germans closed on Moscow, wanted the same thing—a second front in Europe. Winston Churchill didn't. He tallied the number of German divisions in France and feared a direct assault on the Continent would be as devastating as Britain's direct assault on the Somme, where they'd lost sixty thousand men in a single day. Neither the Brits nor the Americans were yet in a position to go head-to-head with the Germans where they were strongest. And so Churchill argued for an end run around Hitler's Fortress Europe, to North Africa, where the compromised Vichy French held sway in the colonies of Morocco, Algeria, and Tunisia. He argued as much in the late spring of 1942 when he visited Roosevelt at Hyde Park and in Washington. Gradually Roosevelt warmed to the idea of an operation known first as Gymnast, then as Torch.

The Torch task force debarked for Europe from Norfolk, Virginia, and Portland, Maine, on October 24 and 25, coordinating with troopships dispatched from England, all bound for landing places on Morocco's Atlantic shore and Algeria's Mediterranean. While the first wave of the invasion zigzagged toward its destination, doing its best to thwart German intelligence, *Plunkett* idled at the 35th Street Pier in Brooklyn, fastened to cleats with six-inch manila rope. Compared to the Navy Yard, few liked 35th Street. It was a merchant shipping facility, dreary and lonely, with a long warehouse lapping out into the stream, and a narrow pier where six other ships of Destroyer Squadron 7, known as DesRon 7 in Navy parlance, made preparations to get underway in the second wave.

There were nine ships total in the squadron, all launched and commissioned around the same time, all about the same size at 1,620 tons, and each the beneficiary of some fame for this and that. *Niblack* had dropped the first depth charges of the war in April of the previous year. *Hilary P. Jones* had rescued survivors of the first U.S. ship sunk by the Germans a year earlier. In September of 1942, *Mayo* and *Madison* helped rescue 1,400 men from a torpedoed troopship. *Plunkett* was the squadron's flagship, which meant the commander of the squadron, the squad dog, kept his quarters and directed the group's activities on a ship the crew had warmed to as the *Charley P*, for their namesake Charles P. Plunkett.

That afternoon of November 1, the crew could sense the imminence of departure, reading signals with a sixth sense they'd refined individually and interpreted as scuttlebutt. They'd been readying the ship for days, the provisions coming aboard in bulk, each new raft of stores dutifully noted in the ship's log. The veal, when it showed up, would come as part of a 172-pound shipment. They'd load 315 pounds of lettuce at a throw, 115 pounds of fresh squash, 330 pounds of tomatoes, 300 pounds of roast beef, 150 pounds of rolled oats, 220 pounds of cornmeal from Quaker Oats, hundreds of pounds of grapefruit and cabbage. A spud locker on the main deck housed 1,500 pounds of potatoes. On it came: canned hams, soda crackers, dry milk, pork sausage, hominy grits, ripe olives, honey, Jell-O, cereal, peanut butter, tomato juice, cranberry sauce, jars of pickles, cornstarch, celery salt, assorted candy, mixed nuts, brown sugar, mustard, fresh eggs, hundreds of pounds of apples. There would be cakes from Drake's, and gallons of ice cream from Good Humor, with the officer of the deck inspecting the arrivals "as to quantity and quality." Jim Feltz, when he came into the service, weighed 117 pounds, partly because his build was naturally slight but also because he was still a kid and growing. On the edge of Operation Torch, writing from the YMCA on Sands Street just outside the Navy Yard, he reported to Betty that he'd gained 30 pounds.

In his first three months aboard *Plunkett*, Jim had convoyed back and forth across the Atlantic twice, each time as a deckhand and each time as part of a troopship escort, ferrying soldiers to the Firth of Clyde in Scotland by way of Iceland. His first time out, cast off to the strains of "Kalamazoo," his stomach plagued him all the way up the Atlantic Seaboard, and then surged forth after Halifax when the ship steered into heavy weather. "I'm going to be sick," he told the officer of the deck one evening. He was up on a wing of the bridge with binoculars, pulling lookout duty, or trying to. "Not on my watch," the officer said, and sent him off the bridge. Jim vomited on the ladder going down the superstructure, heaved on the superstructure deck, then got down to the main deck at the forecastle and chucked up some more, this time at least into the North Atlantic. He was found there by the ship's cook George Schwartz, bearing bread and advice. "Every time you throw up, eat a slice," George told him. It was a far better thing to throw up something than nothing. Jim ate bread the next three days and then, as if by magic, didn't need to eat bread anymore.

Over those first few months as an apprentice seaman, he'd been sleeping in a hammock tied up in the mess, rising in the morning before the first round of breakfast and retiring only after everyone had had supper and, perhaps, a movie. The bunk you were supposed to get on a Navy ship, the putative bunk, was elusive. The crummy sleeping situation notwithstanding, the worst part about being an apprentice seaman was the duty. Jim was constantly painting while at sea, and when the ship came in, he was constantly chipping paint. He'd made it known he wanted into the electrician's department when there was an opening. When a job opened in the forward fire room, and the engineering officer asked if he wanted on that crew, known generally as the black gang, at least until a spot opened in the electrician's department, Jim didn't think twice.

He lugged his sea bag down from a locker in the mess to the engineering department in the rear of the ship. His new berth wasn't all the way to stern; there were deckhands in that compartment, men they sometimes referred to as deck apes when they felt like denigrating them. He climbed down the ladder to the first platform and stepped through a bulkhead door into the torpedo men's tiny compartment, and then into a larger compartment with three aisles and four lengths of bunks stacked three high. His new home was dimly lit, and a record scratched out a plaintive melody, playing off a Victrola shelved on the port side of the compartment, sometimes in fine fettle but sometimes with a voice that slowed strangely to a drawl.

He vaguely recognized all of his new bunkmates. One of the new men in his compartment had eyebrows that were wide and full, not Groucho Marx by any means, but headed in that direction. His smile yanked up slightly to the right, tentatively, and in it there was an implicit recognition that things didn't always turn out for the best. Something about the Mediterranean lurked in his appearance, adding a subtle, swarthy tint to his complexion. This was Irvin "Dutch" Gebhart. Another man had front teeth slightly more protuberant than anyone would have liked. He had a widow's peak so exact it looked drawn, and a certain puffiness under the eyes that lent him the appearance of someone who should have been wearing glasses, except that his eyes were excellent. This was John Gallagher.

Jim had come into the engineering department with a bit of notoriety already established. He was the lookout who'd spotted a periscope in a run over to Scotland a couple months back. With Jim's alarm, the officer of the deck called all hands to general quarters. The bridge jumped on the talk-between-ships phones, the TBS, alerting the convoy to the proximity of a U-boat. The ship moved on the periscope, readying a so-called embarrassing attack by depth charges, but all of the embarrassment was on Jim. The periscope was found out to be the handle of a broom or mop, probably dropped off the deck of one of the other ships in the convoy and floating vertically, a freaky resemblance.

Testing out the accommodation, Jim wedged into the middle bunk in a tier of three, just below Gallagher. His upstairs neighbor weighed a concave shape into the berth, giving Jim about a foot of space over his face and what felt like inches at the midsection. But he may as well have just stretched out in the Waldorf Astoria, such was the upgrade from a hammock in the mess to a bunk in the black gang's compartment.

He quickly learned a few things about his bunkmates. That Gallagher was Catholic and mumbled his prayers out of a little black book he'd received as a kid at confirmation, that he used to press chocolate at a mill on the southern fringe of Boston, that he'd worked in a hardware store before that, and that he'd throw a punch now and then. A few months earlier, he'd mixed it up on shore and was fined $25 for all the fun. Dutch Gebhart's claim to fame was that he was the first man in Delaware to sign up after Pearl Harbor, or so he said. His grandfather had been the chief of police in Wilmington. He'd made gunpowder at Hercules before the war, and he'd worked at DuPont, too. In time, they all had a working appreciation of each other's life outside the tin can. When they didn't have to "turn to," which was the term they used for having to work, or there wasn't a movie to watch again, or shut-eye to catch up on, they talked about home, and girls, and what they wanted to eat, but home first and always.

On the morning of November 2, New Yorkers would awake to news of a major naval victory in action northeast of Guadalcanal, with bomb hits on Japanese carriers and the destruction of more than one hundred planes. Canterbury, England, was digging out after a German bombing run in daylight, the most intensive daytime bombing by the Germans since the Battle of Britain two years earlier. An advertisement in the *New York Times* promised readers they could learn the rumba, the latest dance craze, in just six hours. Arturo Toscanini had just given the first all-American program of his career at Radio City, with Benny Goodman on the clarinet for "Rhapsody in Blue" and the late George Gershwin's mother in the audience.

By the time New Yorkers flapped their papers on this news, *Plunkett* and its squadron were underway. At one o'clock that morning, Ken Brown sounded a special detail and tested the ship's engines. The previous month he'd molted from ensign to lieutenant (junior grade), and with the ship's new CO he'd started standing watch as officer of the deck. Underway on his first watch as OOD, it was night, and they were to start zigzagging as a thwart to enemy submarines. At the moment he was to give the order to set a new course, he was stricken with indecision: Do we turn right, or left? The engineering officer Spangler, on one of his early watches as OOD, had also bungled the zigzag and put *Plunkett* at the vanguard of another convoy entirely. But Ken collected himself in time, called for the change of course, and stayed in formation. This November morning, Ken had the ship's deckhands disconnect the water and telephone lines, and then the half dozen manila lines as a tugboat captain came aboard. *Plunkett*'s captain, Lewis R. Miller, emerged from his stateroom and joined Ken and the ship's navigator.

Miller had just turned forty. Born of a well-established Texas family, he'd come out of the Naval Academy in 1926 with not a single extracurricular interest to his name, but a reputation for philosophizing, for humor, and as a pretty good judge of character. He'd been steering for destroyers since the Academy, preferably one down South somewhere, and preferably one on independent duty. That, he reckoned, would be Utopia. "Just let me see the old sun sinking down and hear the water lapping at my baby's sides." That was Lewy. His type, it was said, formed the backbone of the Navy.

On *Plunkett*, Miller had what he wanted but for the independent duty; his ship was ferrying the squad dog. Coming into middle age now, he cultivated a thin mustache at a time when a mustache was something fancied by effete foreigners, and a commitment to the well-being of his crew. Where Captain Standley hadn't generated much goodwill in the wardroom or on the deck, Miller was another story. Not long after he'd assumed command in September, he'd let the junior officers have their wives on board, not merely for a look around but while the ship was actually *moving*, guided by tugs from a pier on the Hudson to the Brooklyn Navy Yard. Around the same time, he'd called Kenneth P. "Dutch" Heissler to his quarters and told him this: "I want this to be the best-fed ship in the Navy. If you need money to get more, I'll get it."

The new chief commissary steward liked the sound of that. Dutch was a natural wheeler-dealer, and he knew how to provision a ship in such a way that he could trade a little bit of this for a little bit of that when push came to shove. The onetime Iowa farm boy was twenty-eight years old, but already a thirteen-year veteran of the Navy, having lied about his age in order to enlist at fifteen. Dutch's size augmented the lie. He was six-foot-two, and his hands were massive, a prominence that inevitably prompted Dutch to use them again and again. He'd boxed as an amateur, and his nose, repeatedly broken and swollen and broken again, flew his flag as a fighter. One of his nieces claimed a title for him as the middleweight boxing champion of the Navy, and said he'd once fought Jack Dempsey, which was more a matter of family apocrypha than something that happened. But for the complications of the nose, or maybe despite them, Dutch was movie-star handsome, with a broad smile and a Superman-like curl of hair over his forehead. He was new to *Plunkett* that fall, but he was getting off on the right foot. "I like this duty better than I did the [USS] *Augusta*," he wrote to his sister. "A better gang on here, too." A better gang, but a pack of scroungers. Dutch was writing to his sister on some of the nice paper she'd sent him, but he couldn't enclose the letter in one of the matching envelopes. His new shipmates had pilfered those.

At 7:15 that morning, embarked on its first invasion of the war, Jack Simpson lighted the ship and shortly thereafter mustered the entire crew to station. Five men were missing, absent over leave. Jack Collingwood relieved Simpson at 8:00 and moved the ship into the inner screen of a convoy called UGF-2 that included twenty-seven merchant ships in nine columns. UG was the routing designation the Navy gave to convoys moving east from the States to the Mediterranean theater, and F meant it was a fast convoy, steaming at fifteen knots. At eight and nine knots, which was about as much speed as a heavily laden merchant ship could muster, U-boats were more likely to graze along the margins, setting up for a torpedo shot. At fifteen knots, it was infinitely more difficult for a U-boat to land a charge, so much so that U-boats rarely expended the effort.

Plunkett was one of fourteen escort ships screening the nine columns, like a "loose-jointed necklace," the columns about one thousand yards apart, with six hundred yards between the bows and sterns of the vessels. Day after day, *Plunkett* steamed on the outer edge of the convoy, a mile or more from the nearest column of ships, guarding against incursion by U-boats. All the while, the destroyers "looked" for surfaced submarines and aircraft with radar, a newfangled technology that ranked as the greatest technological development of the war to date. And they "listened" for submerged subs with sonar. The convoys zigzagged, each ship following instructions for turns at prescribed times, to stymie the geometry of submariners trying to line up a shot. The sub had to determine the ship's speed, estimate the distance, and then allow for the several minutes it would take for the torpedo to reach its target. Ships that zigged and then zagged unpredictably foiled those calculations. In addition to radar and sonar, *Plunkett* looked out for subs the old-fashioned way, too, with a man on the uppermost decks of the ship, scanning the waters with binoculars.

The first wave of Operation Torch crossed the Atlantic without the Germans knowing. They "knew from ship and troop movements that something was in the wind, but they never guessed what," naval historian Samuel Eliot Morison wrote in his account of the operation. On November 8, when the first wave hit the beaches of French Morocco, *Plunkett*'s crew finally learned they were headed to Casablanca. There was little information about the destination, but for the odd piece picked up here and there about the Barbary Coast and the shores of Tripoli. That was as far as anyone's knowledge extended, but they were thrilled to have a hand in the war at last. The day after the crew learned they'd be wading into the war, the British confirmed a major victory at El Alamein in Egypt, and Churchill mobilized the English language, once again, as a springboard to morale. "Now this is not the end," he said after lunching at the lord mayor's house in London. "It is not even the beginning of the end. But it is, perhaps, the end of the beginning."

Casablanca wasn't on anyone's radar screen in 1942. Americans had a better sense of what was happening in Shanghai, halfway around the world, than Casablanca, a relative near neighbor. Until then, Casablanca and its 250,000 residents had been a preoccupation of the French, like far-flung outposts from Hanoi to Pondicherry to Madagascar. They'd laid out great boulevards and planted public gardens. In the Place de France, they erected a clock tower that looked like a Moorish minaret. When art deco came into vogue, their apartment buildings acquired rounded corners and nautical flourishes. The French hadn't been the first to invade this corner of the Dark Continent. The Arabs had swept into the land of the Berbers more than a thousand years earlier and married into the culture to produce a people known as Moors—an intermingling that precipitated a joke among the men getting their first taste of this destination. What do you get when you cross an Arab with a Berber? Moor for your money. Outside Casablanca, Morocco persisted as it had for hundreds of years. And that's what Jack Simpson wanted to see.

First day in port, he fell into admiration of a motorcycle parked on the mole, then into conversation with an Army captain who also rode a bike in the States. Jack talked at length about his own bike, a Harley-Davidson, and a cross-country trip he'd made from Atlanta to Chicago for the officer's training program at Northwestern University. He bumped into the captain the next day, and the man pointed out another bike. "I got you a bike," he said. "Be careful. And don't get me in trouble."

Now, day after day, there was a bike, courtesy of a kindred spirit,

filled to the cap with gas, and all of French North Africa to explore.
The city itself was tame country after the invasion, a supply depot
and port of debarkation for thousands of U.S. troops now streaming
into the war. The "Ice Cream Front" is what they'd taken to calling
it. But outside the city, here was the North Africa that excited Jack.
The bike was a Harley-Davidson WLA, not all that different from the
WL model he'd been riding at home, olive drab with a knucklehead
seat for one and the same forty-five-inch engine, but outfitted for
service, too. A heavy-duty luggage rack on back meant the bike could
haul a radio if need be, and the scabbard could handle a Thompson
submachine gun. He motored out into country that people were
telling him wasn't exactly the Sahara of everyone's imagination, but
something a little more like Ohio here, and a little bit like California
there. If they'd missed the war here in Casablanca, and they had,
that was clear, then he was looking for desolation as consolation, for
Africa was where civilization was but a rumor of things to come.

Up the coast, he traveled through Fedhala, where the Navy had
set thousands of men ashore in darkness and without incident on
the first day of the invasion. Beyond, the road to Rabat teemed
with cyclists and with locals who seemed too big for their burros.
In Rabat itself, fifty-five miles to the north, were the medieval ruins
at Chellah and a once-mighty wall, now crumbling at its ramparts
but formidable still at the corbels and watchtowers, and evocative
at its Moorish arches. The tracery about one arch retained glazed
turquoise tiling that went back centuries. It was all unaccountably
green and lush about the ruins. He could hear the splash of water
and glimpse orange gardens. Local men napped by springs while
women and children frolicked by the water.

In Salé, where Robinson Crusoe had lived a couple years as a slave three hundred years earlier, the French had applied a lighter hand than at Casablanca. Its terraced houses volleyed the sunlight so powerfully they themselves seemed a source of all that brightness. The blue-white domes of mosques hovered above all, and if a magic carpet were to have swerved past one of those domes, it wouldn't have surprised Jack. The war wasn't here, but he was getting his money's worth of adventure. Here, indeed, there was more for your money.

Exhilarated, Jack emerged one afternoon on the edge of the sea where a cliff jutted into the Atlantic. He cut the motor and listened to the muffled wash of the Atlantic below, and the lightness of wind behind him. There was room for him in all this, and he hollered into it, calling out for his boyhood hounds Blackie and Queenie and Sissie, as he'd called for them in the woods of Georgia a lifetime ago. He called for them, and the cliffs called back to him with echoes that sounded as clear and momentous seventy-five years later as they had one day at the end of the beginning of the war on a lonely cliff in Morocco.

In Casablanca, Jim Feltz wasn't trying to slake any kind of thirst with liberty. He hadn't resorted much to time off the ship since he'd come aboard, preferring instead the $1 his shipmates would give him to stand their watch while they waded out into the thick of it. Jim hadn't turned eighteen yet, and he didn't drink hardly at all, and most of the men were older than he was, more seasoned in vice, more inclined to indulge, and he wouldn't.

One Sunday morning while they were still tied up in the inner harbor, tradition notwithstanding, Jim waded out into the streets of Casablanca with Gallagher and Gebhart, with Ski and Jim McNellis.

You couldn't come to a place like Casablanca, he'd decided, and have nothing to show for having been there. The temperatures were cool, and the air was scented with charcoal. They wore dress blues into the streets, mingling with men wearing red truncated cones on their heads called tarbooshes, others in turbans, others in skullcaps. Every now and then, there'd be a local man in a twill suit, but usually, the local trundled by in a burnoose or some nondescript shift or bloused pantaloons. Most of the women they saw were French, dressed in Sunday finery for Mass. Far more elusive were the local women. The Americans had all been made cognizant of how they were to behave toward Moslem women, but they were still half dreaming there'd be a little bit of the Arabian Nights about these women. Instead, the local women peeked at them from slits in all-white haiks, with everything concealed but for the eyes. But what eyes, the corners massaged with cream, the lashes lustered with oil, the kohl dabbed upon the lids, the pupils the women might enlarge with a dose now and then of belladonna.

The five sailors walked aimlessly all morning, past a French post office with Moorish arches, a crenellated *banque* that looked like a castle, and finally into the Place de France with its resplendent clock tower. They hadn't seen much evidence of Africa since they'd come into the city, not one stinking camel, but that didn't stop them from summoning props to stand with them for a series of pictures in a studio not far from the Place de France. Wearing dress blues in the photographs, the sailors stand in white caps, cocked left or right. They're arrayed in a row and are remarkable for their similarity in height, as if they'd all decided to become friends because they all stood about five-eight. A canteen dangles from Jim McNellis's right arm, and Ski is wearing a cartridge belt since he had duty on shore patrol. They stand for one with a French boy in a black beret, a black turtleneck, an overcoat, and a great grin on his face. Hands clasped at his waist, the French boy is absolutely delighted to stand for this picture, which Gallagher would later caption "11/29/42—Liberty at Casablanca." He's poised between two shipmates, smiling more buoyantly than any of them, a hand on McNellis's shoulder. They took another picture with three local boys in skullcaps and raggedy white hooded cloaks, for the colonial French kid was no proof of Africa at all. When a dark-skinned foreign sailor came into the studio, they dragged this fellow into the picture, a cigarette dangling from his lips. Two U.S. Army chaps in garrison caps stand behind the five men off *Plunkett* and the dark-skinned sailor, out of place, as if Photoshopped into the scene. This was their first great foreign port of the war, and in this Casablanca series they look more legendary than actual, each of these men the product not so much of enlistment as of Hollywood. They'd been to Africa now, and they could prove it.

On Thanksgiving, Dutch Heissler put on the best feed possible, though there wasn't any turkey. At mail call, Jim landed a heap of mail (Betty was writing every day), and read them all on deck, one after the other once he'd put them in chronological order. There was cause for concern. In one, Betty shared news about Ruthene, a girl from Overland who liked Jim and whom Betty sometimes referenced for reasons Jim couldn't quite fathom. He remembered one line from a letter in the summer that stayed with him still, about how "Ruthene is a friend the same as I am." Now she was telling Jim that he "should see her now—what a figure. In fact, she is also very pretty and hasn't lost the sparkle for you either." Something dimmed in the wake of that line. You never knew what was going to come in a letter. Letters from home were often sugar reports, but what was this? Jim dodged a bullet in that letter, and in the next two letters of his chronological journey, she still signed off that she "liked him lots." But it was no better. Then it got better all of a sudden because Betty was also now making plans to come to New York with Jim's mother at Christmas. She told him in one letter, and then confirmed as much in the letters that followed. She'd bought a new red coat. She was no longer going to Tunetown. She was visiting Jim's parents. He stopped worrying about Ruthene.

Gallagher's news was less welcome. His mother had been out singing with a gang his aunt Peggy pulled together, the Looney Band, and they'd been at an old-age home when she'd had a stroke. She was still able to walk somewhat, but they'd made a decision to acquire a wheelchair for her. So now there was this to worry about, on top of what the war would do to his brothers. His brothers Frank and Joe were already in the Army, and his oldest brother, Tom, was waiting to be called. He was 1-A, a Selective Service Act classification that meant he was available for military service, and had decided to wait on the draft since he was already thirty years old and working now as an accountant. "I hope that draft board don't call Tom," John wrote home. "I think three out of one family is plenty." His next-oldest brother, Charlie, had one son, and another baby on the way. He was 3-A, officially deferred from service because of hardship to dependents, and struggling with the pressure to enlist. You were damned if you did, and damned if you didn't. They'd wanted one of the boys home with their mother, as opposed to having all five of them yanked into the service, and Charlie was the heir designate.

Back home at the moment, the country celebrated Thanksgiving as the war production board was considering a 50 percent cut in everyone's annual cocoa ration. Housewives were turning to gelatin to make two pounds of spread with one pound of butter. In New York, a fourteen-year-old boy was home on Lexington Avenue after a three-day trip to Canada, where he'd tried to enlist in the armed forces. And a "rich, suave, exciting and moving tale" was about to debut at the Hollywood Theater in New York. Free French supporters paraded down Fifth Avenue and lofted their flag inside the theater, where they sang the "Marseillaise." It was as much a patriotic rally as the debut of a movie that Warner Bros. had hurried into the theater as coupling on the Allied invasion of North Africa. At 8 p.m. in New York, while *Plunkett* slept, the curtain was drawing open on the world premiere of a new movie starring Humphrey Bogart and Ingrid Bergman called *Casablanca*.

6: STEAMING AS BEFORE

MARCH 1943

Several months before that first German fighter plane swept out of the low-lying Sicilian hills and strafed *Plunkett*, months before they bore down on the Germans at Salerno, before the conflagration of the *Newfoundland*, before the rending of the *Buck* and the calamity at Anzio, more than two hundred of the *Charley P.*'s sailors and their dates and families crowded the Rooftop Ballroom for a Ship's Party at the Hotel St. George in Brooklyn. Tall, narrow windows flanked the sides of the room, rising from waist height to fifteen feet, which was where the ceiling began to arch in a vault. Ornate Corinthian sconces glowed off the walls, and one tall, narrow mirror at the rear reflected the backs of the enlisted men's dress blues. The photographer captured them in a surge of attention, as if all had been up dancing and called to face the bandstand. If you look closely enough, you can hear drummer Gene Krupa in the near distance, and Harry James blowing the trumpet, rolling out the same notes louder and louder, Krupa urging him on, and then the segue to Benny Goodman purling notes on the clarinet as limpid as brook water, piping all the

way up to a magnificent high C before Jess Tracy grabs the baton
and dances over the ivories, all the way to his own high C. It's one
of those pictures you could dwell in for an hour or two, drifting from
personality to personality, each a story in his or her own right, some
more dramatic than others by the looks on their faces. The women
in their fantastic hats and hairdos, their corsages and ribbons, the
men mostly in uniform, all of them exuberant and so engrossed in
this one moment, memorialized in a picture.

There is the elegantly beautiful woman in pearls and a fur
stole and shoulder-length hair standing a sister's distance from an
enlisted man beside her, an older couple behind them. Another
young couple who've forsaken the lens for each other, the enlisted
man turned in profile to gaze upon her. She is facing the camera
but has swerved her eyes up at him, lips pursed. The couples cheek
to cheek. The enlisted man who looks no more than fourteen years
old. Some of the women were USO girls, recruited for the party
and minded by chaperones. You can see as much in their tentative
regard for dates who seem altogether more bullish on their prospects
for the evening. There was a war going on outside of this ballroom,
and this borough, and many of the men in this picture—countless
dozens—would be dead within the year, but they were as alive as
any of us can be for a flash that evening at the Hotel St. George.
The picture's in black-and-white, of course. In fact, it's hard to
believe life was lived in color back then, so conditioned are we to
seeing it in black-and-white.

It's almost as if the world only brightened in color and compli-
cation with Vietnam, and the advent of the Baby Boomers. Before
then everything was black or white, this or that, good or bad. It was
two good nights in a row for Irvin Gebhart, who, after getting two

teeth filled at the dentist's the previous afternoon, had been out to see Benny Goodman on liberty. Afterward, he'd met a bunch of the men from *Plunkett* at Rogers Corner across from Madison Square Garden and drank until there was only time to get back to the ship for 6 a.m. In the photo, he stands shoulder to shoulder with his USO-girl date, and leans his head slightly toward her, a gesture she isn't returning. One or two sailors and dates away, there's Jim Feltz, not shoulder to shoulder with another USO girl, but behind her and closer to the table he sat up from for the picture, because he hadn't been out on the floor dancing. Edward J. Burke is standing front and center, as was customary for the ship's captain, and Dutch Heissler is five places to Burke's right, with a white carnation pinned to the left breast of his uniform and his wife, Ginny, on his left arm. On this March night of 1943, Ken Brown is three rows behind Burke and slightly to the right.

I'd never seen this picture before and didn't know it existed until I'd walked into a room in Jim Feltz's house where he'd memorialized the *Plunkett*. I'd stood a long while, rummaging among the hundreds of faces, and found another young man, toward the front of the crowd, three deep from the first row, leaning in from behind a woman with an awesome crest of permed hair, his hand draped over the shoulder of a young woman nowhere as tentative as Gebhart's. His hair was up and off his forehead, and his eyes were bright with the night, and there was that gap in John Gallagher's teeth, and so much surprise in his face. Because he's looking across the stretch of this ballroom at a camera, but he's looking across decades, too. Aha, you found me!

Coming home from Casablanca, the eponymous movie was still queued up to play matinees and evenings at the Hollywood in New York as *Plunkett* steamed through the submarine net gate by Hoffman Island. Jim Feltz idled topside as the ship came into harbor, awake since before dawn when *Plunkett*'s sonar picked up a sound contact and Ken Brown chased it down. As officer of the deck on the morning watch, Ken decided to drop a few ash cans, and then a half dozen, more on what may or may not have been a U-boat. The three-hundred-pound depth charges sunk at a rate approaching fifteen feet per second and could split a submarine's hull if they detonated within twenty feet of the vessel. Hit or miss, no one could sleep through that, or all of the ship's maneuverings as Ken puttered about the vicinity, looking for oil slicks or wreckage indicating a hit. He wanted confirmation, they all did, for only then would they get to post a silhouette of a submarine on the bridge as a token of their success. But there was nothing. The war was out there, and they were getting close, but they hadn't quite touched it yet. Nor had it touched them.

They'd come into Norfolk thirty-six hours earlier, but Norfolk was no great harbinger of America. Trash banked against the Navy Yard's fences and walls there, and the locals looked only half-awake most of the time. The yard reeked of exhaust fumes, and moreover whatever it was they stored in the warehouses—fruit mostly, it seemed. Indeed, *Plunkett* topped off with apples, oranges, grapefruit, cabbage, and cauliflower before heading up to New York. At the Narrows, the ship steamed between Brooklyn and Staten Island and made straight for the Statue of Liberty, standing tall in relatively welcoming forty-degree weather and fresh winds. Nothing said home like Lady Liberty, and Jim Feltz was about ready to fling himself with relief into the flowing folds of her robes. He'd been away from home for six months already, and though he wouldn't get to Overland this trip, home was coming to him.

On the bridge, Captain Miller was at the conn and Jack Simpson stood nearby as they channeled between Governors Island and Red Hook, and then past Brooklyn Heights. Lower Manhattan loomed off the port beam, its waterfront bristling with piers, its mid-day thrum like a siren song to the crew. Miller was in a lighthearted mood. They'd come back from the first invasion of the war, and there would be people waiting for them in the city. "There's going to be a symphony of bedsprings in town tonight," Miller said.

Outside Wallabout Bay, Miller held the ship in the East River, steady in stream, maneuvering with both engines as he waited for a tug that would take them to its pier. In Norfolk, he'd sidestepped the squadron commander's suggestion he wait on a pilot and made quick work of tying up. New York was different, tricky. After a half-hour wait, *Plunkett*'s tug nestled up against the port beam and nudged the ship broadside to the wind and current. The ship started drifting toward the pier heads, and *Plunkett* queried the tug captain on their pilot. Was he with them? He was not. Meanwhile, *Plunkett* was drifting toward the *Renshaw*, another destroyer tied up at the pier. Miller called for his engines full astern in an attempt to back out of trouble. They struggled nine minutes against the current but lost the battle when the ship's stern swung into the pier head and *Plunkett*'s bow whacked *Renshaw* amidship. The current jostled the ships against each other, until the deckhands ran lines through the bullnose openings in the bows and fastened the ships to mitigate the abrasion. *Renshaw* was hardly damaged, but *Plunkett* had snapped a stanchion and broken a lifeline. There was also some damage to a bilge inside, and a three-inch hole in the bow above the waterline. Twenty minutes after that first nudge into the current, a pilot finally came on board *Plunkett* and called in a team of tugs to bring *Plunkett* to berth. The ship tied up at last, men flew from it on liberties as long as eight days. Some men went home; others checked into hotels for 50 cents a night, preferring a bed to a berth in a Navy yard noisy with incessant hammering; and one other man off *Plunkett*, a sailor named Stripling, checked into the Naval Hospital that night with severe lacerations all over his scalp. You had to fight somewhere.

Two weeks out from Christmas, *Plunkett* was in a festive mood. Ken Brown, who'd spent all of 1942 as the ship's commissary officer, coordinated with Dutch Heissler on a Christmas menu that would feature roast young tom turkey with an oyster dressing, mashed potatoes, Harvard beets, buttered peas, giblet gravy, and cranberry sauce, as well as cigars and cigarettes. They printed a menu, and Captain Miller offered up good wishes in a message they ran on the back: "Let us hope that the spirit of the PLUNKETT will carry us on to victory, that this Christmas will be one of happiness to all, and the New Year will bring us those good things for which we are fighting." Miller, more than most commanding officers, invested in the happiness of his crew, and if his men couldn't be home with their families, they'd at least have a fine meal and a memento of a menu.

In the meantime, there was a Ship's Party scheduled for December 21 at the St. George, not quite two miles from the Navy Yard. The St. George was not only the largest hotel in New York City back then, it may have been the largest in the world. With 2,632 rooms, the hotel was an agglomeration of ambition and opportunity that consumed an entire block of space in Brooklyn Heights several streets in from the East River. Seventeen ballrooms attracted all manner of parties, including *Plunkett*'s in a venue on the rooftop. Venetian blinds concealed the extraordinary view, as per an Army dim-out ordinance that called for veils on windows above fifteen stories.

At the party that evening they learned that Captain Miller was being relieved of command of *Plunkett*, not for what happened with the *Renshaw* in Wallabout Bay five days earlier but for what happened seven days earlier in Norfolk when Miller failed to heed the squadron commander's suggestion that he take on a pilot.

Miller's three months on *Plunkett* had been an antidote to Standley's high-minded tenure, and the prospect of rolling the dice on a new CO was more than some of the crew could bear, especially when the mixers ran out at the Ship's Party, and they started taking their whiskey neat. At some point, some of *Plunkett*'s crew rang the front desk and summoned a boy from Western Union. He showed up, one of those kids in a pillbox hat with a modest beak and red stripes on the shoulders of his uniform jacket. They dictated their message to the boy, a rather lengthy message that pointed out that many men, and some of the officers on *Plunkett*, wanted to keep their captain. Someone tallied the words and called for every man who wanted his name on the telegram to cough up some dough. The telegram boy held his hand out to the drunken crew, and they slapped bills into it. Where was this telegram going? The White House. Who was it going to? Franklin Delano Roosevelt.

Since before they'd left for Casablanca, Bing Crosby's White Christmas had been in the No. 1 spot at the top of the *Billboard* charts, and it was parked there all the way through November and into December.

Christmas at home, like the ones he used to know, was not to be for Gallagher. No matter his mother's shock, or the imminent birth of a niece, he could not get leave. Some of the crew were going home to Boston, and he steered them toward Callahan's, his favorite bar. Callahan's was so much a part of where he was from that he wrote the name of the place, Callahan's Tavern, under the address of his Oakton Avenue home in Jim Feltz's address book. Someday if Jim ever came looking for him, and he wasn't on Oakton Avenue, he might find him there. A few days before Christmas, a small gang of *Plunkett*'s crew entered the brick-front bar with the big plate glass windows and found Charlie Gallagher on station, just as they'd been told they would. They informed Charlie that John had told them to come and say hello to the Weatherstrip, as Charlie called the infant son who'd affected his draft status, who'd kept the draft out, as it were, sealing him off from the war. "Weatherstrip," they told him, and "Callahan's Callahan's Callahan's" were a big part of John's talk. They had to see the place. They had to see the kid. Charlie led them up the hill on Adams Street, retrieving the Weatherstrip on the way, and brought them to the house on Oakton Avenue for a visit with John's mother and sister, who promptly took to the stove to make a meal.

The White House received the telegram sent by the disgruntled *Plunkett* crew and routed that letter into Navy channels, where it wound up eventually on the desk of the squadron commander who quartered on *Plunkett*. Sherman Clark didn't excite much feeling among junior officers on the ship. In general, squadron commanders didn't. He had his own cabin, his own staff, his own dining venue, his own steward, his own agenda, and a unique ability to instill a general feeling of anxiety on the bridge. Mostly, he stayed out of the day-to-day operations, though he was on the bridge at general quarters, and when the ship came into port. Complicating the institutional drag of having someone looking over your shoulder all the time was Clark himself, whose short stature and pompous nature seemed to magnify the feeling against him. At the Naval Academy, they'd called him Shrimp and Cutie, and when he came back from Antwerp, where he'd been coxswain on the remarkable Navy rowing team that won fame and a gold medal on a Belgian canal at the Olympics in 1920, another nickname layered onto the degradation—*Petit*. His boyish looks were an insult to the injury of his modest frame, but this didn't depress him. He evolved in cocky fashion and had ambitions that wouldn't countenance a captain's decision to pass on his order, however ambiguous.

First, the forty-three-year-old squadron commander mustered the ship's enlisted men to his cabin, demanding they show up in dress blues. They crowded into his stateroom. Jim McManus had no idea why they'd been called by the squad dog. That their telegram about Miller to the president had precipitated this summons wasn't flashing on Mac's radar screen until Clark broached the subject. Clark said he was bound to investigate the matter and wanted to know whether the CO had put them up to it.

They all liked Captain Miller, and they couldn't, not one of them, back off their feeling for the CO. It was possible, in retrospect, that whiskey might have had something to do with that enthusiastic telegram, they said. But no, Miller hadn't put them up to it.

Clark dismissed the men, and then called the officers to his room, including Jack Simpson.

"Young man," Clark said, addressing Jack outside the usual and customary form of address. "I don't know where you got the idea that you can just do what you want."

Jack heard him out.

"You do not bypass the chain of command in the Navy," Clark told him. "You go through the procedures that have been established."

He told Jack he was closing the matter then and there. There would be no punishment for this violation. But he'd been warned.

Two days after Captain Miller was detached from *Plunkett* with orders for a new assignment at Newport News, the ship cast off from the 33rd Street Pier in Brooklyn, steamed through the harbor's submarine net before dawn, and took up position as an escort on an eastbound convoy. This one would be a slower proposition than the last, moving east at nine knots, the fastest speed attainable by the slowest ship in the forty-four-vessel convoy. *Plunkett* steamed along its edges at thirteen knots, herding the lumbering, overladen vessels like a cowboy his cattle. The ships were carrying tanks, railroad cars, aircraft, jeeps, gasoline in drums, poison gas, telegraph poles, ammunition, and sundry other materiel to prosecute the war in North Africa. At one point, with one of the ships failing to make nine knots, Ken Brown hailed the master of the merchant ship through the bullhorn, a bridge-operated loudspeaker. He signaled the need for the skipper to pick up the pace. Despite the security of a convoy, the "old shellback masters" loathed being convoyed and let their minders know with "belated turns, unanswered signals and insolent comebacks."

The merchant skipper signaled back to Ken with a gesture that advised *Plunkett*'s officer of the deck to screw off. Ken stared at the man a long moment, remembering Captain Standley's tactic for incentivizing stragglers to speed up—depth charges dropped at the stern of a malingering vessel. But there was a new skipper on board, and no one quite knew the mettle of the man, though they'd been warned.

Shortly after they'd learned they were losing Miller, one of Jack Collingwood's buddies off an old four-pipe destroyer told them they were getting their man Burke—or "that man Burke," as they'd known Edward J. Burke at the Naval Academy. Burke had captained the Navy football team that went down in defeat to Knute Rockne's Fightin' Irish, better known then as the Ramblers, at Soldier Field in 1928, and his team had lost another major game to Army at the Polo Grounds. That loss notwithstanding, Burke was one of thirteen players named to the 1928 College Football All-American Team selected, in part, by the legendary sportswriter Grantland Rice. That same fall, Burke also lost the intercollegiate, light heavyweight title in the final bout of that year's championship. In a profile that Rice wrote in October of 1928, and that was syndicated in newspapers throughout the country, he attributed Eddie Burke's stamina and "never say die" spirit to a "rough and ready" upbringing around the coal breakers of Northeast Pennsylvania. Rice noted that although Eddie didn't have to drive mules underground like some of his peers in coal country, he was surrounded by boys "less fortunate" and was obliged to fight opponents of a far different sort than he faced in the intercollegiate boxing ring. Though modest and soft-spoken, and one "who always lets the other fellow do the talking," Eddie deployed what Rice called a "cyclonic offense." He noted a certain fidgetiness in his twenty-year-old subject, a kid who would just as soon "start out for a hike over a mountain, or to break the bonds of civilization and shove off for wide-open spaces." Rice anticipated far-flung adventures for Eddie, expecting that one day he might "shove off for some little island where the natives are rebellious and need someone to get rough with them."

In the fourteen years since he'd left the Academy, Burke had climbed a few notches to rate a lieutenant commander's stripe. He'd married a woman who stood stately and glamorous in heels, and whose auburn hair and refined beauty were counterpoints to his rudely forged features. The older Eddie Burke got, the more he looked like a union boss, a man who'd dug himself out of the coal mines but wouldn't ever look as if he had. He'd segued from the Academy to service on two battleships, transitioned to submarines for several years in the mid-1930s, then did a stint in the Asiatic fleet in the late 1930s, racking up laudatory comments from his superior officers. The men who reported to Burke were less inclined to commend his abilities and more likely to begrudge the demeanor of a skipper who, when he had to, would physically knock a junior man out of his way on the bridge. One thing became quickly clear to some of the junior officers on *Plunkett*: that if Captain Burke were detached from this ship anytime soon, no one would feel compelled to send any kind of telegram.

After three weeks in Casablanca, *Plunkett* started back to the States with five other ships on February 21. They met a cluster of eleven merchant vessels the following afternoon and then, two days out, rendezvoused with yet a larger group out of Oran. It was a slow crossing, with little more to say officially about it than "steaming as before," a phrase scribbled repeatedly into the ship's deck logs, and that served as euphemism for the tedium that characterized so much of their time on the water. They dropped a depth charge on a school of fish. They practiced firing their 20mm, and their five-inch guns, too. One sailor failed to mind the stand clear signal during one test of the big guns and had his eardrums "broken." The days blurred into one long three-week crawl across the water, segmented by trips to the mess, duty on watch, drudgery, and hours at sleep, or attempted sleep, in the ship's compartments. At night, the men in the engineering department lay down in a soundscape of white noise: the blowers moving fresh air into the lower compartments, the rushing of seawater against the three-eighths-inch steel hull, and, governing all, the reassuring turn of the ship's screws. Jim Feltz labored through an obligatory stint as a mess cook. Irvin Gebhart and Ski slept in one day and were both put on report by Jack Collingwood. While a card game was played by the radio one morning, Gallagher cleaned his locker and later filled out the paperwork for a four-day leave, not liberty. His mother hadn't gotten any better, but she hadn't gotten any worse, either. In letters subsequent to the one that first reported her stroke, he learned more about her evening out with the Looney Band at an old-age home up off Adams Street. Something had gripped her from within, and she'd collapsed to the floor. Her blood pressure ran high, always had, and she'd never followed through on doctor's orders for potassium thiocyanate, or any of the medicines that might have helped relieve the symptoms, not the bromides or barbiturates or bismuth. She carried too much weight for her frame, she wouldn't rest, wouldn't slow down, and wound up for a spell in Boston State Hospital as a result. When she came out, and came home, her mind was intact but her mobility was ruined.

The morning after they docked in Brooklyn, Gallagher crossed the East River to Manhattan and boarded the New Haven Railroad for the five-hour run to Boston. It was a Saturday morning, the cars crowded with service personnel and civilians, all of them now more dependent on public transportation since the country had cold-turkey quit making automobiles after Pearl Harbor.

At South Station in Boston, John shunted from the railway to the streetcar and rode the familiar line into his Dorchester neighborhood. The home at No. 58 reared up out of a cluster of two dozen mature fruit trees—two varieties of peaches, the big Elbertas and a smaller one, too. There were pears, plums, apples, and cherries, both sweet and preserving. A bough from one tree reached so close to one of the kitchen windows they could literally lean out and pick fruit. As kids the children had harvested the sweet cherries and dragged them around the neighborhood in a cart, selling them for ten cents a square. As fast as they could pick them, they could sell them. Nothing was blooming yet as John came upon the house, but they all still stood in the yard by the recently turned earth where his brother Frank had buried another wreck of a car, John's car!, before he went off to the war.

On the porch that evening in March of 1943, a service banner hung in the window with a blue star each for him and Joe and Frank. Otherwise, little had changed in the months he'd been gone. He opened a door that was never locked and stepped into a foyer where a fine oak stairway climbed and turned for the second floor. There was the piano at the foot of the stairs, though none of them could manage much more than "Chopsticks." And there was *The Best Loved Poems of the American People*, with its purple dust jacket, on the telephone table, as if someone might be in need of verse during conversation. Ordinarily of a Saturday evening he'd have spotted his stout mother in the kitchen at work on the cast-iron stove she preferred, her gas stove notwithstanding. Supper on Saturday always included the beans she'd prepare in a crockpot, and the bread she'd baked on Friday. But Martha was bed-bound now, and he'd known he wouldn't greet her downstairs, but upstairs.

The stroke had spared her mind, and the mother he found was as ebullient as the woman who'd taught them how to spell "Mississippi" M-I, crooked letter, crooked letter, I, crooked letter, crooked letter, I, P-P-I, and who once shocked her children by placing these four tiles in a game of Scrabble: F-A-R-T. After Martha's husband died, she supplemented the residual income from her husband's employer with work, first in a nearby laundry when her youngest started school, then at sales in Cambridge, and finally at sales in a dress shop near Oakton Avenue. Until her sons went away to the CCC (Civilian Conservation Corps), she'd enforced a rule that had them home in the house by nine or nine-thirty, even when they were eighteen or nineteen years old. "What could you be doing out?" she'd say. "There's nothing out." She might discipline them by slapping their arms, but she was more likely to invoke the threat of "a thousand mortal sins" as a hedge against bad behavior.

With John's homecoming, and before she'd followed him up the stairs, his sister Helen dialed Charlie and Bernice, summoning them to the house at once. She wouldn't tell them why, just that it wasn't bad news. They gathered in an upstairs bedroom, Helen and Tom, and their sister Gertrude. Charlie and Bernice arrived with the Weatherstrip and the baby Mary, and John took to them at once, the baby first while the eighteen-month-old boy clung to his father's side, unnerved by a man who'd been a regular presence his first six months but who'd been gone since. It had been more than six months since he'd been home, and it seemed incongruous he could actually be here, while the globe was otherwise wracked with great convulsions. In Krakow that day, Amon Goeth and the SS had begun liquidating the city's Jews. Hitler flew back from Smolensk on a plane with a concealed bomb planted by an assassin that didn't explode because the cold air at high altitude froze the acid in the detonator cap. Frank Gallagher was still stateside, as was Joe Gallagher, so there was that much solace for Martha. And now John was home, and talking, catching them up on all the things he couldn't put in his letters. They were writing to him all the time, sending V-Mail. They'd get letters back from him with some parts excised by his censor, *Plunkett*'s engineering officer. For all the good the Navy had done, Charlie pointed out that evening, John still couldn't spell worth a shit, and didn't care much for apostrophes. As an example, he trotted out a classic line from a recent letter. "Hopping to here from you reel soon."

So much had changed since he was last home. The corner was not "what it used to be with all the boys in the Army, Navy, and Marines," John would write, waxing nostalgic for his old gang. He noted similar sea changes up at the Baker Chocolate factory, where he'd stopped to see the fellows still at home and to thank the union steward for mailing him copies of the *Boston Post*, which plopped onto *Plunkett*'s deck at mail call in bundles of fifteen and thirty-five.

His friend, Ruthie, and Frank's girl, Sophie, visited and commented on his appearance, which he later crowed about in a letter: "Thanks for the compliment on my marvelous looks and personality. I wish they were all true."

On John's last evening at home, Tom took out a small guitar he'd taught himself to play. He sang "Let the Rest of the World Go By" in a tremulous falsetto that ached melancholy over all of them. These concluding hours of his visit were inevitable, and they'd all heard them ticking ever louder as the evening approached and his night train to New York beckoned. He was in his dress blues now; they all had to travel in them. With the night deepening, the kids grew cranky, and Charlie announced the need to go back and warm up the apartment. He shook hands in the nonchalant way that brothers will, cognizant of the need to observe the moment with a gesture but cognizant, too, of the fact that a gesture between acquaintances felt somehow strange when applied to a brother. The lump in Charlie's throat prevented any talk, and so he hoisted the Weatherstrip and hurried from the room. A moment later, Bernice bundled Mary and stood to leave. John offered to walk her home, and Bernice demurred. He should stay with his mother. She was on her way across the street anyway to say good night to her mother and father.

She crossed the street to the home she'd moved into as a teenager, and that was bereft now of one son who'd been called up a year earlier, on the same day Joe Gallagher had, and another son who was only waiting for his birthday so he could enlist in the Navy. The Meehans had lost two sons-in-law as well, and the house was crowded with daughters who'd moved back home, each with a child and each of whom was a reminder of Bernice's own fate should

Charlie get called up. Twenty minutes later, with Charlie having had time enough to stir the coals in the boiler down in the cellar, to lie in a bed and bank it for the evening, she kissed her mother and father good night, and started back up Oakton Avenue toward Adams Street. There was snow on the ground, and the temperatures had dropped into the thirties, but it wasn't bitter. Not fifty yards into her trudge up the road, John caught up with her.

"Give me the baby," he said.

He'd had the Weatherstrip and Mary in his arms as long as he'd been home, and this one last chance to feel the heft of a little Gallagher in his arms was more than he could resist. There'd been the pudge of little Charlie in his arms when he'd come along that summer before the war, and Mary with the same thing, a weight, yes, but weight imbued with soul. It was as if he could feel the whole long promise of their lives in his arms as he held them. He wanted one last grasp of family before heading to South Station. They walked without talking as far as the Pierce house, the uncle gurgling baby noises at a niece who was soon asleep. The front of the Pierce house stretched a long way and featured two front doors. It had been there since the 1600s, when Dorchester was still far from the hum of settlement in Boston.

Bernice asked if John minded going back to the war. He told her he didn't. The fact was he minded a lot, but it was only the saying goodbye that he dreaded. Homesickness, like seasickness, no longer plagued him on *Plunkett*. It was the parting of the ways that hurt bad.

Charlie was itching to go now, never mind that hardship deferment. The incongruity of his relative youth (he would be twenty-eight that year) and his presence on the home front was abrasive. He'd recently stopped in a bar room and was set upon by a woman who wanted to know why he wasn't in the service, a confrontation that haunted him and wouldn't ever stop troubling him. The local draft board, they knew, had decided to retain one of the five Gallagher brothers, and it had been decided that Charlie would be the one. John and Frank and Joe were gone, and Tom was 1-A, and Charlie was going to stay 3-A. Bernice knew that he might try to override the draft board's objections, and she believed he would have, except for her. She lived in terror of irrational happenstance, especially the spontaneous combustion of appliances. She'd been afraid to learn how to ride a bike, or drive a car, and she'd been afraid of the two miles between her home and her mother's after marriage, and so she insisted Charlie move them back to Dorchester's Neponset neighborhood. She felt bad for him, but not so bad that she could release her grip.

At the top of Oakton Avenue, she and John looked up to the third floor at 677 Adams Street. The windows were bright, the apartment warmed. Mary's weight was all the more compelling as John walked her up the stairs to the landing. He passed off the baby to Bernice, and told her he wouldn't go in. She smiled and leaned in for a kiss, then went inside. Downstairs, he crossed the streetcar tracks on Adams, and at the corner of an intersection that lacked any appreciable urban appeal or a design that was anything but functional but would be dubbed a "square" one day and named for him, he turned and looked back up to the third floor. His brother Charlie stood in the window, the room warmed to yellow behind him, his figure in silhouette. John hoisted a hand quickly to dispel any more pathos, then turned, drew up the collar of his pea coat, and jogged back up Oakton Avenue.

=

Gallagher returned to the Navy Yard on St. Patrick's Day, in time for yet another Ship's Party at the Hotel St. George in Brooklyn. His date was an attractive moon-faced girl with an engaging smile. A ruffled collar bordered a V-neck that plunged just low enough to make it interesting, and an elastic waist pinched her dress, leaving the pleated lower drape free to swoosh as they jitterbugged the dance floor. One of the USO chaperones introduced Jim to a girl who smiled so brightly her eyes squeezed shut from friendliness. Jim had to own up to the fact that he didn't dance, though he had recently vowed to learn: His girl back home in St. Louis had made him promise.

Jim was a day or two away from receipt of a letter Betty had penned the day before. She was working now at the Wagner Electric Corporation in St. Louis, in an office at the heart of a massive brick plant that made electric motors, transformers, fans, hydraulic brakes, and air brakes. She was at last putting her secretarial school skills to work, and tweaking Jim with jokes she admitted were corny but that she couldn't resist.

"Why did the moron cut off his arm?"

"So he could write shorthand."

Jim had turned eighteen on February 5, and Betty had followed him across another threshold, to seventeen, on March 7. Over Christmas, at the Hotel New Yorker, during the time they'd had alone and after they'd declared their commitment to each other, Jim had said, "If you feel the same way on your birthday, I'll give you a ring."

His words had been echoing for Betty ever since. Seeing him at Christmas, and hearing him say this, crystallized her affection into something she knew was love. When they'd started going out, she didn't like him much. Passion hadn't got them together; her aunt

Mickey had. Jim was just a boy who worked with Mickey at the dime store, and he was company when they went out to the show. She'd kept him at arm's length early on and remembered that she'd been "sorta mean" to him even. Through January and February, writing letter after letter, Betty declared herself without reservation in language that Jim called "mush," and that he himself shied away from and advised Betty to shy away from, too. But she was having none of it. She wrote day after day, a dozen letters to every one she had from him, and she never failed to make a turn toward sweetness and light after she reported the news from home. "To begin the mush, I miss you . . . ," she wrote on a Monday in February when *Plunkett* was moored to the Jetty de Lune in Casablanca, and a record on the Victrola in the engineering department played ten times straight before the complaints finally got someone to shut it off.

Betty reminded him of her birthday in letter after letter and qualified her expectation with a side note that said if there wasn't any ring, she would understand that, too. There wasn't any ring for Betty on March 7. She had no idea where Jim was that day, whether he'd shipped out, or was in New York or Virginia. In fact, *Plunkett* was underway in the Atlantic making thirteen knots in rough seas. He phoned her as soon as he could when the ship docked in Brooklyn. Hearing his voice after more than two months without a letter, she nearly cried. And then he asked her if she felt the same way she said she had at Christmas. Hearing that question, she "nearly passed out." Jim promised to write immediately, and Betty then began a vigil, hoping against hope he might write a letter that had some mush in it. She'd never got a letter like that. Nor had she got any reciprocation to all of her declarations. "You know what," she wrote to him the day before the March 19 party at the St. George, "you never really did say you loved me nor have you wrote it. I tried to get you to say it over the phone, but you wouldn't so I just gave up." Betty rarely succumbed to frustration in her letters. She knew he was in the middle of this big thing, and she was writing about boys coming home wounded to St. Louis, and about others like Jim's friend Bob Bunch who wouldn't come home. And then, on the last day of January in 1943, Betty wrote this: "I hope you aren't one of those 53 that were lost. . . . I don't think you are because, well, it just won't be. Anyway, to me it seems that way but if you were, it is God's will and regardless what happens he will take care of you."

At the St. George that night in March of 1943, the chaperones spirited Gallagher's and Gebhart's girls away with a commitment to the same clock that doomed Prince Charming. Their girls worked at the Kearny Shipyard. They could do it all—rivet steel plates by day, jitterbug by night—but they wouldn't do everything. That Gebhart and Gallagher managed to hang on the entire evening without being prodded back to the ship by junior officers was accomplishment enough. They descended an elevator to the ground floor and emerged onto Clark Street, where the night hardly felt over, though liberty almost was. There would be no further options but for *Plunkett*. Checker cabs advertising fares at 20 cents for the first quarter mile, and a nickel for every quarter mile thereafter, swerved against the curbs and inhaled a half dozen pea-coated sailors at a throw for the three-mile trip back to the Navy Yard. Gallagher and Gebhart hopped into a cab first and were jammed by two more sailors coming in the other side. No one had to tell the cabbie where they were headed. He had steered beneath the Brooklyn Bridge, heading for Sands Street, when some unaccountable fracas broke out in the cab. A fistfight ensued within the confines of the vehicle, as Gallagher and Gebhart mixed it up with the other two passengers.

The night was not yet over—it never was—on Sands Street, which stretched from the head of the Brooklyn Bridge to the gates of the Navy Yard. The bars and grills steamed at full throttle, the street "as vivacious as a country fair," albeit with none of the wholesome pretensions. The uniform and clothing shops had battened down their hatches and stood between the bars like caesuras in the hub-bub. This street was where some sailors hoped to end up when they died. In the meanwhile, the street funneled them toward the gates of the Navy Yard, bracketed by two gatehouses where the Marine Guards were tapping down the hordes of drunk sailors, confiscating bottle after bottle.

Jim Feltz, who would one day strap a plundered German Mauser rifle to the inside of his trousers, feign a stiff leg, and secrete the thing out between these same gates in a throng of sailors bound for liberty, had come back to the ship with a clear head, and a uniform none the worse for wear. He didn't know what to tell Gebhart about his girl from Kearny. Maybe it was because he didn't drink himself into la-la land, or because they all sensed there was a stream of sugar flowing from St. Louis that he would not risk, or because he'd learned the ins and outs of the fire room so fast and with so much authority, but Jim, young as he was, was the man you went to when you had a problem and wanted a willing ear. This reputation was partly a function of not having much advice to give, a reticence that was widely interpreted by drunk men as wisdom. Jim shook his head, nodding. He'd listen, but what the hell could he tell Gebhart?

The Marines patted them down, and they passed into the yard, walking quietly past the somnolent Marines' barracks, the pipe and copper shops, the smithery, up Third Street, with the racket still general all over now. Hammers sounded off everywhere, and the smell of the acetylene torches made breathing an aggravation. Trying to sleep in the Navy Yard was miserable business, and when they didn't have to they wouldn't, preferring the YMCA or, better yet, a hotel in midtown where you could double or triple up in a room for 75 cents a night. But they were all on the ship tonight, tied up at Pier C, and minded by one of the ship's lieutenants (jg), a 1941 graduate of Yale University, John "Jack" Oliver, up on a wing of the bridge, wearing the khaki garrison cap he favored, watching them return.

For those who'd been home, there was the proximity of refreshed memory to savor, the afterglow, the phantom weight of a baby in arms to remember, and all those things said and unsaid. They couldn't know where they'd be headed tomorrow, but one thing Gallagher did know, and that he hadn't aired out on Oakton Avenue, was that he'd got a new job on *Plunkett*, courtesy of Ken Brown. From here on, he'd be a gunner on a 20mm Oerlikon machine gun, mounted in the no. 3 tub on the starboard side of the ship behind the no. 2 stack.

THE MED

PART II

Plunkett wardroom at Christmas 1942. Jack Collingwood is at far left. Ken Brown is at the head of the table. John Jolly is standing at rear (second from right). Jack Simpson is seated at the right with his hand on his chin. His wife, Peggy, is beside him.

7: THORNTON, COLORADO

SEPTEMBER 2016

Within an hour of Karen Brown Fratantaro's return call to me in May, she texted an image of her mother and father, a shot just taken of a couple in their mid-nineties, one on a walker, the other holding his arm, smiling for technology that was science fiction when they married. Ken wore a gray cardigan and a blue polo shirt. His hair was snow-white but comb-ably long, parted left to right. Anne looked seventy-five, not ninety-five, with straw-colored hair and teal-blue eyes all the more remarkable for the seasoning around them. Later, when her daughter Kerry showed me a picture of Anne in the 1940s, I asked how many movies she'd starred in as a young woman. You wouldn't have been able to look like Anne Welte Brown did and escape notice. Modeling, her daughter Kerry Haygood told me, that was what Anne was doing back in the day when she wasn't working for Gerald Murphy at the Mark Cross store on Fifth Avenue in New York. Gerald Murphy? I repeated the name because she'd referenced him as if everyone knew who he was. Yes, she said, and then I remembered him as the model for Dick Diver in F. Scott Fitzgerald's *Tender Is the Night*, a man who "won everyone quickly with an exquisite consideration and politeness that moved so fast and intuitively that it could be examined only in its effect." Gerald, Anne would tell me, was just like that.

On speakerphone in May, the timbre of Ken's voice betrayed his age but evinced at the same time the cadence of a deliberate man. As he recalled for me his memories of *Plunkett*—he never said *the Plunkett*, just as you wouldn't put an article in front of the name of someone you knew—he did so with due respect for attribution of information, and a fidelity to facts. He spoke like a man given to sentences crafted for reports and communications that addressed men at attention. Even at ninety-five, he seemed capable of a stentorian bellow.

Several months after we started talking on the phone, I flew to Denver. Kerry and her husband, Jerry, waited for me at the arrival gate with my name spelled out on a card but for the last five letters of my surname, which had been asterisked out in consideration of privacy. HIPAA might have something to say about me outing you, Kerry told me when I asked about the asterisks. Kerry was in her early sixties, and had just returned from Alaska, where she'd gone to behold its calving glaciers, its whales, the Northern Lights, and the bears, especially the bears. At home, she'd bookmarked a website that trained a camera on brown bears that fished falls in the Katmai National Park, and she was active in chat rooms with other bear spotters. She was tall, with striking green eyes that made you look twice. She was direct and decisive, and you might have divined that her father had been an officer in the military. She didn't hedge anything in conversation. You could develop rapport with her in about two minutes. Jerry was a colonel in the Army, a medical doctor, and more than that, a graduate of the University of Iowa, who'd made over his basement as a shrine to Hawkeyes football.

We drove the highway north to Thornton, a Denver suburb sprung from grassland and farmland in the 1950s and evolved as a town without a center, where the schools and municipal offices and shopping malls and peninsular housing developments were mere appendages to divided eight-lane roadways. Before this trip, I hadn't made any hard and fast commitments about where I was going with my deep dive into *Plunkett's* history, but I knew that meeting Ken Brown, after talking to him as much as I had on the phone, was an opportunity that shouldn't be disregarded. So much has been made of his generation, the so-called greatest generation, that it was hard now to reference them without genuflection, or to say anything about them that didn't tend toward hyperbole. Our regard for them was more religious than grounded. We were led to believe they'd been steeled by the Depression and were capable of withstanding more hardship than Baby Boomers, or any subsequent generation. We rued the possibility of war in our time because the millennials were incapable of switching gears from joysticks to rifles and because, for so many other reasons—their zombie-like regard for their phones, their cosseted childhoods—we found them wanting. To believe this is to deny how woefully unprepared for war we were in 1941 and to ignore what the Brits made of us when we first waded into battle in North Africa.

And yet, the more the greatest generation receded from us, the more we lionized them. Partly, it was the passage of all these years, and that they were still with us. Why not one more tribute. We conflated what they'd done with the enduring, idealized images we retained of men in movies and documentaries who were unequivocally right to do what they'd done in their day. We couldn't feel the same about the guys from Vietnam or the wars in the Middle East, which felt optional, more the prerogative of a political agenda than a matter of national or existential necessity. We'd had to do what was done from 1941 to 1945. In retrospect, but for the curmudgeon, there was no question about that. It was as universally agreed upon as gravity. In 2016, when so much seemed to be coming apart in America, we had that common ground at least.

Jerry steered us into one of Thornton's recently birthed neighborhoods, a development built by KB Homes that advertised itself with a huge balloon at the end of a long tether, an image reminiscent of the barrage balloons floating over the harbors at Palermo and Naples during the war. Ken and Anne were new to Thornton, having arrived the previous year after more than forty years in the same house in La Jolla, where they'd moved after Ken retired from the Navy in 1972.

I met him in the great room of his house. He shuffled toward me on his walker, smiling buoyantly though he'd taken a fall that morning and his arm was bandaged from wrist to elbow. He was a slight man, which was partly a function of age wearing him down but mostly a matter of his natural build. He wore shorts against the heat, and shoes that accommodated the swelling in his feet. He was on the verge of ninety-six, and all the great orbits of his life had spiraled down to this room, by and large, where he and Anne whiled their days. Anne's physical well-being was more the matter of concern at present, and family were coming in this weekend, from Ireland and from California, to say goodbye. Anne had rallied in anticipation, and sat to Ken's right at dinner, their hands when not needed for utensils defaulted to one's upon the other's.

They'd met in early 1944, in New York City, Ken just back from the Mediterranean, from Sicily and Salerno and Anzio, and like many off *Plunkett*, drinking heavily. This one evening he and Jack Collingwood were walking through the Theater District when he spotted a woman with a mass of platinum-blond hair piled up as voluminously as the do on one of the girls made famous by the artist Charles Dana Gibson at the turn of the century, the Gibson Girls. Ken had had just the glimpse of her face going by, the nose pert, the skin unblemished and freshly powdered, the lips engaged in chatter with a girlfriend, debriefing a play they'd just seen. Her radar sensed his distraction, and she swerved her eyes at him for barely a moment in passing. He was just another serviceman out on the town, a dime a dozen these guys. He jerked from a standstill, bereft of a plan, and followed her, driven by the need to do something, anything, or else regret forever after that he'd never tried. He touched the toe of his shoe to the heel of hers, halting her stride and precipitating a new tack that would stay the course for seventy-three years.

Anne Welte had grown up the daughter of an engineer and a nurse on Riverside Drive, in a spacious flat with views of the river. Her mother was from Ireland; her father was from Switzerland and vigilant. When dates brought her home, and her father knew she'd returned, he would cough and knock on the door from the inside if he thought they'd spent too much time on the stoop. On her first date with Ken, he'd started lighting up as usual. As the date deepened and he reached for another cigarette, she issued an ultimatum: This first date would be the last date if smoking was to be part of the program. There was no smoking after that.

The Browns raised five children, losing one as a teenager and another son, an Air Force veteran, a few years before I met them.

Ken had done thirty years in the service, but retiring wasn't how he talked about leaving the Navy. Getting fired, or getting canned, was more often the language he used. His troubles had been complicated irrevocably in Annapolis, or the trade school, as he referred to it, the way people will hide the fact that they've attended Yale by saying they went to school in New Haven. In 1963, he'd been appointed to the Naval Academy as deputy commandant of midshipmen and took it upon himself to mount a campaign against the school's long-established hazing traditions, conducted by upperclassmen "untrained in indoctrination," as Ken put it. He believed there was better use of a plebe's time, but no one else thought so. His campaign to make changes at the storied old school did not go over well, and they canned him by sending him to Vietnam in 1965. Kerry, as a little kid, was so incensed by the move that she and a sister pelted the admiral's house with rocks one night. Anne remembered one of her friends apologizing to her about the transfer, as if her naval officer husband, in failing to come to Ken's side on the hazing issue, was partly to blame for sending him to Vietnam.

Before dinner that evening, Ken and one of his granddaughters and I were chatting to the side of the kitchen. Gemma was closing in on forty and had come out to see grandparents who'd lived close to her until the previous year. She worked as a mental health counselor, and she joined me in a barrage of questions for Ken. Meanwhile, things were heating up in the kitchen, with Kerry at the helm and perhaps in need of a hand. Ken looked from the activity at the stove to the drink in Gemma's hand. "Slug it down," he said, and then directed her to start serving.

It was an old-school moment, and though Gemma seemed fully vested in the twenty-first century, she followed her grandfather's lead cheerfully and without an inkling of visible protest. "He ruled the house," Kerry told me about growing up in Ken Brown's home. "He controlled everything." When she and her sisters were girls, they weren't allowed to sit in the front seat of the car lest an accident "mar a pretty face." Out to breakfast a year later at a place he liked in a little strip mall moored off the highway, I picked up the check when it came. Ken asked for it, and I tried to wave him off casually, reaching for my wallet and meeting eyes with the waiter as if to smoothly and quietly make payment. Ken was having none of it. "Let's not horse around, Jim," he said sternly, reaching for the check, and I offered it up without hesitation.

If through his years in the Academy and his decades as a naval officer, his DNA had lengthened a thread of ineradicable command in his personality, rigidity of thought had not taken root. He didn't have all the answers, and he told me so repeatedly. He questioned everything still and didn't subscribe to doctrine or any political point of view that I could reckon. I steered clear of talk that might lead us into current events, and that might lower a political boom between our perspectives. I listened for Ken's politics. I couldn't help myself, but if I was keeping a vigil over my own opinions, so was he. Except that nothing Ken said led me to believe he marched to the usual beat of a military drummer. When we broke from the breakfast table that morning, and Ken moved his walker toward the door, I noticed for the first time that there was a Sierra Club sticker affixed to his cross-brace.

After three years in Vietnam, one as a naval attaché in Saigon and a second as squadron commander in the Tonkin Gulf, charged with dispatching helicopters to retrieve downed American pilots, the Navy put him out to pasture as an ROTC commandant at the University of New Mexico. His last four years in the Navy were spent drilling students for service at a time when campus unrest was boiling over, and when a man in uniform on campus was a target. Kerry had been so concerned about her father's safety that, somehow, she'd found herself in a meeting with both her father and the president of the university. Growing up in a house where you took a backseat to preserve appearances did not produce a shrinking violet. On the contrary, Kerry told the president that he should shut down a scheduled rock concert on campus if he wanted to preserve peace one particular weekend. Ken laughed over the recollection of his daughter's strident directives, though they hadn't surprised him.

It did surprise me that he didn't seem to harbor any ill will toward the student protesters who constantly disrupted his drilling. There was one student in particular, Manny Smith, who used to run amok amid his parading cadets. Manny did this with the regularity of clockwork, twirling in and among the ranks of ROTC students like a dervish sprung from the San Francisco hippy enclave Haight-Ashbury, tempting a stern response from a naval officer. Ken let him conduct his protest while he himself conducted his cadets. At graduation, Manny sent a note addressed to "Captain Brown," explaining his political opposition to everything Captain Brown stood for but noting as well that he believed Captain Brown to be "an honest man." It was a letter that moved Ken at the time, and moved him still, so much so that there was a long pause before he could finish telling what Manny had written. In all the time I spent talking to Ken, he'd remembered evaluations of his standing by this man only, Manny Smith. There'd been another evaluation about his facility in *Plunkett*'s director control tower, a small chamber—a metal box, really—manned by the gunnery officer and five crew on the highest part of the ship's superstructure. Captain Burke had had something to say about Ken's work in the director, but Ken didn't volunteer what that was, and wouldn't.

Less than a year after my first visit, Anne Brown's condition had deteriorated to the point where relocation to an assisted-living home was now a necessity. Anne and Ken moved out of their home in Thornton for a $9,000-per-month facility that he loathed from the moment he stepped inside. He didn't like how lukewarm the food was when served. He didn't like how they wheeled residents out to flat-screen televisions and parked them for the day. He had ideas about ways they might improve their care. He voiced as much to a supervisor, who reminded him he was not on a Navy ship; they did things differently at that facility.

Anne's situation worsened rapidly, the seizures every day more frequent. One day in August, after I'd sent Ken some notes about *Plunkett*, he phoned as he always did after he went through the documents and my notes. When we'd start talking, I'd frequently deploy the usual pleasantries, referencing the weather and asking after his well-being and Anne's. Ken never treated such questions as anything to skate past. "We're moving from crisis to crisis," he'd say, or something like that, and I gradually stopped with the pleasantries, understanding he felt obliged to answer "how are you" with honesty and substance. We started in on discussion of another ugly scene from the war, involving glide bombs, and Ken's voice thickened and silenced momentarily. I felt bad when I steered close to the bad stuff I'd once again asked him to remember. But that wasn't it. "We lost

Anne yesterday, Jim," he said and then told me he was going to pass the phone to Kerry.

Later in the same day Anne died, they moved Ken out of the facility and back into the house in the KB Homes neighborhood. He'd always said he himself planned to stay around only so long as Mom needed him, then he'd fade away, too. That didn't happen in the wake of Anne's departure and cremation. He was as strong as ever, according to Kerry, though he did admit, when I'd accidentally again asked how he was, to "stumbling and fumbling" through his days. He needed help in the morning, getting underway, but could pretty much manage on his own through the middle part of the day. In the late afternoon, Kerry would stop by to prepare dinner. Jerry would come, and then go home, and Kerry, for the first few weeks after Anne's death, stayed over. There were all kinds of matters to sort, not the least of which was the matter of Anne's headstone. They had a place at a military cemetery in Denver, and they would share a stone over their cremated remains. Ken wanted some language on the stone, but he wouldn't have anything trite. There wasn't much room, and there certainly wouldn't be anything like "In Memory Of." What he decided on in the end was just three words, two of which returning servicemen had encountered all over America upon their return from the war. When he shared the three of them with Kerry—"Bravo Zulu Mom" (translation from Navy parlance: "Well done, Mom") —he told her to be sure she put a comma in there.

At my last visit, in the fall of 2017, the two Shih Tzu poodles Ken had on loan from Kerry worked up a racket as she and I made our way from the garage to the door. They'd been fitted with bark collars, but from behind the door, Ken was shouting for them to quiet down anyway. He'd just turned ninety-seven, but he was indistinguishable from the last time I'd met him. There was the same snow-white hair, the same depth of voice and readiness to smile. Around his neck he wore a medallion that may have been a button to press if he needed help in an emergency.

On a calendar affixed to the stainless-steel refrigerator, I saw my name, "Jim," noted in the squares for the weekend, and a second phrase under my name, "Pest Guy," that was a reference to a man coming to take care of some insect problems but might have been attributed as well to someone coming around asking lots of questions. Ken had been a reluctant participant in my attempts to tell his story, though his reluctance had nothing at all to do with *Plunkett* and what that ship did during the war, but with his own part in all that action, lest anyone think his role was in any way more significant than others'. But I'd read all of his commendations and had been through the deck logs and war diaries and action reports and had seen him up there in the director day after day, night after night, hour after hour, managing the ship's battery of guns. Every shot fired in anger by *Plunkett* had been under his watch, and though there might be something to celebrate in the ship's successes, what Ken dwelled on more were those other times. More resounding in his recollection was the memory of all the things he might have done well, and not those that he had.

We talked for hours that weekend, with Ken standing propped in his walker much of the time. We steamed through days on *Plunkett* but as often as not detoured into other areas. He'd recently watched all of Ken Burns's film on Vietnam, from which he learned things he'd never known and that had prompted him to reconsider his ideas about people and events. He'd worked on occasion with General Westmoreland in Vietnam and said they'd all considered him something of a "superhero" back in the day. Now Ken allowed that there were things he hadn't known about Westmoreland, and that if he had he might have thought differently. He talked about the tribulations of women in the service academies. Where some might believe that a man nearing one hundred, who'd been forged in another era, might object to women at the academies, their presence was not an issue for Ken. What he really objected to was the treatment of these women. He ached for these girls who'd come into the academies, dreaming the big dream that he'd dreamed, and were undone by old-school behavior. His objection to their treatment was not unlike his objection to the treatment of plebes at the trade school more than fifty years ago. See something, say something, was a Ken Brown mantra. His ship's namesake, Charles P. Plunkett, got into "frequent brushes with public opinion." He was a man who did not shy away from saying what he thought, "though politicians and a part of the press vilified him for it." If a destroyer was bound to meld with the personal characteristics of its namesake, so, too, it would seem, was the personality of its gun boss.

On my last night in Thornton, we dined at an Italian restaurant in one of the town's malls, at a table beside six women in their seventies who might have been celebrating a birthday for all the wine and laughter erupting from their tabletop. Jerry and I were each going for the shrimp alfredo, but when Ken emerged from contemplation of the menu with something that was both pedestrian and exotic, bison lasagna, we swerved in that direction, and we three ended up ordering the same thing. Throughout dinner, Ken glanced at the neighboring party as the conviviality pulsed on some shared anecdote. He would glance down at his meal, or draw from his wine, as grimly fixed as a gargoyle. As we finished dinner, Ken told Kerry he wanted her to approach the table and tell the women he'd like to pay for their meal. She rose from our table at once, the daughter of a man who'd spent all his life giving orders at work and at home, and went to them, telling them her father wanted to pay their bill. She explained further that her mother, his wife, had recently died and that their spirits were a real buoy to him this evening. That, Kerry said, and he was also shopping for another wife. They laughed hard at that and lifted their glasses to him, and Ken asked me what Kerry had said. I told him, and he beamed.

Once their bill was settled, and we were waiting on ours, one of the women at the neighboring table stood and came to him, to shake his hand and to embrace him as best she could. The other women idled at their table, quiescent in the aftermath of dinner and this surprise from the neighboring table. When the first woman stepped away from Ken, the second in this party of six communed with her friends in a shared glance, and then rose to make her way to him. One by one in turn they rose, as if from a script written ages ago, and bent at his side.

They did not deign to talk to him from a standing position, but took a knee, each of these women in her seventies, like novitiates, so they could engage with him at eye level. He was old enough to be their father, and I believe that each of them, in turn, recognized that this moment of communion with a man from a generation they'd all lost was pure serendipity. The moment lingered, one of them coming to him after another, and I wondered that we were still capable of this much grace in America, at this table by a window in a restaurant on a still warm October evening.

8: SICILY

JULY 1943

Getting underway, few of the crew ever knew where they were headed. Figuring that out, from communication that leaked out of the radio shack, from scuttlebutt, hunches, and by osmosis, was a rampant enterprise until word came down from the bridge. The day before the Fourth of July, *Plunkett* steamed east toward Gibraltar from Mers el-Kebir, a seaport neighboring Oran in Algeria, to rendezvous with a convoy that included three minelayers. That was interesting and could mean only one thing: that there were plans to lay mines. Somewhere. They shepherded the ships back into Oran and then into Mers el-Kebir, where the Stars and Stripes rippled from the heights of British ships in fraternal acknowledgment of Independence Day. The proximity to all those British ships inspired one of *Plunkett*'s boatswain's mates to borrow some of the cousins' jargon. Instead of calling out, "Sweepers, man your brooms," when it was time to turn to, the would-be bloke piped up, "A clean sweep down bloody well forward and fucking well aft." The profanity appalled the ship's junior officers, who emptied out of the wardroom at once and dressed down the foulmouthed boatswain's mate. It never happened again.

When the big ships moved out of Mers el-Kebir the day after the Fourth of July—the light cruisers *Brooklyn*, *Philadelphia*, and *Birmingham*, as well as the big British ships, an aircraft carrier, and some twenty destroyers—*Plunkett* idled in the rear, and only then got underway as an escort for a convoy puttering north at eight knots. They knew then that wherever they were going, they weren't going to be part of the first wave in. Underway on the 6th, Hap Jolly called the men to the mess, as fraught as ever in the countenance, this time with good reason. He confirmed the scuttlebutt: They were not going to Sardinia, they were going to Sicily as part of the Allied invasion, code-named Operation Husky. They'd missed the hot action off Casablanca, and now it looked as if they'd play second fiddle off Sicily, too. Still, their mission was vital. In addition to the minelayers, *Plunkett*'s convoy included seven cargo ships, known as Liberty ships because they were purpose-built to transport the materiel that would win the war. Each was laden with ammunition that, the executive officer told them, had to get in. "No matter what," Gebhart scribbled in his journal that night.

After Hap confirmed Sicily as their destination, *Plunkett* began to call general quarters at dawn and at dusk, when German bombers were most likely to come at them out of the sun rising and the sun setting. They steamed east past the mountains of Algeria, minding minelayers and merchant ships in this first follow-up convoy to what had shaped up to be the largest invasion force assembled in the history of the world, with more than 3,000 vessels and some

160,000 troops on the verge of opening a Second Front in Europe at last. So momentous was the undertaking that King George had come over from England to see off an invasion force that formed a mile-wide column sixty miles long.

The seas roughened in the hours ahead of D-day on July 10. The spray was battering the gun tubs, and the ships were plunging into holes that challenged the most seasoned of sailors. Battle suppers of steak, eggs, and all the trimmings erupted from the holds of their stomachs, confirming what hadn't been so obvious: that the Med was not a lake compared to the Atlantic but a sea itself. After dark, the conditions no better, the klaxon sounded for another run to general quarters. This time, though, they knew what was coming. Worried that Navy gunners might shoot first and ask questions later, the Army had informed the Navy that friendly transports would be passing by at five hundred feet, headed for drop zones outside Gela on Sicily's southern shore. Topside, the wind was stiff at 35 miles per hour, but overwhelmed by the drone of aircraft, sliding by three planes to a vee in a vast formation blanketing the sky over the ship.

Topside, the men on *Plunkett* cocked their heads for a look at transports so close they might have hit them with spuds. Some of *Plunkett*'s sailors tried counting for a while, reckoning hundreds, and then just marveled at the sky train, stirred suddenly by a feeling of fraternity for these fellow travelers, each of whom was poised to give up everything—their lives, yes, but more than that, their futures. These were men, like themselves, who'd put themselves in harm's way for the welfare of others, a circumstance capable of moving them profoundly.

Before they'd left the States, Gallagher had acquired an official *Our Navy* portrait of *Plunkett* docked in Brooklyn, standing out in a fresh coat of light gray paint. He had Thomas "Cactus Jack" Garner sign his name just under the photographer's insignia on the back. Hugh Francis Geraghty put his name and rating, F1/C (fireman first class) right above the insignia. And then Gallagher kept going, gathering signatures that linked each man to this ship and to him for posterity. "Jim Dale Feltz Mo. F1/C" penned his name, abbreviation of state, and rating in block letters at the top left. Dutchie Gebhart was in there just to the left and below the insignia. As his shipmates congregated on the back of the photo, Gallagher penned his own name, adding "King of the Reserves," but then he scratched that out. He was one among them, and that meant something. He crowded the entire backside with the names of shipmates, eighty-five all told, until there was no room for a man edgewise. No matter what happened, he didn't want to forget them.

In the morning, *Plunkett* called its crew to battle stations well before dawn, as if any of the men needed rousing, as if mulling what was to come had not sowed seeds of trepidation and other feelings apt to keep a man up at night. At the "ugly shock of a summons to judgment," as one destroyer officer referred to the call for general quarters, Ken Brown donned his helmet and a life vest made of kapok, a waxy, silk-cotton fiber harvested from tropical trees. He hurried from his stateroom to the bridge, and then up a ladder on the outside of a round barbette to the fire control director. His battle station was mounted on the highest part of the ship, was shaped like a breadbox of compromised width, and could fit six men, three in back and three more in front before a metal screen at their backs.

As the ship's gun boss, Ken sat in front, on a spring-set knucklehead seat that folded up when he wasn't on it. Jim Bush, his pointer, was immediately to his right, though set slightly lower, and Bing Miller, the trainer, was to the right of Jim. Bonnie Baker was in the rear of the director, on the range finder, and the two radar operators flanked Bonnie. The radar antennas were mounted to the roof of the director, but there was an observation hatch on the upper slope of the breadbox, above Ken's seat, and two telescope ports just below, where Bush and Miller, the pointer and trainer, tracked targets. The director controlled the ship's four five-inch guns, and the gun boss controlled the director.

Just after first light, they sighted a derelict whaleboat, detached from another ship like theirs, the *Swanson*, that had been rammed by another destroyer in a mishap the day before. The Americans had assaulted Sicily's south coast in three sectors on D-day (code-named Dime, Cent, and Joss), and *Plunkett* was now driving into the middle, the Dime sector at Gela. They'd been steaming all night on two boilers, one each in the forward and aft fire rooms. Now, on the edge of Gela, Jack Collingwood called down to Gallagher's aft fire room for the no. 1 boiler. There was no telling how much steam they'd need off Gela. As the burner man lit the boiler, the convoy ceased zigzagging and slowed to the pace of a man walking as Gela reared up in their sights, the city set high on a plateau 150 feet above the sea, little and chalk-gray but imposing. The Greeks had founded the city, and since antiquity it had been renowned for things that fell from the sky: In 456 B.C. an eagle had dropped a tortoise shell from its talons and killed the playwright Aeschylus. In better days, olive groves, vineyards, and wheat fields hemmed in thirty-two thousand residents. Today, with the Allies trying to consolidate their hold on the city from the inside out, and German tanks marshaling in and tightening the noose, Luftwaffe bombers had replaced eagles as the principal threat from the air.

Whether the Allies could hold the beachhead they'd established the day before was still in doubt as *Plunkett* ushered its charges into the roadstead off Gela. The Army Air Force was nowhere to be seen, leaving the skies to the Germans but for spotter planes sprung by two American cruisers. Already Luftwaffe bombers had scored major hits in the Dime sector—on a destroyer, *Maddox*, that sent 203 men and 8 officers to the bottom, and on a landing craft that killed 20 soldiers and a sailor. The Army's standing was just as wobbly. The congested beaches lacked the necessary manpower to empty the landing vessels, and the Navy LSTs (landing ship, tanks) couldn't get the armor off as fast as the Army needed it.

Meanwhile, the Italians and Germans were counterattacking with light (ten-ton) Renault and Fiat tanks, and seventy-five-ton Tiger tank behemoths. Shortly after *Plunkett* arrived, the Army called for naval gunfire and the cruiser *Savannah* dispatched round after round onto tanks two miles outside the city center. The destroyer *Glennon* pumped 193 rounds of five-inch shells into the midst of a counterattack. The Army, which hadn't thought much of the Navy's role as an accessory to what it was doing ashore, gave up that prejudice as Navy shells routed tanks like cue balls that not only scattered formations but detonated one target after another. To be in the midst of all this at last was exhilarating, even if *Plunkett* had yet to weigh in with her own shells.

Enemy planes bore down on the anchorage all day long, drawing great geysers from the harbor when they missed but now and then finding purchase in one of the milling ships. As aircraft came into view, the men in *Plunkett*'s director would turn hopefully to their range finder, Bonnie Baker, whose eyesight was so marvelous that his revelation of things at a distance was as astounding as a magician's trick. But all day long it was the same thing: German, German, German, Italian, German—Messerschmitt and Focke-Wulf fighters and the Heinkel and Dornier and Junkers Ju 88 and Stuka bombers, all of these aircraft, until now, more figments than threats, more familiar to Ken Brown as silhouettes on identification charts he studied in his stateroom, in the wardroom, and in the director. He hadn't been to gunnery school; there hadn't been the luxury of time. After Jolly was made executive officer, he'd inherited Hap's role as the ship's gun boss. Everything he'd learned had been on the job.

Toward late afternoon, one wave of bombers drew a bead on an ammunition ship *Plunkett* had brought in, the *Robert Rowan*, and planted one that exploded in the bowels of the ship. The initial hit scattered the smaller vessels in its apron, but they boomeranged back to evacuate the stricken ship. She smoldered all afternoon and then, the magazines kindled at last, blew in a giant stalk of dark smoke that blossomed into a head of even darker smoke that begot yet another lighter one, the ship's ammunition blazing smoky trails out of the main mass all the while.

From his observation hatch, Ken watched the Liberty ship burn, ruing the operation of Murphy's Law, which allowed the Germans to not only destroy the ship but to disable it in shallow water so it wouldn't sink and be still, but settle on the bay floor and burn as a beacon, beckoning sorties from airfields in the near distance.

Plunkett wrapped up its mine-laying operations after dark, and backed off general quarters to Condition II, which kept some of the gun crews at battle stations. John Oliver darkened the ship well after dark, not sunset as usual—there was too much to do—and Ken settled into his seat in the director, fidgeting for a wedge in that space that would allow some sleep. Five minutes after the ship dimmed, the klaxon brought all of them to full alert at 9:50 p.m., concurrent with the arrival of several enemy dive-bombers. Ken came fully awake at the ship's harsh summons and popped out of the hatch to the god-blasted *Robert Rowan* still burning away. Enemy planes attacked from all sides, hedge-hopping through a roadstead that was smeared here and there suddenly with sheets of red and white tracers. At the same time, higher-flying bombers were dropping magnesium flares that fell like stars parachuting in from the heavens, illuminating ships and men in a sickly yellow light.

At the stern of the ship, Jim Feltz hunkered with the after repair party in a compartment just beneath the fantail, poised to pounce at a moment's notice. It was his group's job to mitigate damage to the ship, whether from shell or bomb, torpedo or near miss. If a ship didn't go down straightaway, like *Maddox* (and the vast majority would not), it was likely the ship would stay afloat for hours on end. Mostly *Plunkett*'s damage control parties trained to fight fire. Until something happened, the after party and the midship repair party, on the main deck by the searchlight, idled at station, as anxious as players on a bench, waiting for the whistle. Jim's compartment was close and tight and dark, dogged down as a matter of maintaining watertight integrity. But the ruckus was more than they could abide in the dark, and so one or the other of them kept popping out of the hole to see what was what.

In the no. 2 gun tub, jutting from the starboard side of the ship like a pugnacious chin, John Gallagher put on a helmet and a kapok life vest. He shoved himself against a brace of C-shaped shoulder rests and cinched a belt across his lower back. His loader, Tom Garner, snapped a sixty-three-pound drum of shells into the breech. Theoretically, they could fire 450 rounds per minute, but in fact, they were limited to the sixty shells contained in each magazine. An entire drum could be emptied in seven-and-a-half seconds. The third man in their tub was a handler, who'd change the gun barrel if it grew too hot, or a talker, who was to maintain contact on headphones with the assistant gunnery officer. Unlike the situation for the gun boss upstairs, and the men in the ship's four gun mounts, the precipitation of their fire was devoid of input from radar and plotting room computers. "You see 'em, you shoot 'em" was the standing order. In the seven minutes after the call to battle stations, they could see nothing near enough to shoot.

In the director, Ken wore headphones that connected him to each of his four gun captains in the five-inch mounts, and the plotting room where men and primitive analog computers coordinated information coming in from the director, from the ship's radar, the ship's course, ship's speed, and weather conditions, to optimize the guns' line of fire. A squawk box they'd rigged in the director linked Ken by voice to the bridge. They were anxious for something to pop on their fire control radar, but nothing had by the time *Plunkett*'s 20mm guns started sputtering after targets. It was three minutes before 10 p.m., and now Ken's headphones crackled with communication that seemed unbelievable: hold fire. They were now getting targets on their fire control radar. The sky was full of burst flares and planes and anti-aircraft fire (ack-ack), and they were in a position to make a difference, and the plotting room—Burke—was telling him to hold his fire.

With the 20mm guns blazing at targets that had to be close, two eggs from a single stick of bombs landed one hundred yards beyond the fantail and concussed the ship like a bowl of Jell-O. A nearby ship was straddled even closer, and its stern literally bounced out of the water.

The ship's 20mm guns and 1.1-inch kept up a counterattack that averaged a shell per second for minute after interminable minute as Burke maneuvered his boat through the roadstead. The gunners knew what had happened to *Maddox*, and they were pushing away a reprisal of a like incident with all the more fury, elevation safety angles on their guns now more suggestion than prohibition. One plane swooped over the forward five-inch gun mount of another destroyer in their squadron, *Niblack*, clearing the ship by ten feet. The machine gunners dipped the angles of their barrels perilously low, riddling whatever they could, including the shield of destroyer *Benson*'s director and its radar, to boot. Friendly fire was nicking personnel and materiel all over the harbor.

For some unaccountable reason and timing borne of the same bad luck that kept *Robert Rowan* smoldering through the night, the Army Air Force had dispatched 144 transports packed with paratroopers for drop zones inland from Gela. There wasn't any need for these planes. The Allies already held the positions these troopers were charged with securing. They were dispatched nevertheless, and the Army made a belated effort to tell the Navy they were coming. Not everyone got the memo.

As *Plunkett*'s 20mm guns sought the low-flying aircraft, Ken could do nothing but stand up out of the observation hatch and watch it all. He'd got the order to hold fire but not the reason for it. The harbor was a tracery of countless red and white streaks, each gossamer thread trailing off as it burned out short of any mark. The bombs came down among the ships, mostly missing and erupting in great geysers of seawater.

While *Plunkett*'s machine guns spewed shells at anything and everything, Ken's legs started trembling unaccountably. When he sat on his knucklehead seat, he stitched anxiety into the plate at his feet. Standing made no difference. His weight did nothing to mitigate this awful new condition. He elbowed himself up out of the hatch, and let his legs dangle, but even dangling they were trembling. The night was now a free-for-all, the 20mm guns chasing enemy planes and rumors of planes. The harbor percolated with the upheavals of five-hundred-pound bombs. The sky was filled with droning aircraft and with the toxic light of magnesium flares, the most unwelcome light he'd ever seen. The parachutes didn't seem to let down the flares so much as hold them up. Ken had been training for this moment for five-and-a-half years, this moment of live ammunition, wondering all the while how he'd *be*. He was getting his answer now in this yellow light, and he hated it.

After twenty-one minutes, *Plunkett*'s machine gunners finally relented, and Burke started steering for *Robert Rowan*. The Army was shuffling its planes into the midst of this German assault like a deck of cards, Burke knew, one kind of silhouette indistinguishable from the other. It was a fiasco, and the best possible thing he could do at the moment was lie to. His five-inch guns weren't part of the problem. There was that, at least, and his machine guns weren't getting anything except, perhaps, other Allied ships. As aircraft flared in the darkness, and plummeted for the sea in fiery streaks, it was understood that the imperiled men were as likely—more than likely—to be American. With no way to know whose planes were whose, he brought *Plunkett* into the pall of smoke fogged off the damaged Liberty ship and cut the ship's engines to wait it out. Shortly before 11 p.m., *Plunkett* was lying to with its stern pointing to the moon.

At 11:30 p.m., Ken was still in the director, his legs quiescent at last, when a U.S. Army transport plane flew over the ship's stern at slow speed and low altitude burning one red light. That one was getting through, but 23 of the 144 transports in all had not, had been downed in a holocaust of friendly fire. John Oliver secured the ship. *Robert Rowan* burned. *Plunkett* hunkered in the pall, shrouded from attack, waiting on dawn, baptized at last and schooled as well in the fog of war.

9: PALERMO

JULY–AUGUST 1943

In the small hours of the morning, lying to near *Gleaves* and *Niblack*, and with *Benson* nursing the repercussions of friendly fire and a near miss, the men on *Plunkett* understood that, all things considered, they were better off here than ashore. Fires burned on the hillsides, and all night long came the dull explosions of shells thumping earth and enemy positions. Lieutenant General George S. Patton was now ashore. It was his Seventh Army they'd landed in Sicily.

Plunkett called everyone to battle stations an hour before dawn, and though the bridge formally released the crew from general quarters a little more than an hour later, in fact few of them shrunk from station, not that day. At dusk, enemy dive-bombers bore down on them again, and Ken slewed his five-inch guns to pump more than a half dozen rounds at targets they'd realized up in the director. He missed, but his legs in the thick of it were fine. He hadn't been afraid, he assured himself now, after flogging himself with the question all day long. It was the stasis that had got to him the night before, the uncertainty of not knowing what to do.

With the mines laid at Gela, their escort work was done, and *Plunkett* nestled up to a convoy headed back to North Africa. When they finally collapsed later that night—Gallagher, Gebhart, Feltz, the whole crew—they tallied their hours at battle stations—thirty-two. It was, they decided, a day they'd never forget.

They steamed back to North Africa, to Algiers this time, a new port for *Plunkett*, and a city that hardly felt like Africa so much as home: The faces were largely white, the architecture familiar. They went out on leave, got drunk, came back late, and had Burke revoke liberties at an eye-for-an-eye pace. Come back twelve hours late, like radioman Aubrey Echols, and lose twelve liberties. Come back an hour-and-a-half late, as machinist Hugh Geraghty did, and lose two: Burke rounded up. He had men at captain's mast for disciplinary hearings so frequently that Miller looked like a pansy by comparison.

If Burke's size and taciturn demeanor didn't continually remind everyone he was a man not to be trifled with, his sparring exhibitions on the fantail reinforced the point. With Dutch Heissler and a couple of the other enlisted men who'd done some boxing, Burke was able to indulge one of his two great athletic passions, ostensibly for exercise, ostensibly as a coach. On *Plunkett*, all comers were welcome. It didn't matter that he was CO and warranted a salute from any of the white hats on that ship. They could squeeze that salute into a fist and have at it on the fantail. Burke would pull off his shirt and note as much to the men ringed up on the fantail: "My shirt's off," he'd tell them. "Come at me. Don't hold back."

As the sparring sessions grew more frequent, Captain Burke began to wonder whether one of his junior officers, a much slighter man who'd worked on the school's stunt committee and newspaper, and who had entirely too much to say as far as the CO was concerned, might entertain a bit of exercise on the fantail. Ken Brown, after Burke proposed a bit of the sweet science, bobbed and let the suggestion go right overhead. The next time Burke started talking about the gloves, Ken weaved. This was how it went: Burke encouraging Brown to submit to a little exercise on the fantail, and Brown offering unsolicited advice to Burke on how he thought the ship should be run.

On Sicily, the Allies gained control of their assault beaches by the end of that second full day and charged inland. Patton plunged in three directions at once: to the west for Marsala, into the mountainous interior, and over the island's shoulder toward the capital at Palermo. The Germans and Italians, having failed to stop the Allies on the beaches, fought rearguard actions. Now all they wanted to do was get off the island with as many men and as much materiel as they could.

The losses on the Cent assault beach were relatively light, with 12 sailors missing and 164 wounded at the end of the first day; they were heavier on Joss, with 28 sailors killed and 118 wounded, and downright dispiriting on Dime, owing largely to the loss of *Maddox*.

Their putative Allies, the Brits, were claiming all kinds of credit for the success of the landings on Sicily. The men on *Plunkett* heard as much on the BBC, which had reported that the Royal Navy, the Marines, and the Canadians had come ashore and beat back the island's defense. From a distance, the Brits were the noble men who'd persevered at Dunkirk and took to the skies against all odds over London. Up close, they were limeys. The evening after they'd come into Algiers a second time, Feltz and Gebhart had hopped back aboard from liberty with minutes to spare, when a brawl erupted on a neighboring dock between British and American sailors. They watched from choice seats topside, a fight so brutal it looked like a gang fight.

With the real combat now roiling inland on Sicily, the ship's calls to general quarters receded like a tide, and again the men on *Plunkett* turned to tasks as mundane as cleaning boilers and evaporators. Burke inspected the crew's compartments and their mess and their persons, too. He didn't like how unkempt their hair was getting. The ship didn't have a barber, but there was one man on board who was both Italian and an aspiring actor who sometimes put on a show in the ship's mess. He'd do.

The first few times John B. Stango cut hair, the results were as entertaining and talked about as his theatrical acts were not, but he settled into the job, and in time even the most fastidious sailors were trooping to his chair.

Body odor was another matter. One of the chief petty officers, speaking for a number of the crew, prevailed upon Jim McManus to bring the matter up with a gunner's mate called Pop for his prematurely gray hair. They could no longer stand the mate's body odor or the stench of his clothes.

"Why don't you tell him?" McManus said. "You're the chief."

"Come on, Dooley," as they'd taken to calling McManus, "with your charming Irish ways, you can do it."

McManus approached Pop when he was alone one day and sauntered into the delicate subject with a query about how frequently Pop took a bath when he was a civilian.

"Once a week," the Navy reserve sailor told him. "Saturday night."

McManus told him that in the *regular* Navy they took showers every day. They changed their underwear every day, rinsing skivvies and socks in saltwater and hanging them on blowers to dry, if need be. If you didn't, you'd run the risk of being called a "scrounge."

"Okay, I can do that," Pop said.

In the same way that men deteriorate from lack of attention, so, too, the ship. As the first lieutenant in charge of the repair parties, keeping rust at bay was a priority for Jack Simpson. One day in North Africa, he trooped ashore looking for paint with a crew from one of his damage control parties, a bunch he referred to as the Dead End Kids for their roots on New York City's streets, similar to the gang in the popular movie series. He drew a bead on a supply tent where, presumably, they'd have as many gallons as *Plunkett* needed. The tent's supply officer, who was young and invested with authority, called out to Jack that he had ten gallons to spare. Jack could take it or leave it. But ten gallons was tantamount to throwing dust in the air, Jack knew. One of the Dead End Kids had an idea, and briefed Jack while the supply officer bustled out of earshot in the massive tent.

"You keep him talking, Mr. Simpson," the sailor told him. "If you hear any noise, don't pay any attention."

The Kids slipped around to the back of the tent and either put a hole or found a gap in the canvas. Jack couldn't be sure and wouldn't ask. In any case, the Kids spirited so much paint out the back way, Jack found he had twice as much as he needed.

Jack liked the Kids and took pride in how, with discipline and the assumption of responsibility, they were shaping up as capable men. He liked many of his fellow officers—not all of them— and he respected Burke. What Jack had seen of Burke so far was impressive. The man knew how to handle a ship, and Jack sensed his steel wouldn't buckle. They were no longer steaming on a happy ship, and they had broached the action he'd wanted all along, but he still wanted the Pacific, as well as one of the Fletcher-class destroyers the Navy was now minting. These new ships were 25 percent bigger than *Plunkett*'s class, cost a million dollars more to build, and achieved top speed at 40–44 mph. They'd started commissioning them six months after Pearl Harbor, and Jack Simpson wanted on one. Through Burke, he formally requested transfer to the Pacific, on a Fletcher-class destroyer operating in a carrier task force. When word filtered down to the white hats that the first lieutenant was bucking for a transfer, he acquired a nickname snatched from the popular newspaper comic *The Toonerville Trolley*: Suitcase Simpson.

At mail call, John Gallagher learned how they'd transported his mother earlier that summer, from the bedroom where she'd been recuperating since the stroke to the foyer downstairs by the front door so that she might participate more actively in the life of the house. She was carried in a wheelchair, with Charlie on one end and Tom the other, and Martha piloting all the way down, shrieking at every turn and calling out to whoever wasn't actually on the chair, as if additional help might be needed. It was a scene right out of a slapstick comedy, and John could picture how Charlie and Tom would have handled it, gravely, and all the more gravely each time their mother's shrieks put the convoy in jeopardy.

Home never felt so close as it did when he was reading one of the letters that came in from his brothers and sisters. What was learned about that sacred place leached out of the envelopes and hallowed the surrounding hawsers, hatches, sponsons, bulkheads, and wherever else he'd segregated himself for the read. V-Mail, a small facsimile of an actual letter, used by the military to save shipping space, was mostly what Gallagher got from home, from Charlie and Helen, his most faithful correspondents, reporting from Oakton Avenue.

Some of the letters he read aloud to his shipmates, like those he got from Frank's girl, Sophie, a woman Tom Garner called the "Boston reporter" for all the news she embedded in her missives. They called Tom "Cactus Jack" because he shared a surname with Franklin Roosevelt's first vice president, John Nance Garner, who was from Texas, and sort of prickly, just like Tom. *Plunkett*'s Garner was from Camden, New Jersey, twenty-four-years-old, built low-to-the-ground and solid, but with a face more cherubic than rough. Sophie, he told John one day, ought to quit her job at the Baker Chocolate Factory and get a job on one of those newspapers John was always reading.

Occasionally when it wasn't V-Mail but an actual enveloped letter, a photograph might sprinkle from the folded pages and join his collection of personal pictures. There was one of Frank, him, his mother, and Charlie standing in the backyard on Easter Sunday in 1937, the sons in buttoned-up jackets and ties, a fedora perched on John's head, an outsize saucer of a rig on his mother's head. Another pictured his father in his traveling clothes, just before he came home from the sanitarium at Saranac, a picture that was haunting for the buoyancy so clearly evident in his father's demeanor, his jaunty perch upon the porch of his cure cottage, the impatient clasp of his hands: *Just get me home.*

John learned, too, that Frank had shipped out after more than a year's training in the States. Where he was going, no one knew. Frank had tried to get into the paratroops, and then tried to get into tanks, but they made him a medic, perhaps because he was on the verge of thirty and was no longer susceptible to the unbridled impulses the military banked on in younger men. The Army taught him how to identify every bone in a man's body, and then sent him to Mark Clark and the Fifth Army. He was considered a "pill roller" by the uninitiated; by the time the war was over, Frank would be known as Doc to the men he served with.

After nearly two weeks on Sicily Patton's troops took Palermo, and the Navy moved in to establish a new base. The place was a mess. There was no water, no light, and no power in the city. The city's residents were streaming back from shelter in the outskirts to set up housekeeping in the rubble of bombed-out homes, a "bedraggled and gaunt and pitiful" people. Fifty ships lay submerged in the harbor, and the Navy called in the same salvage operator who'd cleaned up Casablanca. By the time *Plunkett* steamed in on July 31, they'd cleared half the shipping berths, and readied the city for tens of thousands of soldiers the Allies planned to land there the following month.

Plunkett had come into Palermo with seven troop transports, ferrying the 9th Infantry Division, and left them idling that night in the outer harbor. In the director, they sat through the evening, imagining baseball games they weren't seeing, and college football now that they were coming into August. There'd been a rumor making the rounds on *Plunkett*—that when Burke played on the team, Navy hadn't won a single game. Ken didn't have any inside information on Burke's performance at the Academy, but he didn't dispel the rumors; in fact, he believed he was doing more to abet them than stifle them.

In the months they'd been with Burke, none of the casual conversation at the wardroom table had plumbed one another's history, even so far as the superficial depths of what they'd done at the Academy. Jack Simpson was right. They weren't a happy ship. Jack had been obliged to run his request for a transfer through Burke, who was loath to move on the motion, but Jack was insistent. Ken and Jack were no longer roommates, not since Ken had become the ship's gunnery officer and acquired his own stateroom—his own except for the commissary crates he now roomed with. But he would be sorry to lose Jack's company. Some men on *Plunkett*, like Jack Collingwood and Jack Simpson, were men whose proximity you wanted for as long as possible.

On the last night of July, *Plunkett* anchored southeast of the entrance to Palermo's harbor, fixed between the breakwater light and the city's massive opera house, the largest in Italy. Their Liberty ships and the soldiers of the 9th Infantry rode out the night at anchorage. Shortly after Ensign Russ Wright called the morning watch at 4 a.m., German fighters dropped flares over the harbor, illuminating ships off *Plunkett*'s port bow. A long arrow of fire sprang from a nearby mountainside and directed bombers to the harbor in the darkness. Forty-eight of the Luftwaffe's planes somehow eluded Allied radar and swept down on the anchored ships, launching a surprise attack on the anchorage that was redolent of what had happened at Pearl Harbor. Bombs followed the flares onto targets all over the inner harbor, initiating noise and violence the likes of which the Allies had yet to see from German aircraft.

One bomb fell near railroad cars loaded with ammunition, sparking a fire that kept growing and getting louder as more and more ammunition exploded. Another bomb landed squarely on a British freighter. Another obliterated an LST. The ship's new squadron commander, George L. Menocal, called for *Plunkett* to put up a smoke screen around the troop transports. Anti-aircraft fire streaked the inner harbor and erupted sporadically in the outer harbor as *Plunkett*'s boiler rooms churned smoke out of its two funnels.

At general quarters, Jack Simpson was stationed near the wardroom—was all but tethered to it—but floated throughout the ship to assess readiness. With the ship's funnels pouring smoke, Jack was headed to the radio shack by the no. 1 stack when his right ankle suddenly seared with pain. He looked down to see a trench of opened leather on his shoe. One of the machinist's mates nearby, Frederikson, hit the deck at the same time and as promptly sat back up and reached for his left temple, smeared now with blood. Another machinist's mate, Lewellen, had his dungarees shredded with shrapnel at the calf.

Wave after wave of aircraft dove on the ships, eluding proximity to *Plunkett* until just after dawn, when four planes swerved on the ship from the inner harbor. All six machine guns and the 1.1-inch erupted at once. The targets were now blipping all over the fire control radar and within Bonnie's range finder. Ken took command of the battery and started sending up shells from one gun or another every five seconds. In his slewing sight, he tracked one plane flying erratically through the curtain of anti-aircraft fire, wobbling its wings from side to side in a curious fashion. He was bearing down on the target when suddenly it was gone—gone without fire, without evidence of disintegration, without explanation, the weirdest thing.

He asked Bonnie if that plane, that bogey, was theirs, and Bonnie said it was not. Had Bonnie seen the markings? Bonnie said he had. Ken asked if he was sure. Bonnie said he was. The silhouette? German. They'd all been through recognition training sessions with 35mm black-and-white slides, but the difference between a German Junkers Ju 88, say, and an American C-47 was a nuance difficult to parse in low light.

But then Ken looked back into the airspace where he'd last seen the plane wobbling its wings in a way he'd never suspect of a German bomber. They'd been having all sorts of problems coordinating communication between Allied aircraft and Navy ships off Sicily; in fact, there was no communication. The Air Force wouldn't let Navy commanders communicate directly with the planes for fear the Navy might try to control them. So Allied ships and planes were forced to operate independent of one another's perspective in battle.

Up in the wardroom, Jack was complaining to the ship's doctor, David Bates, about the very good pair of shoes he'd lost to whatever it was that ripped through them. To hear Jack talk was to believe the man was more concerned about the shoes than the shrapnel in his ankle. He didn't know what hit him, whether it was friendly or foreign. "There wasn't any mailing address on it," he said.

Bates was a tall man, as broad as a lineman, with a square face and a receding hairline. He was a general practitioner, Brooklyn-born but more of the borough that produced Whitman and the bridge than second- and third-generation immigrants. He asked Jack if he wanted any morphine for the extraction. The first lieutenant said no. The doctor said good, he wasn't giving him any anyway, and yanked out the embedded metal. The doctor also told Jack, before he hopped off the wardroom table and went back on duty, that he had a wound that would qualify him for a Purple Heart. Jack shook his head nope: not for that.

In three minutes, they'd gone at the Germans with more than sixty rounds of the five-inch guns, nearly two hundred of the 1.1-inch, and more than seven hundred rounds of 20mm. In that predawn barrage, two enemy planes had been shot down by other ships.

The only thing that made sense to Ken in the wake of that plane's disappearance was this: that the aircraft took the full blast from the exploding five-inch projectile and more or less disintegrated. And that the shell came from his ship, his battery. That was the only explanation.

Bonnie's eyes were terrific, Ken was thinking, the best. But this perspective would not dislodge what he deep down believed to be true, no matter how hard he tried to see things as Bonnie had.

That night some of *Plunkett*'s crew went ashore, and the Brits were all over them, confirming what Ken feared. "You shot down a friendly aircraft," the Brits said. "One of ours."

10: THE BOOT

AUGUST 1943

Friendly fire was the elephant in the wardroom. After the invasion of Sicily at Gela, the beast lumbered into the memory banks of officers who commanded batteries that took out twenty-three Allied troop transports, and squatted. Ken did not have to dwell on what part *Plunkett* might have played in that "screwup"—they'd got word and had checked fire—but now he had that plane over Palermo with the "wobbling" wings to haunt him.

It was August now. After months of little to no drama and calls to general quarters that were routine and uneventful, there had been since Gela three weeks earlier the possibility of something at large every dawn and every dusk, and sometimes in between. Days and nights marked by action that Irvin Gebhart declared early on he would never forget merged into a stream of shore bombardments, nights at general quarters, and exhilarating bursts of action like the time they went after marauding Italian motor torpedo boats. "We gave them a run for their money," Gebhart declared after *Plunkett* finally gave up the chase.

German bombers were picking off destroyers all around them. As *Plunkett* patrolled the entrance to Palermo Harbor two days after their arrival, the ship's crew watched German bombers work over the anchorage for an hour, dropping sticks of bombs that blew up targets from materiel on the piers to ships, including the destroyer *Shubrick*. Two bombs in a stick of three straddled that ship, and one hit, penetrating the main deck and detonating between an engine room and fire room. Nine died immediately, and seven of the seventeen wounded would die later, some from the skin-boiling effects of six hundred pounds of pressurized steam spurting from ruptured lines. A Junkers Ju 88 straddled another destroyer, *Mayrant*, killing two destroyer men and wounding thirteen, including the president's son Franklin Delano Roosevelt, Jr. Some destroyers would go down suddenly, like *Maddox* at Gela, but more often than not, like *Mayrant* and *Shubrick*, they'd take a hit, stay afloat, and leave the damage control parties to cope as best they could. It was becoming clear, too, that the "sympathetic" consequences were as much to dread as the initial explosion—the scythes of steam that could literally slice off a limb; the ship's own depth charges, if not set to safe, exploding at prescribed depths when the ship went down; the magazines in the bowels of a ship kindled by an enemy bomb and erupting with a ferocity that was oftentimes exponential to the initial hit. Sympathy hurt.

Some men went into shell shock, such as the sailors on *Shubrick* who'd collected parts of their torpedo officer under the tubes on the main deck, on the after stack of the ship itself, and on the machine guns, too. Officers succumbed to the yank of madness as well. One of the stories making the rounds on *Plunkett* that early August concerned a ship in their squadron that had shot up one of their own seagoing tugs, by accident. The CO believed he'd been wounded in the action. He called for a pharmacist's mate to put him down for a Purple Heart, but the wound, as Jim McManus had it, turned out to be an "infected pimple." By the time Dooley finished shaping his story, they'd had to remove the CO from the ship in a straitjacket. There'd been a pharmacist's mate on *Plunkett* who'd crowed about the ferocity of the war in the Pacific, where he'd been, and who denigrated the European theater as a sideshow. Traumatized by the action he then experienced on *Plunkett*, he, too, was removed from the ship in a straitjacket, according to McManus. Dooley had a knack for turning up the heat on a story and subscribing to the wildest possibility as explanation. When the black gang emerged from the engine rooms and fire rooms after general quarters, and asked Mac for details on what they could only hear below deck, Mac would describe the trajectories of bombs that didn't merely straddle *Plunkett* but would slant between the stacks of the ship.

Two weeks after General Patton took Palermo and set his sights on Messina, orders dispatched *Plunkett* to Ustica, an island thirty-seven miles north of Palermo that harbored an enemy penal camp and a concentration camp for political prisoners. What kind of opposition they'd meet was vaguely surmised. They might meet 80 Italian soldiers with three light machine guns and, possibly, 108 German soldiers with heavy machine guns, though it was believed the Germans had already fled. *Plunkett*'s squadron commander, George Menocal, was to "demand and accept without conditions the enemy military force there stationed."

The ship steamed out of Palermo in the morning with a British major—who would take charge of the island after its surrender— and the island's Italian mayor on board. As a matter of public consumption, the Italians were still fighting alongside the Germans, but a nascent government was already maneuvering with the Allies to swap sides, a move that wouldn't be made official for another month. In the meantime, Ustica was enemy-occupied territory, and had to surrender.

Plunkett and *Gleaves* took station off either bow side of a "love charlie item," as *Plunkett*'s orders referenced the landing craft, infantry (LCI). If there were prisoners to be had on Ustica, they'd ferry them back. After three hours' steaming, the two destroyers and the LCI neared their destination at Santa Maria Bay and sounded general quarters. The island was the top of an extinct volcano and had been named *Ustica* (burnt) by the Romans for the black rocks dominating its expanse. There wasn't much water on the island, but that didn't stop Mussolini from cramming the place with thousands of political prisoners, including Slavs and homosexuals who wasted away in the early years of the war from malnutrition and tuberculosis.

Twenty minutes after coming into the bay, *Plunkett* lowered the squadron commander's gig with Bill Maners, a lieutenant on the squadron commander's staff, and eight enlisted men, three of whom could speak Italian. They motored for the town's mole under a white flag. As the gig pushed off, Ken stood in the director with his five-inch battery trained on the island. The British officer and the island's mayor, the *podesta,* idled on one wing of the bridge with Burke, and watched the gig motor toward shore, its canopy fluttering with the breeze. Maners stood behind the squadron commander, who was gripping one of the canopy's poles. His arm might have been shaking from the wind, but Maners didn't think so. The squadron commander hadn't earned much admiration from the crew. While Burke strode onto the exposed wings of the bridge during air raids that were becoming a regular part of their daily fare, scuttlebutt was the squad dog sought shelter under tables in the wheelhouse.

As soon as *Plunkett*'s gig made the mole, a group of men, including the garrison's Italian commander, met them waving white sheets. They were hungry, they said, patting their stomachs. They were thirsty. They'd been rationing water since Palermo had fallen, and there were eleven hundred civilians on the island. They had no medical supplies. The Germans were long gone, having decamped on the day the Allies invaded Sicily. The Italians were glad the Americans had come. And so they surrendered.

A signalman in the landing party broke out his flags and communicated the surrender by semaphore. The British major and the *podesta* now made preparations to land. Jim Feltz, who'd been repositioned at general quarters from the hole in the fantail to a repair party topside at midship, looked to one of the signalmen for a translation.

They'd embarked on this mission with zeal, like men from the Age of Discovery bent on subjugation, or better yet, the Pacific, where the islands bristled with enemy. This was the *Plunkett*'s moment, they'd thought, conjuring visions of dauntless men storming ashore, but the whole thing had petered out as a farce.

Remembering the signalman's pronouncement, Jim recorded the day's anticlimactic depths with a simple phrase in his diary: "We just took a island."

With the Allies now in command of Palermo, and the Germans long since persuaded that the only thing to do about Sicily was get off it, the chase was on. The Germans slogged across the northern reach of the island, heading for an escape valve onto the European mainland at Messina, fighting rearguard actions against Patton's troops all the way. Patton had come into war as a skeptic of the Navy's effectiveness to complement the Army's efforts. Just prior to the landings in North Africa the previous fall, he'd said he doubted the Navy could land troops on schedule. The Navy proved him wrong, landing as planned at Casablanca, Fedhala, and Oran. Then, at Gela, with Patton's troops pinned down by swarms of German and Italian tanks, he watched Navy guns pummel enemy positions. He'd become a believer.

A week after they'd arrived in Palermo, *Plunkett* and the ships of its squadron and the larger task force sortied for points along the shallow scooped northern coast of Sicily to conduct a series of leapfrog landings. *Plunkett* screened cruisers and other destroyers, who'd soften up the shores for Patton's troops, and then Ken Brown's battery would weigh in with its five-inch guns. On deck with the midship repair party, Jim Feltz watched his ship's guns bear down on the tanks and trucks of the retreating Germans. He didn't much care that they were at general quarters night after night. He liked that they were engaged behind enemy lines, and he liked that they'd crept up on the Germans without the enemy knowing it.

The first of their leapfrog landings, at Terranova, was especially gratifying to the crew, who tuned in to the radio the next day and learned they'd "made out very good," as Gebhart put it. He concluded that what they were doing to the Germans now with these surprise leapfrog landings was the "slickest trick" they'd pulled off since the Allies had dropped a dead-tramp decoy off the coast of Spain and then gobsmacked the Germans on Sicily. One night they went out to duel with one of the Germans' 88mm guns, mounted on a train car. The 88's reputation as a tank-killer and a plane-downer preceded *Plunkett*'s sortie. They knew what it was to go up against a Ju 88, but this 88 was like going into the ring against a southpaw: You couldn't know what to expect. By the time *Plunkett* moved into position for its assault, they learned the Army had knocked out the big gun. "Thank God for that," Jim declared that night.

Two hours after getting underway from Palermo on August 7, *Plunkett* was making eighteen knots, steaming off the starboard bow of the cruiser *Philadelphia*, when one of the lookouts spotted something in the water two miles distant. Jack Collingwood was at the conn, and he changed course to investigate. He steamed up to the edge of a generous buffer between his ship and what turned out to be a small yellow life raft with a CO_2 canister strapped at the rear, occupied by a single man, a German.

Finding men in the water, dead or alive, was something they were getting used to. On the Atlantic Seaboard, they'd been merchant marines, undone by U-boats. After the invasion at Gela, their squadron picked up a dead German airman. They took his papers and, dipping colors, buried him at sea. They were adversaries, but up close, they were men like themselves whose end warranted some gesture of respect.

Jack Simpson had been up all night, standing watch as officer of the deck from midnight until 4 a.m., had been deprived of shut-eye again for general quarters from 5:05 a.m. to 6:29 a.m, and had only just now had the opportunity to dive down for some deep sleep, when the bridge roused him. As first lieutenant, it would be his job to retrieve the man from the raft.

Jack and a crew of enlisted men, including Jim McManus, lowered one of the ship's whaleboats and motored for the raft. They'd taken their first island, and now they were about to take their first German prisoner. As the boat closed on the raft, Jack leveled his pistol at the survivor who, it became clear to Jack, was prepared to offer no resistance. One of *Plunkett*'s crew extended a bow hook to the prisoner, and he surrendered his weapon to the hook. The German airman didn't speak English, but Jack could hear thankfulness and relief in the young man's voice as he climbed into the whaleboat, mumbling something.

Jim McManus wasn't about to remember the capture of this German prisoner with this little drama. For Jim, errant captains came off their ships in straitjackets and "sons of the Führer" wouldn't surrender until they tried to kill you first. When *Plunkett*'s whaleboat got to the raft, what Jim remembered was that the airman had pulled his gun on the crew. But the pistol clicked and wouldn't fire because the saltwater had taken its toll on the firing mechanism.

Whether Jim's version or Jack's version was closer to the bone of truth, one thing was clear: Everyone wanted the airman's gun. As soon as they'd pulled the hook with the gun back into the whaleboat, the coxswain said, "I'll have that pistol." Then Jack Simpson, according to McManus, pulled rank on the coxswain and, like a character in a B-grade farce, said, "*I'll* have that pistol."

Back on the ship, McManus noted that the *captain* would have that pistol. Burke took possession of the gun and summoned one of the crew who spoke German, Irving Diamond, from the ship's store. They learned the twenty-one-year-old German sergeant, Karl Sebald, had been in the water for five days. He'd been flying a Junkers Ju 88 as an observer during a raid on Palermo. The plane had crashed after a steep dive over the anchorage, and two of the plane's crew had drowned.

John Putis, the ship's chief pharmacist's mate, treated the pilot for shock, exposure, and injuries he received in the crash, and they quartered him in Ken's stateroom, with Diamond as guard. When they discharged the pilot to an Army ambulance in Palermo later that afternoon, Sebald removed his wristwatch and gave it to Putis in gratitude. The war was over for the German sergeant, but the odyssey of his pistol had only just begun.

The desire for plunder that had fired the Achaeans sitting by the ships near Troy was no less fervent among *Plunkett*'s crew. A gun was the preeminent trophy. A few days after the capture, Captain Burke called McManus to the bridge, asking the gun captain if he might do anything about this pistol that wouldn't fire. McManus was establishing a reputation for himself on *Plunkett* as the go-to man for guns needing repair. He had a knack for zeroing in on problems, from faulty valves to gunked-up barrels, and the captain knew it.

Mac and one of the ship's torpedomen took the airman's pistol apart, cleaned it, oiled it, and got it to fire. Turning the gun back over to Burke, McManus suggested the captain clean and oil the gun several more times in the coming week, until all of the rust was gone. Another gunner's mate later offered to clean the captain's pistol and left the gun to drip dry in an ammunition storage room. That's when it went missing. Burke ordered inspections of all the gunner's mates' lockers, and then called for a moratorium on movies, hoping that might help incentivize the gun's return. It did not. The suspicion fell most heavily on McManus, who was now the beneficiary of taunt after taunt: "What'd you do with the old man's pistol, Dooley?"

By the middle of August, Karl Sebald's gun was buried in John "Annie" Oakley's cache, though no one knew it at the time. Burke couldn't sustain his prohibition against movies and he relented after several days. They took in a show on the afternoon of the 16th, capping an eight-day stretch of shore bombardments and amphibious landings. After that movie, as the men began scattering for watches, they learned Sicily had fallen.

The Allied campaign for Sicily concluded thirty-eight days after the Operation Husky landings on the south coast. The British and the Americans had suffered an equal number of men killed, 2,700 for the Brits and 2,800 for the Americans. One of every five American dead was a sailor. There wasn't any formal capitulation of the island to the Allies, but Sicilian ports and airfields were now in Allied hands. With plans for the invasion of France still ten months from fruition, the next major Allied move would be to the Italian mainland. *Plunkett* was about to strike the first blow.

The ship's work—Burke's role in particular—on the Husky landings, the leapfrog landings, and the Ustica surrender merited commendation from Rear Admiral Lyal A. Davidson, who had managed shore bombardments from his flagship, the cruiser *Philadelphia*. "Your calm judgment, untiring devotion to duty and prompt appreciation of your tasks under difficult and hazardous conditions contributed materially to the early fall of Messina," Davidson wrote to Burke. The elevated language notwithstanding, it was a pat on the back, nothing more.

Since he'd come out of the Academy, Burke's commanding officers had rated him as a man fit for promotion, whether for command of submarines or an expedition, a squadron or a classroom. More than any other attribute, he impressed his superior officers with his ability to carry on under any and all circumstances. He wasn't going to be put down. No one expressed reservation about his ability to succeed. He was levelheaded and quick to react in emergencies. "He is the type I would particularly desire to have serve under me during war conditions," one of his submarine commanders noted early on. Under Burke's command, said one of *Plunkett*'s squadron commanders, the ship was a beautifully run destroyer.

As soon as they'd heard Sicily had fallen, *Plunkett* got underway in the early evening to sweep the northwest coast of the island. Through the small hours of the morning, the crew stood at general quarters while the ship zigzagged at twenty-seven knots. There was nothing to be had of the sweep. The Germans and their Italian allies were gone, and *Plunkett* started back toward Palermo, relieving the crew from battle stations just a few hours before dawn.

Burke left the ship in the morning, motoring away to conference with Rear Admiral Davidson and the commanding officers of two cruisers and three other destroyers. When he returned that afternoon, he carried orders for a shore bombardment of the Italian coast. They would fire one hundred shells onto a railroad bridge at Gioia Tauro, an assignment that would fall to Ken Brown up in the director.

Plans on the table, Burke looked at Ken. "Don't try to tell me how to do this," he said.

Ken hadn't said anything, but Burke had an idea he needed to pre-empt input from Brown.

They steamed on all four boilers for the Italian coast under a gondolier's moon, together with the cruisers *Philadelphia* and *Boise*, and destroyers *Gleaves*, *Niblack*, and *Benson*. The crew came to general quarters for a couple of hours after dark, stood down for an hour, and were back at battle stations again just before midnight.

From the observation hatch of the director, Ken looked out at the Italian coast, which was little more than a smudge to the east. A searchlight on Point Scilla groped for targets on the open water, but *Plunkett* was out of range now, having dropped one of the cruisers and the other two destroyers to move farther north with *Philadelphia* and *Benson*.

On each of *Plunkett*'s four five-inch guns, one of his captains stood by, waiting on word from the gun boss as Burke moved *Plunkett* into position. At the end of the day, this was *Plunkett*'s principal purpose. Say what you will about convoys and screening, the ship was first and foremost a floating gun platform, light and nimble to be sure, and not nearly the kind of platform that a battlewagon was with its sixteen-inch guns, but a platform nevertheless. All war was a matter of putting ordnance on a target. It all boiled down to that.

Seven men crowded the turret at each mount—a pointer, a trainer, a fuse setter, a projector man, a powder man, the gun captain, and a hot shell man who wore asbestos gloves and whose job it was to yank the brass shell casings from the breach and toss them out the hatch onto the deck. Below them in the handling room, four more men prepped the shells and powder, and below them in the magazine, four or five men would pass up the powder and the fifty-two-pound shells. Moving as fast as they could move, the crews could send up twenty shells per minute.

A 1:30 a.m., *Plunkett* ceased zigzagging and steamed at fifteen knots to its firing area. Twenty minutes later, Burke called up to the director, and Ken signaled his men to commence firing. *Niblack* and *Philadelphia* uncorked their gunnery as well, and soon the Italian mainland was under fire—the first time American ships had ever bombed continental Europe.

Ken kept his gun captains firing at a slow but steady pace as he worked on the bridge at Gioia Tauro, hoping to inhibit an Axis escape. Eventually, a fire sprung from all that shelling. He believed he'd found his target, and he brought his guns to bear on that faint light. Six or seven minutes into the bombardment, Burke called up from the bridge, asking how many rounds he'd fired.

Ken heard the question, and his mind blanked for a moment as he considered his response. He looked at his trainer, and unconsciously pumped his thumb, as if he had a clicker. How many shells? he mouthed silently.

His trainer shrugged.

Ken told Burke he didn't know.

Burke told him to find out.

Find out, Ken thought. How was he supposed to find out? And what the hell was it about commanding officers that they wanted you to count everything, from cans of peas to five-inch shells?

Ken called down to Jim McManus in gun no. 3. He wanted Mac's hot shell man out on the deck, counting spent shells?

Mac couldn't believe the request.

Then Ken called Richardson in gun no. 2, Wikstrom in no. 1, and Jaffee in no. 4. While the hot shell men hopped out of their hatches and started counting, *Philadelphia* and *Benson* continued to pound the Italian coast. Ken knew he had to deliver a hundred shells, and he had an idea when to stop. It was going to be a sixth sense that got him there in lieu of technology.

In the yawning gap of silence from *Plunkett* Burke was back on the squawk box, asking what the hell was going on. Why weren't they firing?

Ken told him they were counting shells.

Now Burke couldn't believe it, and his order for the gunnery officer to resume firing, as if he were a nitwit who needed to be told what to do every step of the way, cut Ken to the bone. He didn't think Burke knew much about gunnery; if anyone should have been told what's what, it was Burke. And so Brown couldn't help what he said next, or the way he said it, the way he declared compliance.

"Aye aye, sir," he said, the first aye and then the other aye each sounding with an inflection that was anything but routine. He'd swerved a boatload of other communication into those three words. And the other men in the director knew it. So did the men on the bridge, Ken's voice sounding loud and clear on the squawk box.

The gun boss set his captains to firing again, and a few minutes later, at 2:02 a.m., they were done. The hot shell men scrambled out of their hatches and tallied the 109 shells they'd fired. Burke called for steam and started *Plunkett* into a zigzag at twenty-five knots.

Fifteen minutes later, they skirted the searchlight at Point Scilla, and shortly afterward, *Plunkett* secured from general quarters and Ken came down off the director.

Burke was waiting for him on the bridge. "Brown," he said to Ken. "Go to your quarters. And stay there. For the next five days."

II: READYING

AUGUST–SEPTEMBER 1943

In time, pretty much everyone on *Plunkett* had a nickname. There was Steamboat Jackson, Shanghai Pierce and Fish Head Pierce, Bad John Hall, Jocko Rushlow, Heave-around Hayward, Hobo Hobbs, Fearless George, Beep-Beep Mangosun, Doodlebug Meade, Skunky Kline, Skid-shoes, and sundry Pops, Fats, Shortys, and Skinnys. If you had a surname that suggested a feminine moniker, you got one, thus John Oakley was always Annie, and Ozzie Baker was always Bonnie, for the singer Bonnie Baker, who'd had a hit with "Oh Johnny, Oh Johnny, Oh" in 1939. Officers weren't immune to the dubbing. Jack Oliver was Pluto, because he never said much but always seemed to be around and was a bit distant. The crew called Collingwood Smiling Jack for his disposition. Jim McManus's first two initials were J.P., and because someone had a record by a guy named J. P. Dooley, Mac was Dooley to many.

While Ken Brown was banished to his room, oblivious to the wider world's cognizance of what they'd done, the *New York Times* reported the action in a headline above the fold on page one: "U.S.

Warships Shell Toe of Italy." The *Times* didn't name any of the six ships that smashed trucks, bridges, and railroads as Axis troops tried to escape north. The action wasn't pivotal or decisive, and hasn't merited much attention in the history books, but they'd taken note, like a shot across the bow, in Berlin and Tokyo.

Five days after the shelling, liberated at last, Ken walked past a chow line of men headed into the mess. As scuttlebutt always ensured, dawn hadn't broken after they'd shelled Gioia Tauro before all of the crew knew Burke had put Brown in hack. Now, after all those days in the can of his stateroom, he was out among them in the sun, moving past the chow line, and one of the enlisted men called out, "Mr. Brown, what kind of bird are you?"

Ken knew he was being set up, and that sometimes you had to let the white hats do what they would. He stopped and looked at the chow line, waiting on the inevitable elbow in the ribs. Soon enough, there it was: "A jail bird." Jailbird Brown.

Palermo, in the wake of the Seventh Army's arrival, was a mess. Rubble lined the streets, banked against buildings as if deposited by the surge of a river. The bombing had shorn some buildings of their facades, leaving here and there a room intact and somewhat functional for inhabitants who'd sit down to domestic business as if the wall was still there. On liberty now, Jim Feltz would not eat in the city. He'd seen too many bedraggled queues of people on the dock, waiting for *Plunkett*'s stewards to jettison the ship's trash. He didn't have the stomach to digest food away from people who were lining up for his ship's scraps. For a bar of chocolate now, or for soap, desperate women would now let men come calling. *Plunkett*'s storekeeper, Irv Diamond, stockpiled a little something for the weekend and doled it out to sailors leaving the ship with tins of rations and plans for a little relief. Dr. David Bates ensured the ship's store was well provisioned on that front, understanding that when "ye touched at the islands," and any landmass was like to be an island, even in war, there'd be "fornication."

Without anything for the weekend, Jim made his way from the dock to the Red Cross Club, past trollies stranded by the side of the road, their overhead lines severed by Allied bombing. Soldiers from an engineering battalion worked on one mound of rubble with pneumatic drills like prospectors. People moved through the city, carrying tubs of water and furniture. There was so much to feel bad about, the little kids unmoored from their homes especially, some so young and alone but for a clutched doll, that seeing them that way induced an emotional vertigo. Jim tried not to explore the possibility of his own end. There was no percentage in thinking about that. But then he'd get a letter from Betty, telling of the fifty-three men who "were lost" and how she feared he might be one of them, and the thought would flash in his brain: He might not survive this war. Another letter he'd received from her recently detailed her visit to a fortune-teller, who knew she was in love with a sailor in the Atlantic. He was in the Med now, not the Atlantic, so there was cause to not believe any of what Betty was about to reveal. But this fortune-teller also knew her father's name and various, peculiar words he used in conversation—his "common words." She saw Betty waiting for the sailor. But when the sailor came home, he turned his back on her and took another girl. There was no bottom to Betty's sorrow. She cried a lot, though she wouldn't let anyone know why she was crying. Eventually, the sailor apologized, and asked her to take him back.

But her pride was wounded and she would not. So the sailor married the other girl. Betty was also auditioning for a part in a dance show at the Chase Hotel. She didn't think she'd get the part, but in this were the seeds of an end to everything. All Jim had to do was think about his failure to jitterbug, or the colonel back in St. Louis with his common words, and the misery would set in.

The apocalyptic cityscape complicated his gloom, but he wouldn't bring it up with Cliff Dornburg, who'd joined him for the jaunt to the Red Cross Club. With the likes of Cliff, you didn't talk about such stuff, unless it was partly in jest. Cliff was a boatswain's mate from Mount Washington just outside Pittsburgh, twenty years old and going steady with a girl named Betty. He'd come aboard in March and had been one of the new guys until they hit Gela. After Gela, all the new guys were old guys.

What Jim really wanted to think about en route to the Red Cross Club was a doughnut. They had them at the Red Cross Clubs, and he would eat there. They walked in on a scene that was as cheery as any place could be in such ruins. In the lounge, idyllic pictures of bucolic American countryside—fall foliage in New England and dairy cows at pasture in Wisconsin—tethered them to that other world. If you were lucky in such a club, one of the Red Cross girls would retreat to a corner of the lounge and powder her nose, and you might ask her to do it again. Jim had his doughnut, and they listened to music, and after a while Jim and Cliff found themselves drawn to a table with a Ouija board, crowded with a mix of sailors and soldiers. The servicemen were all over the board, asking the insane questions that percolated in men just emerging from adolescence.

Am I gonna get laid tonight?

Of course, said the Ouija board.

Is it gonna be by another man?

The planchette, answering in the affirmative, scattered these guys momentarily in laughter, only to have them boomerang back into the huddle with more fun stuff.

Before Jim knew what he was doing, he squeezed in a question silently, figuring if the board could see into the future, it also had the means of sensing his question. He asked whether he'd survive the war.

The heart-shaped planchette went to the upper right corner of the board: No.

He felt blindsided by what he realized now was an asinine mistake. Why had he asked a question like that when all he really wanted out of this night was a doughnut, and maybe a couple of new jokes? He'd had enemy aircraft dive on his ship all over the Tyrrhenian Sea, himself completely exposed topside in the mid-ship repair party, and he'd never felt then what he was feeling now.

He could have wandered then into a game of Parcheesi, or cards, or browsed records. Instead, another irrepressible question asserted itself—*When?*—and Jim hoped against hope the next answer on the board would give up the name of an Italian vixen. The board started to spell out a word with an "O"—*let it be Olivia*—but the second letter was "C," and then a "T," and then a long, direct slide down the board to the number 9, and Jim had his answer: "OCT 9," the day he'd die.

The men who did indulge a meal off ship in Palermo, who succumbed to the temptation of fresh fruit and vegetables, no matter what was said about the local practice of using night soil as fertilizer, sometimes paid the price and threw it all back up. Reminders trailed the men going off on liberty—*don't eat any raw fruit or vegetables*—but this was the Mediterranean, and the siren song of fresh food over-whelmed the dirge issuing from the commissary's lockers. At mess one day, Jim had started to work on a side of black-eyed peas when he noticed the black eyes moving. No one else noticed anything, and he wondered at the dimwittedness of his mates. Recently, he'd been the one to discover that the engineering compartment was infested with bedbugs; everyone else just figured they were itchy. Jim took his tray in to George Schwartz and pointed out the weevils. George shut down the mess line and called in Dutch Heissler to look at the bottom of his barrel. They were scraping it.

On Jack Simpson's orders, the ship's paymaster gave Dutch money for provisions, and he ambled away with a detachment of men from one of Jack's repair parties. Even as Jack authorized the foraging expedition, he didn't have a good feeling about the outcome. Dutch could work wonders on a provisioning run to a supply depot, or the Liberty ships. He could wheel and deal with peers on other cans who'd just topped off and the chockablock freighters that had plenty of everything. The crew loved Dutch for this, and because he was the kind of man who'd stay up all night with the cooks to bake bread, not because he had to but because he was vested in the stores he procured, as well as the men he fed: He wanted it done right. But Dutch was also a tattooed hard-ass who went toe to toe with Burke on the fantail, who cheated at cards and craps, and who could drink himself into oblivion, and Jack wondered whether it'd be the good Dutch out there on the island of Sicily, or the mercurial Dutch, operating out there without any decent restraint. It was both.

Long after Dutch was due back, he was not back. There weren't any Germans on Sicily. The last of eighty-eight thousand fighters had been spirited off the island while *Plunkett* was shelling Gioia Tauro, concluding a mass evacuation the likes of which had not been achieved since Dunkirk. But there were plenty of Sicilians left on Sicily, and that was the problem. Standing on a wing of the bridge, Jack Simpson heard the sounds of the returning repair party from a distance, heard songs in Italian, for some of the men who'd gone out with Dutch could speak Italian and those who couldn't by now thought they could. When *Plunkett* finally did see them, they also saw wheeled wooden carts filled with food, and in one or two of the carts, a couple of the ship's men too drunk to walk.

At the gangplank, in a voice thickened by wine, Dutch called up to report that they'd had some success. They'd secured food, and they'd managed to do so without having to expend any of the ship's money. The Sicilians had greeted them as liberators and wouldn't let them pay for anything.

Jack's Dead End Kids, reeling with the same Sicilian vintage, started hustling their provisions up the gangplank. One of the Kids tottered off the side and plunged into the drink. Someone deadpanned the obvious, "man overboard," and the splashed sailor's voice billowed up from below, small, happy, and oblivious: "Where is he? I'll get him while I'm down here."

A week or two later, Jack "Suitcase" Simpson's orders came in: The Navy was detaching him from *Plunkett* for reassignment to a new Fletcher-class destroyer, bound for the Pacific. Burke informed Jack of the opportunity at hand, and then told him he wouldn't let him go.

Jack absorbed this revelation in silence. After eight months in Burke's company, watching the man bull his way around the bridge, he knew that you did not meet Burke head-on in opposition. Jack hadn't expected Burke to detach him immediately, but within a reasonable period of time. Burke's position defied that expectation. Destroyer officers, especially, put a premium on the talent they had and were more reluctant than most to part company.

The skipper told him they were headed into combat, and the first lieutenant could not be spared. Jack wondered where they'd been. It seemed they were in combat all the time now. There were the aerial assaults at the sides of the day, the small, nimble German E-boats prowling at night, and submarines, too. At night on the wings of the bridge now they'd look out at a phosphorescent tack bearing down on the ship, and they'd catch their breath over the possibility of it being a torpedo.

"You have responsibilities on this ship," Burke told him. "I don't have another damage control officer."

"You have two very good damage control teams," Jack said. He'd trained them.

"I can't let you go," Burke said.

In late August, *Plunkett* steamed to Mers el-Kebir while plans brewed for Operation Avalanche, the invasion of the Italian boot. This invasion, as with the invasions of North Africa and Sicily, was very much an extension of Winston Churchill's will, and his insistence on striking "here, there and everywhere in the Mediterranean," which the Americans thought "hopelessly romantic." The Brits, led by Churchill, wanted Italy out of the war before a cross-channel invasion. The prime minister believed that sundering the Axis would "cause a chill of loneliness over the German people." Because he'd wanted to attack the soft underbelly of Hitler's Fortress Europe, the Allies focused on Sicily, and then Salerno, and at last, before the Americans finally got what they wanted with a cross-channel invasion, Anzio. Every time *Plunkett* got underway, there was the possibility this was it, the first invasion of the European mainland, as on the morning they formed a scouting line outside Mers el-Kebir with three other destroyers and zigzagged up the coast to Arzew, screening troop transports. Soon enough word filtered down that this would be practice for an amphibious landing. Eleven new men joined the crew on the 1st of September, and the ship detached two seasoned crewmen on the 3rd, and then three more on the 4th. None of these detachments budged Burke on Simpson.

While the new men settled aboard, *Plunkett*'s crew took to liberty like kids at musical chairs, knowing all passes could be revoked at a moment's notice. On one outing, Irvin Gebhart was paging through the guest register at the Red Cross Club in Mers el-Kebir, running his eyes down the list of place names, when he saw his hometown, Hockessin, Delaware. His eyes swerved left to the name "Pvt. Leonard Gebhart." He'd last seen his brother nine months earlier, in January when Leonard had picked him up in Wilmington on a forty-eight-hour leave. He knew his brother had joined the Army in the meantime, but he hadn't any idea he was in North Africa. The last batch of letters from home had said nothing about Leonard's location. With guidance from the Red Cross and a Navy chaplain, he plotted the moves on a trip out to the Fifth Army's staging area, but duty was a hurdle, first the practice run up onto the beaches east of Oran, then the practice shore bombardment, and then watch after watch. Finally, he finagled a so-called Special Liberty and hitched a ride thirty miles to Len's camp, where he shocked his younger brother and then collaborated with him on a letter about the reunion to their mother. She received it three weeks later, on her birthday. It was, she said, "the best present she got."

Knowing the Fifth Army was in Arzew, John Gallagher also decided to rattle the dice cup. His brother Frank was in the Fifth Army, like Gebhart's brother, and so John hopped on a motor transport and traveled likewise from Mers el-Kebir to Arzew. It had been more than a year-and-a-half since he'd seen Frank. The letters he'd been getting from home provided scant detail on Frank's whereabouts since his brother left the States in April. Because Frank was in the Fifth Army, that meant he had not gone into Sicily but that he would be in on the invasion of the Italian mainland. Frank was two-and-a-half years older than John, and the wildest of the five Gallagher brothers.

Like John, Frank had set his sights on the Navy first, but he'd dallied. He'd turned twenty-eight a few weeks after Pearl Harbor and had a good thing going at the MTA. The war could wait. The Army couldn't. They drafted him before he could claim a bunk on a boat. After a year in the States, Frank had come over in April on what had once been a luxury ocean liner, the SS *Mariposa*, five thousand men in all, medical units mostly and some of the Tuskegee Airmen, the famous group of African-American pilots, too. They'd come in through Casablanca, where Frank had seen the disabled *Jean Bart*, and where he started taking pictures like a tourist with a boxy Kodak Brownie. Within two weeks of his arrival in North Africa, the Germans surrendered, leaving

Frank to muck around Morocco all summer, first along the coast at Casablanca, Rabat, and Salé and then inland to Meknes and Oujda on the Algerian border. With the invasion of the European mainland brewing, his 52nd Medical Battalion had motored up to Arzew for amphibious training and was camped inland from the coast at St. Lew.

John waded into an infantry base where they'd pitched two-man pup tents on a sandy, rock-strewn African plain. That setup was yet another reminder that the Navy, with its spring bunks and heads that flowed with seawater, was the better option. He found Frank holed up in one of the Army's pitiful canvas tents, and was able to lord it over him, his older brother on his hands and knees like a rat while he lived large on a destroyer. He also had had something Frank had not by then, a taste of war, acquired at Gela and seasoned by Palermo, by leapfrog landings and shore bombardments. He'd already taken the war to mainland Europe while Frank was crawling in and out of his miserable little shelter in the rear.

He let Frank have it on that plain: the scent of cordite when *Plunkett*'s battery was pumping shells at German fighters, how the concussion of the guns could very well threaten the seams of your shirt, they pounded so hard. There were the hazards of friendly fire to talk about, and the numbers of Army Air Force planes that had flamed and splashed at Gela. They were capturing islands, *Plunkett* was, and German airmen, and what was Frank up to?

At home, Johnny had buttoned things up more decidedly than either Frank or Charlie. John was the Gallagher brother who bought the car; Charlie was the brother who'd steal the car; and Frank was the one who'd wreck the car and engineer its burial in the yard on Oakton Avenue. Why Frank did that instead of towing it to a junkyard, no one knew. John always had money, always had his clothes cleaned and ready for wear, and was always engaged in a rearguard action, calling for support from their mother, as one or the other of his brothers stole out of the house in one of his pressed shirts.

The buried cars (there was more than one in the yard), the pressed shirts, the stories they told again and again. The time their brother Joey fell into the little creek behind the cottage in Green Harbor and Tom sprinted across the yard to dive in and retrieve the toddler in his little Lord Fauntleroy outfit. The ancient, one-legged relative who used to visit when they were boys and regale them with stories of sailing ships in the Navy back in the 1870s and 1880s. The sledding down the bumps on Oakton Avenue. And that other time Johnny took to the back kitchen stairway on a sled of tin, urged to make a run down by Charlie one day in the early 1920s, and how Johnny did just that. There had been a rush of sound, at great volume and with elements familiar and obscene: of tin, and wood, and a staccato rip of noise that concluded with a clatter, a thump of weight, and a shout as Johnny landed at the bottom of the stairs. Tom ran for Doc Littlefield because that's what he could do, faster than anyone. And Johnny lay in his mother's lap, the fear on her face as stark as the bottom of the bay floor when the tide was out. Johnny lay there, waiting for stitches, not crying, holding it all together. He was that day, Frank reminded him with the authority of an older brother, a tough little Irishman.

This was where they ended up that morning in Africa, talking about home, about Martha's condition and what worried them, but moreover about the things they wanted to get back to—the fruit trees, Charlie's kids, that house, and perhaps even their most faithful correspondents. In the same way that Frank's relationship with Sophie was deepening (and would all the way to marriage when he returned), John was also growing closer to Ruthie, one of his crowd from the corner. "I know I am lucky having such a nice girl wait for my return" was how he put it then. Still, he couldn't imagine any wedding bells in the near future, at least not while he was still in the Navy. "I am still King of the Reserves," he declared.

At last, they stood to memorialize their reunion with something they could send home. Frank handed his Brownie to one of the men in his unit, and the brothers stood side by side, John with his arms akimbo, Frank with one hand on a hip and the other hung straight. Frank was in his khakis and a garrison cap, and looked sternly at the lens, as if affronted by the photographer, as if he hadn't asked the man for this favor, while John was in his dress whites and made do with a lazy smile on a face darkened by so many hours topside at general quarters. They'd both canted their hats at jaunty angles from the right down to the left. It was still early in the morning, and their slender shadows stretched a long way behind them. When he developed the picture, Frank deployed a fine scrivener's hand to the white border at bottom, writing "Africa Sept. 1943."

It was the latter part of the first week in September, and they were several days away from embarkation. They'd practiced their landings at Arzew, and when they pulled anchor the next time, the crew of *Plunkett* knew they'd be going in. Reunion over, John bummed a ride on an Army transport back to the ship, and that Saturday, September 4, he went to Mass aboard one of the other destroyers in their squadron, the *Benson*. Then on Sunday, and despite the fact that he'd fulfilled his obligation as a Catholic to attend Mass once a week, he went to Mass again, on the dock at Mers el-Kebir. At

11:50 a.m. Ken Brown rang the forward fire room and had Jim Feltz's crew fire up the no. 1 boiler. At noon, they were still moored as before, but at 12:52 p.m., with Smiling Jack Collingwood at the conn, they got underway to land the first American troops on the European mainland.

12: SALERNO

SEPTEMBER 1943

Underway on the early afternoon of September 5, Hap Jolly gathered the crew in the mess and confirmed that this time it was for real, the invasion of the Italian mainland. They'd be going into Salerno in the early morning of the 9th, with a pit stop at Bizerte in Tunisia on the way.

They steamed out of Mers el-Kebir and then Oran in a complement of twelve destroyers, screening nineteen troop transports and three cruisers. In Bizerte, they tied up to the repair ship *Delta* for several hours while technicians righted their radar. One of *Plunkett*'s machinist's mates, Ken Sahlin, might have said something then about his troubles while they idled next to *Delta*, but Murphy's Law had them hell-bent for Salerno when Jack Simpson learned there was a major operation brewing in the wardroom, and that members of the repair party would be needed.

Dr. Bates was used to fielding complaints about stomach troubles, which he could sometimes trace to George Schwartz, who might serve weevils with his black-eyed peas, or Dutch Heissler, whose wheeling and dealing as provisioner didn't necessarily include quality control. But the machinist's mate's situation—his nausea, fever, rigid muscles in the lower right abdomen—was clearly a bigger deal. The symptoms called for extraction.

As officer of the deck, Jack put the ship at general quarters before leaving the bridge at 8 p.m. and reporting to the wardroom, where Bates was setting up for something he'd never done before—an appendectomy. He hadn't cut anyone since he'd tucked into a cadaver back in med school, but there wasn't any choice. One hundred eighty German planes had stormed Bizerte just hours before their pit stop to fix the radar, and who could say what awaited them on the shores of Salerno? They were bounding over swells at twenty knots, and that appendix had to come out.

At the wardroom, Jack mustered a complement to Bates's pharmacist's mates with some of his repair party, including Heissler. Dutch seemed to be capable of handling anything, and the doctor needed a team that could keep their heads. They strapped Sahlin to the wardroom table, and then rigged a harness for Bates. One of the pharmacist's mates was reading out of a medical book that detailed what was needed—sulfa tablets, hemostats, scalpel blades, catgut, cans of ether, retractors. Not every ship had retractors, and when they did not but needed them anyway, they'd bend back spoons from the mess. Harnessed, Bates doled out jobs to his team.

"Count the swabs," he said to Jack. "Count them going in and count them coming out."

One of the pharmacist's mates started reading a how-to section on an appendectomy, and Bates dug in. It was long after sunset now, and *Plunkett* was in the convoy's vanguard, the lead ship. If anything were to come down on this convoy in darkness, it would come down on *Plunkett* first.

With the first can of ether administered, Bates made his first incision and started for the appendix. He wasn't a man to shy away from something he'd never done before. Later in life, as a general practitioner in northeastern Connecticut, he'd open the chest of a local justice of the peace with a scalpel, saw through the sternum, and perform open cardiac massage in a last-ditch effort to save the man's life. Emergency surgery was not new to him by then, but this kind of thing was all new to Bates as they headed into Salerno. White masks covered the crews' mouths and noses. Everything was happening in slow motion, each step placed as deliberately as a thief's in the night, hoping to keep the floors from creaking while they waited out each of *Plunkett*'s shifts in the sea. Bates finally went after the appendix with his fingers, fiddling for it down behind the cecum. He knew it as soon as he had it, and there it was, the distal tip black and gangrenous and ready to burst. Bates called for finger-nail clippers he'd had boiled in water and torpedo juice (alcohol), and he snipped off the offending little organ. He doused the stump with carbolic acid, cauterizing it, and then used sulfa, which they'd ground to powder from tablets and baked in the ship's oven, and sprinkled that about the peritoneal cavity as a hedge against spores. With that, he double-checked the cavity for the gauze, confirmed the count with Simpson, and started sewing up the three-inch incision. They'd been more than two hours at it.

Appendix extracted, *Plunkett* steamed into the warp of a 642-ship armada bound for the shores at Salerno, there to deposit fifty-five thousand men. Topside at dusk on the 8th, right after they'd been secured from general quarters, the crew got word that Italy had surrendered. General Eisenhower had declared as much in a broadcast on Radio Algiers. The Italians hadn't yet admitted to the armistice, but the crew trusted Eisenhower.

Notions about what this all meant began to ricochet among the white hats. The Salerno landings were to be a milk run. They were invading Italy, and the Italians had quit. Irvin Gebhart flexed his muscles and said, "They must have known we were on our way." On the *Mayo* they believed "the war was over." One of the men in the black gang on *Niblack* was less sanguine but confused. "Who is going to fight who when our guys land on the beach?" asked Joseph Donahue. The complacency didn't last long. Enemy planes bore down on their convoy a couple of hours after the announcement, and *Plunkett* spent nearly an hour laying a smoke screen to hide the troops in the transports. That evening, Jim Feltz scribbled a furtive note in his journal: "Italy gave up. But we still half [*sic*] to push the Germans out."

Clear of the smoke screen, Jim stood with five or six other men in the midship repair party near the after deckhouse, just below the searchlight, as they steamed to within a mile-and-a-half of the Licosa Light at the southern reach of the Gulf of Salerno. It was a warm and moonless night, and the sky blazed with a million stars—the firmament, as the poets called it—each prickling of light sowing dreams of another world. In ancient days, Ulysses had sailed these waters tied to the mast while a siren called Leucosia beckoned from shore. She beckoned this evening, seducing them with songs of home, and Jim was listening. His thoughts drifted back to the dime store, the drudgery of all that work redeemed by the halcyon light of recollection. He envisioned the store's front three bays, lit and merchandised with product, the middle bay separated from its neighbors by two inset doorways. After parking behind the greasy spoon, he'd always come in the back way for work, but he walked through the front door this evening, and there was Mickey, hunched over the glass shelf on her forearms, and Betty nearby, twisting a tube of lipstick between her thumb and forefinger. Just for a moment, there was a tremendous vividness to the recollection, and Jim yearned for reinstatement, as miraculous as that was, wondering that he ever wanted anything else but the dime store. In the one letter he'd had from Mickey after he enlisted, she'd written that she'd never been able to understand why he'd joined. That wasn't a question he ever asked himself. However fervently he dreamed of something as mundane as cutting another piece of glass for one of Mr. Siegal's shelves, he knew that night that he was exactly where he was supposed to be.

As the 8th ticked into the 9th, there wasn't supposed to be room for any quiet reflection before Avalanche, as the landings had been code-named. The Navy should have been pounding targets on shore. They'd been agitating for a license to do just that. But the Army thought they might spring a tactical surprise on the gulf's defenders. They'd achieved surprise in North Africa, and, thanks to the man who never was, surprised them again with Operation Husky on Sicily. But the barbarians knew the Allies wanted the port of Naples, and it didn't take hard math to swing one arm of a compass from Allied positions in Sicily onto the beaches of Salerno. While Army commanders dreamed of surprise, the Germans were moving a Panzer division onto the Salerno plain and crowding their airfields with bombers. They were positioning their 88mm and machine guns. They were ready.

Gebhart's brother Leonard went in at H hour, 3 a.m. on the 9th. Gallagher suspected the same of his brother Frank, except that Frank's ship, *Durban Castle*, was idling at a pier at Mers el-Kebir, held back because they'd had trouble getting water. Frank wouldn't hit Red Beach near the old Greek temples at Paestum for another six days.

The first wave moved in, then the second, over inshore waters with "gentle swells like quiet breathing of untroubled sleep." Waiting on the whites of their enemies' eyes, the Germans finally unsheathed on the third wave and came down on the invaders with a ferocity comparable to the Japanese defense at Tarawa two months later. The Germans had mined all of the beaches, and were resolved to annihilate the Allies and throw them into the sea. Mortars, 88mm shells, and machine guns pummeled the assault beaches, and then the Luftwaffe swept in to strafe and bomb. All the while, as per the Army's request, the Navy guns were silent. On one of the southern-most beaches, a German loudspeaker actually taunted the invading Americans: "Come on in and give up. We have you covered!" Two hours after sunrise, Navy gunners connected with their spotters in the air and fire control parties on shore and finally joined the battle. By the end of the day, they'd engaged 132 enemy targets and kept annihilation of the Army at bay, for that day, at least.

Through the first two days of the invasion, *Plunkett* patrolled an eight-by nine-mile rectangle of sea, guarding the southern approach to the gulf. On the northern stretch of its patrol, *Plunkett* was still ten miles south of the assault beaches at Paestum, where the Luftwaffe was in the midst of nearly 450 sorties. They dove on ships to the north of *Plunkett*'s position. They strafed the beach and bombed it.

German E-boats sniped at the fringes of the transport area, but not from the south. Ken Brown didn't get to weigh in with his battery until the end of D-day plus one, and then to no effect.

Nearly forty-eight hours after the initial landings, Jack Simpson watched from the bridge as an orange flash blazed suddenly on the near horizon. Orange was a color you never wanted to see in the wake of a hit, for that was the color of one of your own ammunition magazines exploding. *Plunkett* couldn't identify the vessel from that distance, but the chatter was rampant in the wake of the explosion. It was another destroyer, *Rowan*, ruptured most likely by a torpedo dispatched from an E-boat or maybe a submarine. No one would ever know for sure. The ship sunk in forty seconds, killing 202 men and officers. Talk about the *Rowan*'s fate was all over the map the next day. Irv Gebhart was saying only seven had survived. Jim Feltz countered that eighty-three men had survived. In fact the number of survivors was seventy-one. At Gela, they'd got *Maddox*. At Salerno now, it was *Rowan*. It was almost as if one destroyer had to be given up to the gods of war per invasion, with complementary hits that would take out a dozen destroyer men here, another dozen there.

Hours after *Rowan* went down, *Plunkett* was called into the transport area to screen cruisers *Philadelphia* and *Savannah*. On D-day, these cruisers had pounded German tanks, infantry, observation posts, and artillery batteries with six-inch shells, summoned by fire control parties on shore and by spotters in float planes launched from the cruisers. At nine-thirty in the morning, Jack Oliver got word that a dozen enemy planes were approaching from the north and rang general quarters. Ten minutes later, the planes bore down on the two cruisers. From the director's observation hatch, Ken looked at *Savannah*, which had been lying to, a sitting duck, and was now getting underway. His battery was to do nothing, as word had just come in from the bridge that Allied fighters were on the way, as if they were fighting the same war as the Navy.

A thousand yards to *Plunkett*'s stern, one of the bombs nearly struck *Philadelphia*, and the ship dialed up more steam for evasive action. Then Ken saw something he'd never seen before, a projectile in descent, not waggling, not like a bomb, but more like a shell, and not only a shell, but one with a mind of its own. The bomb sported fins and rocket boosters and had been dropped from a high-level bomber at eighteen thousand feet—dropped but not forgotten. The plane's crew guided the bomb with radio control, steering a 660-pounder dubbed Fritz-X for the six-hundred-foot-long target on the surface below. Ken watched the glide bomb hit *Savannah*, just forward of the bridge. The bomb barreled through the top of a gun turret, and then through one deck after another—five decks in all is what they reckoned on *Plunkett*—and exploded in a lower handling room. The blast vented through the tunnel the bomb had carved for itself, and sideways, too, opening a thirty-foot hole in the hull.

Few in the Navy, let alone on *Plunkett*, had ever seen a bomb like this, and its debut at Salerno inspired a little doggerel from one of *Plunkett*'s junior officers, Russ Wright: "The engagement was quite a session / We learned there of CHOO-CHOO's—they made quite an impression." It was the largest bomb to hit a Navy ship during the Second World War.

A few minutes after *Savannah* was hit, Allied planes showed up—a day late and a dollar short as usual, thought Ken. Burke headed for *Savannah*, where the damage control parties had sprung to action right after the blast, dogging down bulkhead doors between compartments to staunch flooding. The ship's engineers diverted fuel oil from one compartment to another, playing chess with disaster. All the while the crew fought fire as the ship listed degree by degree to port, and its bow settled twelve feet, until its forecastle was nearly awash.

It was September 11, and the day had only just begun. On *Plunkett*, the boatswain's whistle shrilled again in the late morning as enemy aircraft attacked, and again just after noon when bombs started hitting the beach off their starboard side; in mid-afternoon as more enemy aircraft winged in; in late afternoon with enemy planes coming in from the north; in the early evening as the Luftwaffe swooped in again and Ken Brown dispatched three rounds before friendly fighters took charge.

A little before 7 p.m., the task force commander called for *Plunkett* to join a screen for *Savannah*. The crippled cruiser's black gang had worked throughout the day, surviving one aerial assault after another, to get the ship's power plant back online. They were now capable of getting underway.

Burke called general quarters—for the seventh time that day—and then for twenty-seven knots as he set the ship's course on a 240-degree bearing for station at *Savannah*'s starboard bow. It was late afternoon now, the sun twenty minutes shy of the horizon in the Gulf of Salerno. For the poet Henry Wadsworth Longfellow, writing of this place sixty years earlier, this stretch of the Italian coast had been an "enchanted land," the strand not a beachhead but a "sickle of white sand," the waters not a transport area but "the blue Salernian bay." The potential for poetry seemed a distant thing to men reverberating with the klaxon's call, and who knew that two hundred had gone down with *Rowan* that morning, and that there were uncounted dead on *Savannah* but many: that had been clear from the wrath of the explosion they'd seen—dozens, maybe hundreds.

At twenty-seven knots, *Plunkett* was at full steam. Her colors flew straight off the gaff and churned a wake as roiling as anger, that seemed as much a consequence of her fury as the turn of her screws. The bay was full of clustered ships, some lying to, all bracing for the next assault, as *Savannah* set a heading for Malta.

As Burke dialed down the ship's speed to twelve knots and took station in the screen at 7:07 p.m., a curious thing happened all across the transport area as *Savannah* at last got underway, heading south. The sun was minutes away from setting and favoring its subjects with that soft, luminous light peculiar to September. Gallagher in his gun tub, Feltz with the midship repair party on the main deck, Brown up out of his observation hatch in the director, Burke on a wing of the bridge, they could all see the crews on other ships in the transport area—hundreds and hundreds of men—aligning themselves at the rails of their vessels with an alacrity reminiscent of shards compelled by a magnet. It was an overwhelming spectacle, like something choreographed on Broadway, the men bidden by fanfare, compelled by the sacrament of communion. The white hats stood at the rails all over the decks. The officers stood among them. Each man was holding a salute as *Savannah* passed by, trying for Malta with a thirty-foot hole in her hull and a tally of dead that had already climbed past two hundred.

The British hospital ship, HMHS *Newfoundland*, was a 406-foot-long steamer, launched in 1924 as a packet boat running mail between Liverpool and Boston with stops at St. John and Halifax. She was all white and had a wide green band of paint running around the hull but for big red crosses at intervals. While Navy ships darkened at dusk, hospital ships flipped the switches on everything they had. Green lights festooned the deck like decorations on a Christmas tree, alerting would-be bombers to the ship's mission, which was supposed to be a deterrent. The Hague Conventions prohibited attacks on hospital ships, but that prohibition wasn't always an effective shield. Nor was it any kind of buffer for ships lit by their glow. As heartening as it was to know there was a hospital ship in the task force, *Plunkett* hated to see them come into a transport area.

There were 103 American nurses on board *Newfoundland*, bound for hospital tents on the beachhead at Paestum. They'd embarked from Tunisia one day after the Salerno landings, gung ho and pleased by the prospect of being the first American nurses to set foot on the European mainland. But the beachhead was hot and getting hotter as six hundred German tanks bore down on the Allies that Sunday, and now there was no telling how long, or whether, the beachhead could hold against the German counterattack.

Concerned about too much light in the transport area off Salerno, the task force commander ordered *Newfoundland* and three other brilliantly lit ships way back offshore—twenty miles out—where they were to mill about until it was safe to discharge personnel. A little after five o'clock the following morning, a German pilot dropped a bomb that hit *Newfoundland* just behind the bridge. A British wireless officer heard the German pilot announce the strike over his radio, whether with contrition or glee, it's hard to say:

"I've hit a hospital ship . . . she's on fire . . . sure to sink."

Fifteen British nurses, officers, and crew died in the explosion; the American nurses, who'd been sleeping in the hospital wards, struggled out from under blown debris and piled into lifeboats.

Nearly an hour after the bomb hit, the task force ordered *Plunkett* to *Newfoundland*.

Captain Burke had only two boilers on-line that morning, but he made the most of them at twenty-five knots. Within a half hour he had the burning ship in his sights and picked up his pace slightly for the final fifteen-minute run to the stricken vessel. The bomb had hit on the boat deck just behind the bridge. Its main funnel was still standing, though swayed by the blast, and one of its deckhouses was tilted into a ruptured crater spewing smoke. The survivors had decamped already for the nearby hospital ships, and the destroyer *Mayo* was drawn up alongside *Newfoundland*'s port quarter.

Burke decided to take *Plunkett* bow to bow with the burning hospital ship and stood by the helmsman to direct the delicate maneuverings.

The squadron commander voiced another idea. He wanted *Plunkett* to stay clear of the burning ship. *Mayo* was already up against the hospital boat. What more could *Plunkett* do?

It was seven-fifteen in the morning, and the officer of the deck, Jack Oliver, decided then that that moment would be a good one to make a note in the deck logs: "Commenced steaming on various courses at various speeds, preparing to go alongside the burning ship."

The squadron commander's preference sounded to Burke like an order, as the previous squadron commander's suggestion to Lewis Miller that they take on a pilot in Norfolk had been an order, defiance of which could very well lead to sacking. Except that this was his ship, not the squad dog's. That was how Burke saw it.

He maintained course for *Newfoundland*'s bow. Jack Simpson was already in the wheelhouse, as keyed up as the last man in a relay, waiting for the baton. As *Plunkett*'s first lieutenant, his repair parties took the lead when it came to fighting fire.

Jack didn't think much of this squad dog, not since he'd seen the man duck under a table during an aerial assault and heard about how he'd quaked all the way into Ustica on the whaleboat. Now this man had found cause to fear the possibilities of a burning hospital ship. He was like one of those Civil War generals who always overestimated what he was up against and so elected to stand down. It was embarrassing.

If the squad dog was afraid of a sympathetic explosion as the fire raged about the nether parts of the hospital ship, Burke knew he needn't be. This was a hospital ship and didn't have any magazines.

Still, the commander wanted *Plunkett* to stay clear.

Burke didn't know what it was to stand down, hang back, or do anything but go toe to toe when a threat was imminent. There was nothing for him to do now but remind the squadron commander he was CO of this ship, a declarative fact fraught with no more urgency of voice than recognition of the sky as blue. Relieve me if you have to, Burke told him. Otherwise, *Plunkett* was going in.

Minutes later, the destroyer's port bow caressed the port bow of the burning hospital ship, and Jim Feltz swashbuckled over the rails onto the burning deck, gripping the nozzle of a fire hose. Jack Simpson clambered after him, then several hose men, then the auxiliaries with forcible entry tools, the corpsmen, and an electrician's mate. The nurses' leather suitcases and olive canvas bags were strewn all over the deck for the nurses had left everything deposited there the day before, anticipating disembarkation.

Jack had graduated from two Navy firefighting schools and was trying to fall back on what they'd taught him, wondering whether any of it was applicable, or if he'd come up against a fire that defied the rules. He looked from the bow to the superstructure, where smoke was venting from innumerable hatches, blown bulkheads, and ruptured decks like a geyser field. The source of the fire had to be somewhere beneath where the bomb hit, and he led his hoses in that direction.

Meanwhile, Jim had checked pressure on his nozzle, glanced across the relatively stable forecastle, and loosed a fog of water into the wreckage. He felt for heat through the soles of his shoes, if that was possible, and moved on smoke pouring out of a hold that had lost its hatch with the concussion of the blast. The textbooks had distinguished between the likes of Class A fires, and Class B, and Class C, and there were protocols for fighting different kinds of fires. Should they be running foam into those hatches, or water? No one knew for sure, so they just poured on what they had at hand—water.

It didn't seem to Jim that the ship's circuitry could be responsible for as much smoke billowing out of her guts, but what did he know. All the fire he'd fought had been orchestrated in Brooklyn and Norfolk, in mocked-up deckhouses and engineering compartments they'd set ablaze and run the men through, as much to sap them of fear as for any technological expertise they might gain from the schooling. Jim knew to fight electric fires with CO_2; ammunition, bedding, wood, paint, and other such combustibles with water; and fuel oil with foam. Beyond that, he knew how to point a nozzle when he was on point, and how to cradle a 1.5-inch hose when he was trailing the lead man. At the blown hatch, he looked down into an inferno that took his breath away. How was anything they could do going to put out *that*? He tilted his nozzle into the hold and switched the lever from fog to stream.

While Jim and his crew funneled water into the smoking holds, another party from *Plunkett* salvaged the nurses' luggage, passing suitcases off the forecastle and into a chain for the fantail. *Newfoundland* edged deeper into its starboard list, and an hour and twenty minutes after he'd dispatched his firefighters, Burke called them back. *Newfoundland*'s master boarded *Plunkett* with the men, and Burke learned that the ship's medical supplies alone constituted the need to do everything possible to save the ship. He mustered the crew on station to be sure they'd left no one behind, and then, two hours after nosing in, shoved off to try for a better angle of attack on the fire.

Like a wrestler adjusting his grip, *Plunkett* sidled back up against the burning boat with as many hose and nozzle men as they had, arrayed along the rail, streaming water on the ship. That didn't seem to do much, so Burke sent fifteen men and officers back onto the burning ship.

It was Monday and turning blacker by the hour. On the Salerno beachhead, German tanks had broken through American lines. Britain's General Montgomery—"Slow Motion Monty"—had been lackadaisical about his advance up the Italian boot, and General Clark was readying an evacuation order for tens of thousands of Americans. Dunkirk was on everybody's mind, and the Navy raged against the possibility. "We have never done this," said one rear admiral.

An hour into the second detail's attempt to get a handle on *Newfoundland*'s fire, the salvage tub *Moreno* showed up to render assistance. The tug was to distressed vessels what a medic is to a fallen soldier, and *Plunkett* deferred to *Moreno*'s expertise.

That afternoon, with *Plunkett* circling the burning ship to guard against a predatory sub, the crew scribbled notes to the nurses and stuffed them into their luggage. Jim wrote a short note, saying he was happy to help save this luggage—he struggled for any more eloquence than just that—and shoved the slip, with his mailing address, into the case. Though he'd maintained his fidelity to Betty, the fortune-teller had seemed to doom their future. He wasn't happy about the prognostication, but on the other hand, that fortune-teller at least had him surviving the war.

The uncertainty on the beachhead trembled as well in the set piece happening offshore. *Moreno* fought the fire and rigged the hospital ship for towing. *Moreno*'s commodore had salvaged wrecks and impediments in harbors from Casablanca to Palermo. If he could save this one vessel from going down, so much the better.

The task force commander called *Mayo* back to the beachhead, leaving *Plunkett* to maintain the vigil. Burke sent a whaleboat out in the afternoon to sink a flotsam of lifeboats and life rafts that would otherwise have floated on as a distraction to other ships in the task force. After general quarters at dusk, they sunk quietly into the night, rousing once near midnight when German planes attacked ships that had come in on Operation Avalanche.

Ken Brown squatted in the director afterward, obliged to that roost by the ship's modified Condition II (battle stations for select gun crews only), and moreover by brooding he couldn't help. He had screwed up badly when they'd bombed the boot, smarting off to the captain from a compulsion that percolated as naturally within him as breathing. He'd deserved the sacking, he'd admit as much. If he'd done right by the shore bombardments on the leapfrog landings, that hardly mattered as much to him as that aircraft in the harbor in Palermo, which haunted him as a Spitfire, no matter what Bonnie said about its German provenance. Nor could he forget his stitching legs at Gela, and what that nervous energy said about his mettle as gun boss. They'd lobbed but a single salvo since they'd come in on Avalanche. Maybe that's why they had been relegated to the fringe of the action. *Plunkett*'s battery wasn't getting it done. He wasn't getting it done.

Getting to sleep in the director at general quarters was never an easy proposition, especially when there was plenty to think about. He could count sheep; he could do that all the way to one hundred. But it was no use this evening, for any of them, wedged as they were into that tiny box, steaming fraught circles around *Newfoundland* at fifteen knots. They sighted an unidentified plane in the small hours of the morning, sliding by to starboard at low altitude. They couldn't identify it, one way or the other, and so didn't touch it. Lapsed back into another bid for slumber, they struggled for decent shut-eye, as they frequently did in the director and sometimes tried to redress with a song. It would be just the one man at first, a little something for himself, a snatch of verse that dwelled within him and that he'd retrieved as a way to deal with the melancholy or deepen it. Someone else hummed along with the verse, encouraging the singer into a chorus that a couple of them picked up. It would be a small song, carried by an undercurrent of yearning and homesickness, and expertly rendered by no means, the acoustics of the director all wrong, and it couldn't be heard outside the confines of their little perch on the Tyrrhenian Sea, except for the echoes of this song, of so many of those songs, melded by memory and reverberating across the decades. *Dinah, won't you blow. Dinah, won't you blow. Dinah, won't you blow your ho-o-orn.*

In the morning, *Plunkett* picked up a sound contact on a vessel that may have wanted to add insult to *Newfoundland*'s injury. They dropped a pattern of five depth charges, but nothing turned up. Though the officers fighting to save the ship believed it could be saved, the task force decided that afternoon to have it sunk. They wanted the destroyer back on the beachhead.

Plunkett edged away from the now doomed ship, and Ken's battery tightened its grip on the burning vessel. He thought these orders to scuttle the hospital ship were premature, and he was of half a mind to let Burke know what he thought. Except that he fired that first shell without protest. Burke stood on one wing of the bridge, watching as each shell put another straw on the camel's back. He gauged the reaction to each new hit, wondering whether it had had enough. It went on like that for forty-five minutes. Ken marveled at the seaworthiness of the old mail packet. After the forty-seventh shell hit, at 10 p.m., Burke called him off. The hospital ship was listing badly and seemed to be slowly sinking. *Plunkett* secured its crew from battle stations ten minutes after the firing stopped. They idled topside, watching twenty more minutes as *Newfoundland* finally succumbed.

Shortly after the ship was lighted the next morning, *Plunkett* steamed into the swept channel at thirteen knots, bound for the transport area off Salerno and a British ship with a funny name that would top off their fuel. Thanks to hundreds of dropped paratroopers over the previous two nights and incessant naval gunfire, the pressure on the beachhead had lightened at last. After *Plunkett* secured the men from general quarters at dawn, the crew started for breakfast at the mess hall. They were slouched against the bulkheads, awaiting their turn for Schwartzie's fixings, when Jack Simpson responded to a red alert. The men sprang for general quarters and braced against an aerial assault that began eight minutes after the klaxon had sounded.

Ken Brown popped from his hatch to scan the skies as Focke-Wulf 190 fighter bombers burst from the sun. *Plunkett*'s machine guns opened on the low-level bombers, and Ken gripped the slewing sight as the director readied a salvo.

"Mr. Brown," torpedoman Frank Vyskocil shouted from the torpedo director between the stacks. "Mr. Brown, there's an aircraft overhead."

Ken looked off the port side.

"There are two aircraft," Vyskocil yelled.

Ken looked but couldn't see it.

"No, it's one," Vyskocil said. "It's one and he's dropped something."

Ken saw the thing then, a flicker of green on an angle of descent that he computed against the speed and bearing of his own ship and decided was lethal. It was a glide bomb, one of the choo choos chugging under the command of a German in a plane overhead.

"Take cover," Ken shouted.

There wasn't time to take cover, or any place to take it really. But something had to be said. He said it but didn't move.

A hundred yards away, dozens of Army stevedores had been teasing cargo from the holds of a Liberty ship, *James Marshall*, and loading it into the maw of a landing craft. The radio-guided bomb flashed by *Plunkett* and drilled *James Marshall*'s boat deck, exploding. The blast sprung bodies airborne in obscene arcs of flight, and fire flashed all over topside.

Burke called in to the bridge for more steam, and in an instant, *Plunkett* dug into the sea like a fighter who's sensed an opportunity. The skipper thrived on competition, with an offense like a cyclone of jabs, hooks, and crosses. But all of his offense was in the hands of Ken Brown, and he had nothing to do but run. Hard right. Hard left. Full steam.

Amidship, Jim Feltz hunkered by a bulwark beneath the torpedo tubes, watching a landing craft hustle through the tumult at seven knots like a fat man who knows he has to hurry. He doesn't know where or how, but he knows why. Men clung to the edges of their vessel, its empty berthing space as wide open as an invitation. Jim's repair party was as vulnerable as the men in the LCT, but they enjoyed the illusion of protection afforded by the bulwark and the proximity of the deckhouse behind them. There were bombs falling all over the roadstead, and for whatever reason, Jim gripped this one landing craft with his sight. Until he blinked. Or maybe he didn't blink. All he knew after the fact was that whatever he saw was right then and forever banished from his sight because the landing craft simply "disappeared." That was Jim's euphemism for what he didn't want to remember because what actually happened was this: Another bomb, dropped from one of the high-level bombers, whacked LCT-241 and so completely obliterated it and the seventeen men it carried that the Navy could only presume it was sunk.

With fire now raging on the *James Marshall*, and panicking men flinging themselves into the sea to swim for the beach, four of the Fw 190s swept on *Plunkett* low and fast. Burke now had the ship at flank speed, maneuvering at twenty-five knots on two boilers. Ken dispatched a single salvo with the five-inch battery, and the machine guns and 1.1-inch maintained fire. Burke called for a rudder change, putting the helm over hard to port as one of the German bombs streaked for the ship. The bomb dove into the ship's wake 150 yards from the stern, a second or two shy of its mark.

The dive-bomber circled back to come in low and tight on the port beam, like a taunt. The no. 2 and no. 4 machine guns each emptied a full canister into the Fw 190, the tracers making no mistake about it. The plane absorbed the shells without evidence of injury. It was the damnedest thing. They could plant shells in the fuselage of a plane, and sometimes it wouldn't even cough back smoke.

As quick as they'd come, the planes were gone, all of the action contained within five minutes—the *James Marshall* hit, the bombing runs on *Plunkett*, the ship to flank speed, the expenditure of 194 rounds of the 20mm and 55 rounds of the 1.1-inch. Burke slowed the ship to five knots and, like a shepherd to his sheep, crawled in among the merchant ships should the bombers circle back over this part of the transport area. They did not, and by 9 a.m., *Plunkett* was siphoning fifty-one thousand gallons of fuel oil off the British tanker *Dertwendale*. In the faux leather oxblood diary that Cliff Dornburg was keeping of his time on *Plunkett*, he jotted five words to sum up the day: "Near dead by dive bombers."

The day was not over. Jack Simpson was on the bridge as officer of the deck when the *James Marshall* was hit and *Plunkett* was dive-bombed, and he dutifully penciled the details into the ship's log after the fact. Having Jack in the box quite often meant something was about to pop. In his stints as officer of the deck and as first lieutenant, Jack found himself more often than not a witness to or a player in matters of consequence and calamity. He'd put his name on that telegram to

Roosevelt, asking the president to retain Miller as *Plunkett*'s CO. He was at the conn when they first sighted Africa in the fall. At Gela, he'd been officer of the deck when German planes roared into the roadstead and started bombing the transports. He was one of the first three men on *Plunkett* wounded in action. He went out to retrieve the downed German pilot. He'd counted the swabs coming out of Ken Sahlin. He'd led men onto the *Newfoundland* to fight the fire. He'd watched the *Rowan* explode at Salerno and noted the time he saw the flash at 0132. If there was a pivotal moment on board *Plunkett*, Jack Simpson invariably found himself at the fulcrum, shouldering some of the burden. No wonder Burke wouldn't let him go.

So when the lookouts spotted several dead men floating two hours after they'd finished fueling off the *Dertwentdale* and had begun patrolling Able sector, it was Jack Simpson who lowered one of the ship's whaleboats and, together with Dr. Bates and a damage control party, went out to investigate.

Burke didn't stick around. He resumed his patrol, always within sight of the detached gig, leaving Jack and Bates to putter from one floating man to another, some of whom were intact, some of whom were not. There wasn't any mystery to why these men had not stayed down with their ship. Each had bloated completely out of his clothes, as well as his necklace of dog tags, and was buoyed now by the gas of decomposition.

They retrieved seven bodies in all and then sat with them in the cockpit of the whaleboat, Jack and Bates and the crew, while *Plunkett* continued its survey of Able sector. At last, after too much time in a cockpit roiling with the stench of decomposition, *Charley P.* steamed within reach, and hoisted the gig.

They laid the bodies out on the fantail between the depth charge projector and the bulwark. They'd looked for clues to the individual identities of these men, but all they could know for sure was that the bodies were male. The miasma—what else to call it?—was overwhelming, like rotten cabbage.

Though *Savannah* had also lost two hundred men, they surmised these men were off the destroyer *Rowan*. That ship had been steaming at such a high rate of speed that when the explosion ripped open its hull, the ship took on water like a fiend. As water rushed in, presumably, men washed out.

They'd worked alongside *Rowan* on the leapfrog landings, and had seen these men, or their downed shipmates, moving topside as silhouettes in the dark off the northern coast of Sicily, or in the light of day on a nest in Palermo. Now here they were, and there but for the grace of God, they knew.

The grace of God would be called for now, because there was no way Burke was going to indulge the luxury of further attempts at identification. *Plunkett* didn't have a chaplain on board, but one of the ship's reserve officers was a Southerner, and he had a Bible.

They retrieved canvas for shrouds and fifty-two-pound shells to weigh the men down. There was some discussion about what to do next, for the dead men had to be relieved of the gas but nobody wanted to do it. So Jack Simpson, the Southerner, did it, because he was also first lieutenant. Jack didn't have a Navy-issue knife but had fashioned one for himself in the ship's engine rooms, grinding one of the files until it was white hot, dunking it in colder water to set the shape, then grinding and dunking again until he got it the way he wanted it.

Jack knelt before the first bloated sailor and slipped his blade into the man's gut, venting gas so wretched that a sympathetic ventilation of his own gut was now a possibility. The first lieutenant stood and turned away from the body a moment, collecting himself. The Med sparkled sunlight off swells that made for a head of land that was no sanctuary. It wasn't enough to address only the gut; each lobe of the lungs must be vented. It was a thing you wanted done quickly, but hurrying such enterprise would be tantamount to blasphemy, for this was the end of a man who had a mother out in the world perhaps, or a wife or a child. He angled the tip of his blade at the rib cage between the armpit and nipple, and then leaned on the hilt to pierce the skin. Surprisingly, it took very little pressure to get into the space between the lining of the lung and the lung itself. He could almost feel a pop at the entry, and there was an audible rush of air as the gas was exhausted. There were prayers stirring within Jack as he conducted this ministration, psalms susurrating from his lips at barely discernible volume and with no need for articulation. This was between Jack and the man for whom he had to do this. The man deflated to a semblance of his former self, and the pharmacist's mates negotiated the remains into a canvas sack. The gunner's mates contributed two fifty-two-pound shells per canvas.

Burke stood by in stony silence, bearing witness to the administration of each man. *Plunkett*'s crew not otherwise on watch mustered themselves at the fantail, no boatswain's whistle needed. A crew of six emerged from below deck in dress whites to man the sides of a board that would usher each man to burial. The other sailors stood by in dungarees, some with hands clasped at the rear, some with slumped posture, and all with bowed heads as Jack Simpson's gentle, rhythmic voice with its rounded vowels and dropped r's said the words that concluded as such: "God, we give these men up to you and the depths of the sea."

One by one, each of the seven was brought to the board and draped with an American flag. Jack repeated the rites, and each of the retrieved dead was balanced on the upper cable of the guardrail between the depth charge projector and a rack of ash cans, and slid feetfirst, two five-inch shells leading the way into the Tyrrhenian Sea at 40° 21" N and 14° 43.5" E. It was 4:40 in the afternoon.

In the small hours of the morning, an unidentified plane flew over the ship at low altitude, and *Plunkett*'s machine guns opened fire. With his 20mm stabbing blindly in the dark, and Ken now cognizant of a positive blip they'd just picked up on the surface radar, a tidal wave of adrenaline overwhelmed the director as the men broke from slumber. Up out of his hatch, Ken twisted around to the right and the left, trying to read something, anything, from the 20mm tracers, but the gunners were acting on hunches, the worst possible information. Their lines of fire unspooled in the weak light, each falling off in an impotent little comma of failure. Not for the first time he wondered what else he might do to refine the decision-making in the ship's gun tubs. The 1.1-inch remained silent.

The hell with it, Ken thought. They've got something. He called down to his gun captains and told them to load. Jim and Bing kept up a low mutter that firmed up suddenly when the blip showed on their screens. All they had to do was grip that thing a moment and get that info down to the Mark 1 computer so they could read its course and speed, and then bang.

Bing was onto the plane for a minute, and though it was a shot in the dark, Ken let it go. A salvo spewed from the muzzles and went silent. The 20mm went quiet, and they listened. To nothing.

At dawn they stood general quarters for an hour, tried for some breakfast, and ran back to battle stations for a red alert on enemy planes coming in from the east. *Plunkett* was too far from the assault to offer up any gunfire, but at least had the satisfaction of seeing three planes flare out of their trajectories, downed by naval gunfire.

Ken exercised his mounts after breakfast, training them through a full circle and making sure the elevation hooked up neatly to the director. They'd recently had a problem with the air pressure in the no. 4 gun. Someone had neglected to tighten a valve, and an air leak caused the gun to fall out of battery when they tried elevating it. McManus and Richardson, another one of the ship's gun captains, took to the mount with crowbars and got an air line into it, and 1,550 pounds of pressure again. Now, on full automatic, Ken had complete confidence in the battery as he slewed the works, as if each of the guns channeled directly into his grips on the sight. There was some extra sense at work, some preternatural feeling of confidence in the outcome.

Plunkett fell in behind *Philadelphia*'s stern as the cruiser steamed into position to lend fire support to a naval assault now crushing German forces on shore. Dr. Bates puttered away in one of the gigs to help a man who'd been injured on a minesweeper. There was a red alert that came to nothing in the late morning, and Ken sent the men down to the mess at lunch.

Just then, a bomb exploded off *Plunkett*'s stern and Ken sprung from the hatch as the bridge called general quarters. He looked for targets, but the dome over *Plunkett* was a void. They had to wonder if what had come down on them was one of these new kinds of bombs, like the one that got *Savannah*, a choo choo bomb. How else to explain the absence of an airplane?

Twenty minutes after they were secured, a red alert had them hopping again, this time as Fw 190s sped out from shore. The lookouts spied two of them in their binoculars, coming on high and fast.

They nailed them on the fire control radar, and Bonnie had them on the range finder. Ken took the battery to thirty-eight degrees and, twenty seconds after they'd spotted the planes, let the guns go straight off the port beam.

The port machine guns and 1.1-inch drew beads on the same planes, one of which was now coming under fire by ships in the vicinity, the other veering toward *Plunkett*'s bow. The ship's battery tracked after the one bomber, and the barrels cranked up to fifty degrees.

In each of the ship's four five-inch gun mounts, the men braced for another burst—the pointer, the trainer, the fuse setter, hot shell man, projector man, powder man, and gun captain, all squeezed into that impossibly tight space like fraternity boys in a telephone booth.

Plunkett's guns boomed, and a shell burst near a plane that immediately peeled away in distress, heading back the way it had come but in jeopardy. There wasn't the luxury of tracking this one to confirm its fate. Burke had the ship's speed up and down, dashing erratically as he tried to stay one step ahead of the Folke-Wulfs.

The planes coursed over the fire control radar, and Ken swiveled after them, loosing one salvo after another. They only had the one plane to deal with now. With his guns pointing up again at fifty degrees, Ken's battery discharged another salvo and flames burst from the barrels. Almost simultaneously, a parachute blossomed away from the plunging aircraft.

It was the kind of moment that might rouse a huzzah from the men on deck, or the antics of players in an end zone, but of this first downed plane there was only tacit acknowledgment on *Plunkett*'s deck, as if they'd been there before. The ship was moving too fast, there was too much to do. This was combat, and each one of them, all the way down to the men in the bowels of the ship, was in the thick of it, all equally vulnerable, all in it together. On a destroyer in combat, they all walked point.

The following afternoon, they were screening *Philadelphia* as the cruiser pounded targets on shore, and two more Focke-Wulfs again came in off the port bow. They'd just learned that Slow Motion Monty's Eighth Army had finally connected with Mark Clark's Fifth Army, adding another layer of security to the Salerno beachhead. With the Fw 190s angling for approach, Burke kicked the ship into a surge again, sloughing this immediate threat with the finesse of a running back. Ken didn't sweat that. The ship's computer was faster than Burke. The gun boss tracked his targets for twenty-four seconds before calling up the first salvo. At the one-minute mark in this new action, he watched two shells burst near one of the Folke-Wulfs, and then watched a shell burst right on the target. By the time he pulled his eyes from his sights, and looked for confirmation with the naked eye, it was gone. Disappeared. Vanished.

Once the skies cleared over their heads, the crew allowed themselves to pump fists in the recollection of what they'd done. "We knocked out two," Gebhart kept saying. On the more sober bridge, they confirmed one and said a second was possible, but Gebhart, no matter his battle station below deck, was convinced of the second.

Jim Feltz watched the bombers dive other ships in the roadstead. He watched geysers erupt sometimes by the hulls of near misses and other times in the middle of nowhere. The Germans, this master race of people, looked more to him like the Keystone Kops, flying hither and thither. "They're guessing, by golly," he thought.

After Gela, Palermo, and now Salerno, watching the Luftwaffe in action, sometimes too close for comfort but as frequently from a near distance that gave him a perspective and that allowed him to run a little math, Jim wondered a thing that he wouldn't sound out to anyone, that seemed treasonous even to think: Why wouldn't the Luftwaffe concentrate on just a single ship?

1

In his senior year at the U.S. Naval Academy in 1928–1929, Edward J. Burke captained the Midshipman team that confronted Knute Rockne's Notre Dame Ramblers before one of the largest sports crowds in history at Soldier Field in Chicago. Here he's staring down the Rambler captain at left.

2

Frank, John, Martha, and Charlie Gallagher in their backyard in the Dorchester neighborhood of Boston in 1937, probably at Easter. Before the war, Frank worked as a streetcar driver and John was a machinist in a chocolate factory.

3

Ken Brown grew up in Glen Ellyn, Illinois, as the son of a man with outsized ambitions for his youngest. Attending the U.S. Naval Academy wasn't Ken's idea but his father's: "I was going along for the ride.

4   5

Ken Brown, on his Youngster Cruise, a Naval Academy summer ritual for plebes who have completed their first year. He distinguished himself at Annapolis with a "yen for kidding" but that characteristic didn't seem to compromise his emergence as one of the Navy's most able gunnery officers.

As a representative of a new class of American destroyers, USS *Plunkett* (DD-431) made the cover of *Popular Science* in March of 1941. Before the country's entry into World War II, the magazine celebrated destroyers for their ability to transport heavily armed Marine detachments to hot spots in the Caribbean.

6

Brown graduated from the Academy with the class of 1942, though the war hurried up graduation to December 19, 1941.

7

In 1941, Jack Simpson rode a Harley-Davidson motorcycle from Atlanta to Chicago to complete his training as a Naval Reserve officer. Later, he rode an Army Harley on trips through French North Africa.

8   9

Simpson requested duty in the Pacific at the outset of war, anticipating that the most significant naval engagements would take place in the Pacific theater. He would get there eventually, but not before he saw plenty of action in the European theater.

Jim Feltz persuaded to his mother to sign his enlistment papers shortly after he turned 17 in 1942. After training at the Great Lakes Naval Training Center, he was dispatched to New York City where he volunteered for duty on the USS *Plunkett*.

10

Home from boot training at Newport in Rhode Island, John Gallagher stood for a photo in the backyard of his family home shortly before he crossed town to board *Plunkett* on January 24, 1942, two years to the day before the ship went into action at Anzio off the western coast of Italy.

11

Plunkett as she looked on the day Jim Feltz joined her at the Brooklyn Navy Yard. Note Ken Brown's fire control director perched on the round barbette at the highest part of the ship's superstructure.

Christmas
1942

U. S. S. PLUNKETT
431

.. *Menu* ..

CREAM OF TOMATO SOUP

OLIVES	CELERY HEARTS
HOT ROLLS	MIXED NUTS
LETTUCE AND TOMATO SALAD	

ROAST YOUNG TOM TURKEY
OYSTER DRESSING	CRANBERRY SAUCE
MASHED POTATOES	GIBLET GRAVY
HARVARD BEETS	BUTTERED PEAS

| APPLE PIE | ICE CREAM |
| HARD CANDIES | FRESH FRUITS |

CIGARETTES AND CIGARS

COFFEE

K. B. BROWN
Lt. (jg) U. S. N.
Commissary Officer

K. P. HEISSLER
CCSTD.
U. S. N.

12

Menu for Christmas dinner on *Plunkett*, courtesy of Ken Brown and Dutch Heissler.

14

Plunkett had a number of Ship's Parties at the Hotel St. George in downtown Brooklyn—on December 18 and 21, 1942, March 19, 1943, and March 11, 1944. The hotel was then the largest in New York City. Captain Edward Burke is front and center here, with his wife Adele to his right. Dutch Heissler is in front at left, with his wife Ginny to his left. Gallagher, Brown, Feltz, and Irvin "Dutch" Gebhart are also in this crowd.

15

In the spring of 1943, John Gallagher started gathering signatures of his shipmates on the back of an "Our Navy" photo of *Plunkett*. This image hung on the wall beside his purple heart on Oakton Avenue for fifty years.

16

17 *africa* Sept 1943

After *Plunkett*'s first day in combat off the coast of Sicily on July 11, 1943, Irvin Gebhart wrote this in a journal he kept, surreptitiously, throughout the war: "Arrived in Gela. Landed troops. Had planes attack all day. We fired back at them. A day I will never forget."

Frank and John Gallagher met twice during the war. The first time was outside Oran in Algeria on the eve of the Salerno invasion, aka Operation Avalanche, in September 1943. There is no picture to memorialize their second meeting on *Plunkett* on the eve of the Anzio invasion. It was the last the brothers would ever see of each other.

18

19

Tom Garner was in the gun tub at Anzio with Gallagher, serving as his loader. He was wounded two ways at Anzio, physically and mentally. He'd told his wife that he'd seen one of his buddies mortally wounded at Anzio—indeed, that he'd "melted into his gun." Jim McManus was asked to visit Garner in the hospital. Garner was so traumatized by what happened at Anzio that he couldn't speak for three days. He killed himself in 1968.

Plunkett "splashing" one of the three or four German aircraft they shot down at Anzio. The watercolor was commissioned by Ken Brown for a ship's reunion in the 1990s, with 431 prints authorized.

20

En route to Palermo, a ship's photographer took a dozen images of the damage. They were to remain classified for decades. John Oliver (in garrison cap at right) inspects the wreckage in the vicinity of the blast hole. John Gallagher's gun tub is draped with float netting at top center.

21

'2

23

Anti-aircraft fire on the Anzio beachhead. Frank Gallagher was there and took this photo on the evening of January 24, 1944. It was under this same aerial assault that *Plunkett* was hit.

The ship buried two dozen of its confirmed dead at a cemetery in Palermo. Most were disinterred and returned to the United States after the war. Seven men were buried again at the Sicily-Rome American Military Cemetery in Nettuno.

After applying too late for their blood tests and thus missing the chance for a wedding on 4/4/44, Jim Feltz married Betty Kneemiller in New York City on April 5, 1944.

After the death of his wife, Feltz stopped sleeping in their bedroom. He sleeps now in an easy chair (not pictured) in this room that he keeps as a shrine to *Plunkett*.

John Gallagher's gravestone at the Sicily-Rome American Military Cemetery in Nettuno, which neighbors Anzio. When the staff there know family will be visiting, they brighten the name on the stone with sand from the Anzio beachhead. The January 24 date on Gallagher's stone is probably wrong. As Gebhart notes in his journal, his shipmate died at 0100 on January 25.

THE DUSK

PART III

Captain James P. Clay and Captain Edward J. Burke on *Plunkett* shortly before the invasion at Anzio.

13: OVERLAND, MISSOURI

OCTOBER 2017

In St. Charles, Missouri, I checked into a hotel in the river town's historic district. The building was all brick, like so many of the nineteenth-century structures lining the street, and they'd tried to make the new construction look more august by chiseling the concrete foundation to mimic granite, but its sterile, utilitarian lobby and a plastic display case of chocolate chip cookies on the reception counter belied attempts at time travel. After the receptionist gave me my room card, I asked what St. Charles was most famous for, and he promptly said Lewis and Clark, as if I'd pressed a button and there was my answer.

"They started here," he told me proudly.

I nodded, knowing from childhood they'd launched from St. Louis and figuring St. Charles could probably lay claim to some of the credit.

Then he tilted his head to the side and shook it slightly. "But I'm not sure where they ended up."

I looked to see if there was a joke coming, but he seemed genuinely puzzled, so I offered up a guess, as if I wasn't sure, either. "Oregon?"

"Oregon, that's right," he said.

For as long as I'd been talking to Jim Feltz, we talked infrequently of anything but the likes of Salerno, Sicily, Casablanca, Anzio, Brooklyn, and Overland back in the day, so much so that I had a hard time inserting him into the present. On the way in from the airport, I'd driven for St. Charles on I-70, past one big box store after another, and then past a Trane factory and a Hewlett-Packard plant. It wasn't all about commerce, for there among the titans of retail sales and manufacturing was faithchurchstlouis.com, a massive warehouse of a store that might have once been a supersize Walmart but was trading in souls now, or trying to, and recruiting new members with its URL in big bold lettering strung along a facade that fronted the highway. High on a bluff over the Missouri was an Ameristar, whatever that was, sounding more like a third-rate television brand than what it looked like and actually was, a casino. I-70 heaved up beyond the big boxes to crest the Missouri, and there was the casino, laid out along the river with a lot of faux, old-style lighting and ample room for cars. In this thoroughly modern mix of commerce and industrial-weight soul-saving, it was hard to imagine there was room enough for men like Jim Feltz, who'd come of age at a time when they rigged Victrolas in their cars for music and when the dollar store was an essential part of the shopping experience, not symptomatic of what was desperate and tawdry about America.

Waiting for Jim in the lobby, on the verge of meeting him face-to-face for the first time, I tried mapping from the one image I had of him from 1942, in that Casablanca picture, to what he might look like today, aging him like one of those time-lapse exercises online. He pulled up to the front of my hotel in a late-model Ford

Escape SUV and stepped down out of the car to say hello. His hair was sparse but comb-able, and his mouth had sunk some with age, and yanked slightly to the side, that "crooked Feltz grin," as his sister put it in a letter she'd written to him in 1942. He weighed probably what he weighed in the Navy. In fact, no matter how much older men resemble no one so much as one another, Jim clearly looked like an older version of the seventeen-year-old sailor who'd stood in that studio in Casablanca with my great-uncle in November of 1942.

That night at dinner in Lewis & Clark's on South Main Street, he told me he hadn't talked much about the war after the war. He'd started a truck parts business that did well all the way through the fifties, sixties, seventies, and into the eighties. He hadn't been hiding anything; he just wasn't talking about it, and he recalled how even his closest customers, when they found out he'd served on a destroyer during the war, were surprised that such a vital experience wasn't part of what they knew about Jim. His reticence thawed all of a sudden in 1982 when he decided to go to one of the ship's first reunions. He never missed another, and as late as 2017 he was hoping for one last hurrah at a Tin Can Sailors reunion in Buffalo.

In the same way Jim hadn't maintained his ties to *Plunkett* for so long, he likewise hadn't dwelled much on one other setting he talked about a lot: the dollar store. Because I wanted to see the store, he'd traveled to his hometown the day before my arrival for some reconnaissance. He'd parked and set out on the Woodson Road, looking up and down at the old brick buildings, but he couldn't quite recall which had been Siegal's. He'd gone into stores and asked questions, hoping to locate the old five-and-dime. One man took him outside and showed him a newer building in between two older buildings, and then Jim got his bearings and figured he'd located Siegal's. Still he wasn't sure.

In the morning, after a breakfast of buttermilk pancakes and bacon, we drove to Overland and parked on Woodson, just up from the big intersection at Midway that had once been run through with streetcars and was now dominated by a QuikTrip convenience store fronted by banks of gas pumps. On either side of Woodson, the storefronts of Overland's hub were shaded by primary-colored canopies and signage so small we couldn't tell what sort of businesses had set up in town except for the Medicine Shoppe Pharmacy. It was as if the discreet signage was in cahoots with the nonessential nature of the business within. On the ground floor of the most architecturally compelling building on Woodson was the Game Haven. Still, there was a hardware store in town, its windows filled with classic Radio Flyer toy wagons, its aisles stocked with the nuts and bolts of anything built since 1868 that needed fixing, unless, perhaps, it was built after 2000. Jim had talked to the owner of the hardware the day before, and orienting himself on George's Diner, where they were still flipping burgers, he believed his dollar store was today a tax office.

Jim and I headed into George's for a drink. It was noon, and we took seats on stools at a low lunch counter. I'd asked Jim if he might have preferred a chair with a back at one of the several high tables along the windows, and he shook his head, noting that high tables weren't something they used to have back then. That wasn't why Jim didn't want to sit there. He just didn't relish climbing up into the chair.

He asked the fry cook if she'd sell us hamburgers for 10 cents apiece, the place was that much of a throwback. The sixty-four-year-old cook smiled and said she wished she could. Her hair was long and gray, and her voice sounded older than she looked. She asked Jim how old he was, and he told her. One of the men at the high tables suggested we check out a Facebook page that posted lots of old pictures. I told him I'd seen that page, and expanded on Jim's note about Overland, noting that he'd grown up here and that my story was really about a Navy destroyer that Jim had served on during the war. A burly man who might have come off a Harley nodded approvingly of the references made to Jim's service. And then another man came in, and the fry cook asked him how old he was. The newcomer, Charlie, seemed sideswiped by the question, but rallied and told us he was ninety-three years old and had grown up in Overland.

"Wasn't you in the Army, Charlie?" the fry cook asked.

"I was a combat medic," he said.

Jim asked where he served, and Charlie told us he'd been in North Africa first, having been drafted in '42. He said nothing about Italy, but noted he was part of the invasion of Southern France.

Charlie had been born on Tudor Street, where Jim lived when he worked at the dime store. They were only a year apart in age, and they must have passed each other a hundred times as kids, but they didn't try to bridge any of the people they might have known in common. Instead, Jim was talking about the bakery on Woodson and the laundry, and Charlie nodded along, noting that the hardware store was where the laundry used to be. They mentioned the movie theater, and Woolworth's, and Jim said he was trying to get a fix on where the dime store was. Charlie said it was just up from the hardware store, where the Game Haven is today. Jim shook his head, sure of himself. No, that building was too new.

After our drink, we drove back down Argyle, where Jim had lived, and then Olden, where the Feltzes had rented, and where he'd got drunk as a five-year-old who didn't know what he was drinking when he'd drawn beer from a keg the morning after a block party. He pointed out where so many creeks had run, and I began to think that Overland might have been a veritable Venice back in the day. Then one of the town's historians, who'd gotten wind of our search, phoned and told me she'd worked at the same store for Mr. Siegal right after she'd graduated from high school in 1950, and she had a picture of the place all lit up at Christmas in 1939. She told us to come on over.

The historian, Shirley Needy, showed us several three-ring binders of historical pictures of Overland that included one of the Overland Dollar Store, as it was known in 1939, with additional signage saying they sold goods from 5 cents to a dollar. Two doors opened from sidewalk alcoves into the store. Its windows were chockablock with "dependable merchandise," featuring dolls most prominently. Draperies of holiday lights hung from the upper floors of a building that today houses the Game Haven on its ground floor.

Jim didn't protest the evidence and said it made perfect sense that the dollar store was that far down Woodson from George's. Siegal's had closed the year after Shirley started working there, undone by some new commercial developments just outside town. Her pictures detailed Woodson in 1939 and 1940 at Christmas and on Frontier Day, when thousands of people, it looked like, had turned out into the streets for the celebration. There was another of Midland and Woodson with two trolleys passing; another of an appliance store interior with its white ranges and refrigerators and steel Westinghouse cabinetry; a clothing store with a pressed tin ceiling and collared shirts for 98 cents. There was another, too, of five suited men gathered at a circular table where one of them was signing a document concerning Overland Day in 1939. Another of the men, with dark hair receding and combed back like Nixon's, was Mr. Siegal looking just as Jim remembered him.

We drove back into town and walked into the Game Haven, where huge flat screens hung from walls all the way back on either side of the old dime store. Plush sofas were set before the screens. Only one of them was occupied, by a woman, perhaps a store employee, halfheartedly playing a game that involved zombies. Jim was in his old country now, and 100 percent sure this was the place. He showed me where the cosmetic counter had been, Mickey's counter, and the candy section, and the door into his storeroom. He walked the room all the way to the back and up again, talking almost to himself as he lifted his cane to point out the way things had been, oblivious to modern distraction. I could hear screeching as something fell from a great height during the one video game in full throttle, and then an electronic beat as the game's characters went on the march, the explosions of small arms fire and the bellows of things lunging around them. Even with his hearing aids Jim literally couldn't hear the game, and even if he could, I doubt he'd have taken a dim view. Like Ken Brown, and counter to what I half expected to hear from these men of another era, Jim didn't bemoan the drift of time and didn't talk about how much better it all was back in the day. I don't know if it was a function of their age, if as you climbed through your nineties you shed all the dissatisfaction that might weigh you down, or whether there was something in their individual makeups that precluded the development of a curmudgeon.

I watched Jim walk around the old dime store with a smile, flipping through the pictures in his memory. He was happy, and for some time on the way back out, he stopped and stood silently where he'd told me Mickey's old makeup counter was. He stood in that space, the way he'd stood there seventy-seven years earlier at sixteen years of age, with the whole of his life ahead of him and a slightly older woman telling him that Howell was the place her niece was from, Betty Kneemiller.

He'd lost her now, and his three sons, upending the expectation and the hope that his children would bury their parents and his wife would bury her husband. Cancer had gripped him twice, and he'd beat it twice. Maybe the war had put that fight in him, maybe he, like his ship, was capable of sustaining a hit and steaming on. But that explanation was far too mawkish, even for my sentimental self. Jim didn't dwell out loud on what he'd lost and had resigned himself to whatever will be will be. But there was one thing he hadn't ever been able to reconcile himself to, that had haunted him for decades and would never be still within him. It was something my family had done.

14: THE FALL

OCTOBER–DECEMBER 1943

The gush of letters from Betty Kneemiller dribbled off to a trickle through summer and into the fall of 1943. There hadn't been anything in July. Two came Jim's way in August, and there was one in September with news that Mickey had broken her engagement to Joe Jaye for reasons that went unsaid and that might have had everything to do with the war, or perhaps reservations her family had about his being an Italian fellow. Some things could not be overcome. Families could be like that. Betty had quit her job, and all of the girls at the dime store had quit theirs, too. They "got wise to themselves," Betty had written, and found new jobs that paid much better, understanding there was more important work to do elsewhere, and that it wasn't necessary to make "Jack for a Jerk." About Jim, she'd written, "I still call you mine, but I'm not as definite on that being the truth."

There was no telling what he'd read in the next letter, and mail call became something to both pine for and dread—just like October. One day in Palermo, he received a letter from a nurse off the

Newfoundland, who thanked him for his part in the recovery of her possessions. "You're a luggage-saver," she wrote. That was all. There wasn't any return address, and nowhere to write back, but consolation, at least, in the fact that he'd got a reply.

Gallagher's news that fall wasn't as welcome. The Army had called up his oldest brother, Tom, which meant his mother was putting a fourth blue star in her window.

"They would get him sooner or later anyway," John wrote home, after getting the news. "I am glad he took the Army for it's ten times better for a guy than the navy."

John had had no news from Frank since Salerno. All he knew for sure was that the men on the far right flank, where Frank went ashore on Red Beach near Paestum, had caught it worse than anyone. Whatever apprehension he harbored over his brother's situation, he kept that to himself. Writing home, he said nothing of the nine thousand Allied casualties in the ten-day struggle for Salerno or what he'd heard about the assaults on Monte Cassino or the fighting along the Rapido and Volturno Rivers.

"I know about where Frank is and am pretty sure I will meet him again if they give us liberty," he wrote to Sophie. "Tell [my mother], Frank is in a swell place and not to worry. I am OK also but would love to hit the States and have my ration of good American beer."

In the meantime, there might be beer in Palermo, and if not then vino. But first he had to get Jimmy Feltz to cover his watch in the aft fire room. Jim was spending a lot of time in the hole these days, blindfolded no less, and his grasp of the ship's power plant was firm, and impressive. Would he do it?

They'd been neighbors for a year now, Jim in the bunk just beneath John's, and had come into a familiarity born of close quarters and shared experience. Jim could recognize Gallagher from the peculiar depression of the man's weight in the berth above him, as telltale as a silhouette, and from the modulation of John's breathing in sleep. They'd waded ashore on liberty together, from Norfolk to North Africa, bumming about like tourists, shooting bull all the while. Once, after a new man had come into their quarters, drunk and catching flak for the perm he'd put in his hair, the man had pulled a knife on Jim. John rolled out of his bunk, literally, and collapsed on top of the threat, laughing all the way. John was always smiling, as happy-go-lucky as they come, without an enemy on the ship.

Sure, Jim told him that afternoon in Palermo, I'll watch your fire room.

The ship was nestled up to two other destroyers on the dock at Palermo, with the no. 4 boiler in the aft fire room supplying power to the other idle cans. The aft fire room was an operational twin to his own but as different in appearance as a nonidentical twin. He climbed through the hatch and started down the ladder, understanding right away he had a problem. Something down in the hole was clacking in rhythm and loudly.

He descended past the top-watch, who'd be the only other man in the hole with him for the next four hours. At the bilge plates, the bump man he was relieving started up the rungs as soon as Jim relieved him.

"Gland's loose in the water pump," he told Jim, looking over his shoulder, but it should hold for now.

The hell it would, Jim thought.

Shutting down that pump would have shut down power to *Plunkett*, and the other two cans, and it would take at least two hours to bring power back.

Jim went over to the auxiliary pump and looked at the thing. Two ears, each pinned with a five-inch bolt, held down the pump, except that they weren't doing a very good job. The gland was loose, the packing bore out, and every time the piston came down, the gland moved and clacked.

"Go get the chief," Jim called up to the top-watch. "Tell him we got to switch fire rooms 'cause this gland's going to bust off."

He looked back to the pump, the racket louder now. The gap that shouldn't have existed was a half inch, maybe three-quarters. There was no way of tightening that thing while they were running 150 pounds of steam.

He'd been down in the hole for the better part of a year, and could listen through the myriad hisses, clacks, and roars of the fire room for the discordant note. He knew how things fit together, and how to keep them together, and what there was to do came effortlessly to him now. He was going to have to shut that pump down and get some caulking in there, some hemp rope, and then tighten it.

The top-watch hadn't been gone a minute when Jim decided he might not have another minute. He got on the phones and rang the bridge. "I'm shutting down," he yelled.

The gland beat him to it. No longer able to hold against the action of the piston, the gland blew, and steam spewed from the pump at 150 pounds, which wasn't 600 pounds—a jet of high-pressure steam powerful enough to cut your arm off—but harsh enough. The steam filled the room magically fast. Steam at 600 pounds of pressure would fill the fire room at 500 degrees in 4.5 seconds. They'd timed their escape runs up the ladders from the burners, and the best anyone ever managed was 6.5 seconds.

Jim scrambled up the eight rungs to the grating on the upper level and went for the water first. He spun the wheel, shutting down the supply of water, then looked to the steam drum, which was hardly visible in the fogged room. There were 250 valves in the fire room.

His dungarees and T-shirt were soaked already and scalding hot. He grabbed the wheel on the drum and spun that with both hands, shutting down the steam. The fire room was now as unnavigable as a cloud, and the only bearings he had were a matter of knowing where the drum was in relation to the ladder. But how many steps? He stretched out his arms as tentatively as a man in the dark and stepped forward. The heat burned his hands, and they started shaking wildly. Before he could see it, he felt it, the two narrow, flat rungs of each step up the ladder, the metal wet and hot. He grabbed an upper rung, felt his foot slip, and compensated by pulling himself up. One by one, nine more rungs to the top, where the hatch was shut when he started but opening now as the deck crew realized they were having a problem.

Jim levered himself out in a burst of white exhaust and rolled away from the hatch like a man on fire. The heat on his exposed skin seared all of sudden, the darkest hour just before dawn. He drew his knees to his chest, sitting up, and only then opened eyes he'd clenched on his way up the ladder. His hands were still there, but beet-red. He looked up to see Gallagher in his dress blues, ready for liberty, with his arms crossed over his chest, grinning at what may have ranked as the funniest thing he'd ever seen.

"You blew up my fire room," he said.

―――

That fall, the Navy officially commended Burke for his work on the leapfrog landings and awarded him the Legion of Merit for the Salerno invasion, referencing what *Plunkett* did to repel aerial assault, what they did to render the *Newfoundland* salvable, and what they did to screen the transport area and cruisers. The language of the commendations was elevated but somewhat stock—"fearless leadership" and "gallantry and intrepidity"—and at times pointed: "Commander Burke contributed in large measure to the repulse of strong enemy counterattacks at the Salerno beachhead and the protection of assault shipping during unloading operations in support of the invasion forces." The squadron commander, James P. Clay, who had taken over from Menocal that fall after service in the Pacific, was immediately impressed by what he found after a short time aboard. "I consider the *Plunkett* one of the most efficient DDs in the U.S. Navy because of the leadership and alertness of Com'd'r Burke."

Nights now, *Plunkett* was running patrols to Ustica, that island they'd taken, and the Aeolian Islands, prowling for U-boats and E-boats. One night, they picked up a surface radar contact at sixty-five hundred yards. Jack Oliver called general quarters and cranked the bell for twenty-five knots to close on the target.

When they'd secured earlier, the bridge kept half the ship at battle stations, including Ken Brown and his crew in the director and Jim McManus's crew in gun no. 3. Mac was taking a break and sleeping through the summons when a shipfitter shook him awake and told him the gun boss wanted him on the phones.

Mac hustled up to the no. 3 gun and climbed into the turret. His fuse setter was approximating a horrible Boston accent, pretending to be him as they tried to sort a problem with the rammer. Mac pulled on the phones to hear Ken Brown sounding at high volume: "McManus, get that goddamned gun trained out and loaded."

They couldn't have any light in no. 3 because of its canvas tarp, so Mac made do with the glow shed by a breach light and deployed a trick he knew, and that everyone in the mount knew he knew, to keep the gun from jamming.

"Don't shoot till I give you the word," Ken said.

Plunkett dialed down off its twenty-five knots as they closed on the vessel. Ken was out of his hatch, phones on with a direct line to the assistant gunnery officer who was on the torpedo deck, ready to fire.

All of the guns and the torpedoes were now trained on the target. The thirty-six-inch searchlight was blasting a tunnel of light through the darkness. Lying to five hundred yards off the port beam was an Italian fishing vessel, all of the men topside and waving anything white.

The Allies had taken Naples on October 1, but not before the retreating Germans had blown up the spaghetti factories. They'd polluted the water. They'd torched the city's archives. They were desperate times, and one of every three women in the city was prostituting herself to men who had a tin of food to fork over.

The ship escorted convoys into Naples as the Allies worked their way up the boot from the beachhead in Salerno. They conducted night patrols and lit things up with their searchlight—local fishing vessels, British ships that didn't respond to their challenges, and wreckage, which they'd sink with their machine guns. If aerial assault had been the principal threat through the summer, the maneuverings of U-boats were to be guarded against that fall.

Regularly now, they dropped depth charges on sound contacts but turned up nothing.

If they weren't on patrol in the Tyrrhenian Sea, they were in Mers el-Kebir or Naples or Palermo, where they got their teeth filled and sat for movies projected onto seawalls, some of them, like *The Fleet's In*, again and again. "Very good show," Gebhart wrote after one viewing of *The Fleet's In*. "That makes the sixth time I saw it." The men went to beer parties and tried to make hay with colonial French girls. The officers did their own drinking in their own clubs, and like sleep itself, the advent of night was no longer the main impetus for a drink: Being off watch or off your battle station was.

Ken Brown returned to the ship one afternoon after a couple hours' liberty, sailing a sheet or two to the wind, but not all three, not now when the whistle was liable to kindle the klaxon off the bridge any time of day or night. You could afford to get tight, but not wedged in. Still, Ken was literally wedged in this afternoon. In addition to his work as gunnery officer, he was still handling the commissary, the job like a hangover. He'd had stores hauled on that afternoon, cigarettes and candy and sundry supplies better left under lock and key. Not that you had thieves on *Plunkett*. With the exception of the missing German pistol, and a loaf of fresh bread that might go missing at night when the bakers weren't looking and the snipes were hungry, everything stayed exactly where they left it. Destroyers were like that. But cigarettes and candy in unlocked space? That was too much temptation, and so Ken stored the crates in his stateroom. He returned to a bunk shelved with stores, and he transferred them all to the floor. The room was so crowded, he wondered, heading down for the count, whether he'd left enough room for oxygen. It was October 9.

In the forward fire room, Jim Feltz was just trying to get through the day. They'd come in from a Lipari patrol and had been more or less moored as before since they refueled. Half the crew had been perched at general quarters all the while, which he didn't necessarily like, but it couldn't be helped. At three o'clock they got word from the bridge to fire up the no. 2 boiler.

Why we firing up? Jim wanted to know.

The burner man removed a tip with the smallest orifice, put it in the barrel, and shoved it back in the burner. No one asked why they were firing up. They were getting underway. That was life.

Jim lit the torch and shoved it deep in a hole at the bottom of the boiler box, and they had combustion. You'd think we might just sit tight for a while, he thought. Except that rarely happened.

The anchor chain started hauling, and *Plunkett* was underway. A minute later, the bridge rang down to engineering for the no. 1 and no. 3 boilers.

In the after fire room, Gallagher fired his two boilers, and a half hour later, with instructions from the bridge, he cut each of them in on the main line. The boiler boxes breathed out suddenly, a funny thing that seemed so unlikely for carbon steel and never ceased to surprise any of them. A bell rang in the engine room, and the dial on the ship's speed jumped from standard to full. The burner men replaced the tips on their barrels, enabling more flame and higher heat and more steam. The bridge rang again, and they went to the tray for still-larger tips, and now they were at flank, a call that hadn't ever come down to the fire rooms when they had four boilers lit.

The ship leveled into a smooth run, bow up and proud, stern buried, digging for speed. The boilers roared as the burners spewed oil that fashioned a conical flame at twenty-eight hundred degrees.

Normally, a fire room was no louder than a truck at 40 mph, but now they were submersed in a steady roar that made communication by voice all but impossible. With no more to give, and no more to say, Gallagher settled into the run, listening to his boilers and to the propellers thumping all they had. Word had come down to them soon after they'd cut in their two burners. Another destroyer, the *Buck*, had been torpedoed some hours earlier, and they were going out after survivors.

His watch over, Jim climbed out of the hatch and made his way to the fantail for a look at the ship's rooster tail. A towering wall of water chased them like some sort of biblical portent, capable of breaking over the deck should the ship suddenly give up a few knots. They'd never run at flank on all four boilers, not off Sicily, not off Salerno, not in evasive action against the Luftwaffe.

Plunkett ran at flank for more than two hours, and then throttled down to twenty knots as they came into the vicinity of *Buck*'s bad luck, forty-three miles southwest of the Italian mainland at Point Licosa. The disconcerting crank of the manila line on the davits finally roused Ken from the deepest sleep he'd had in a while. Staring off his bunk, he waited for the data to come in. What time it was. What day it was. Where the hell he was. Sometimes you just couldn't be sure of anything in a stateroom on a ship at sea. But something was up. He swung out of bed, grabbed his hat, and found himself barricaded into his room, the crates having shifted during the run out. He removed the stores to his bed and got up to the bridge.

"Why didn't you wake me?" he asked Collingwood. Outside the bridge windows, he could barely make out the bow guns for all the fog.

"We couldn't open the door," Jack said.

A nearby British ship, HMS *Dehli*, reported they had one survivor on board. *Gleaves* had better news. They'd flashed visuals to *Plunkett* to say they'd picked up two officers and forty men thus far. At 7:50 p.m., they sighted an object in the water off to starboard, and the first lieutenant took out the ship's whaleboat to investigate. Minutes later, they cranked the whaleboat back up with *Buck*'s assistant engineer on board, a lieutenant (jg) from Needham, Massachusetts, named James Anderson. In the wardroom, they treated Anderson for lacerations on his ankle and his head and noted the distinct possibility of internal injuries. Then he started talking. He told them they'd picked up a radar contact at about five thousand yards just after midnight. The *Buck* rang general quarters, and Anderson went topside to his battle station on the ship's platform just ahead of the forward stack. The bridge rang full ahead, and they charged after the contact, black smoke spewing from the ship's funnels, looking out for a challenge from the unknown vessel. It never came. Just as the ship came up to speed, an ensign on one of the *Buck*'s 40mm guns felt the ship hesitate, as if she'd had a collision. She had, with a torpedo that slammed into the starboard side of the ship near the forward fire room and exploded. The pressure in the ships' steam lines fell from 560 pounds to nothing, but she retained power for a spell.

"I was blown over the side by the explosion," Anderson told *Plunkett*'s officers.

The explosion knocked down an ensign on the 40mm gun and raked him with flying debris while a foot of water surged over the deck. The ensign got to his feet and ran to the fantail, yelling for the crew to set all of the depth charges to safe. He glanced back for sight of the stacks or the bridge and saw neither. Either the ship was cut in half, or smoke and steam from the forward fire room blocked the view. Another lieutenant was now on the fantail, also calling for all of the depth charges to be set to safe, so they would not explode if the ship sunk.

In the forward engine room, the crew secured live steam leaks and made their way up top past a blazing fire room where they believed one of the boilers had exploded. The rent in the midst of the ship levered the stern quickly aloft to a forty-five-degree angle.

The need to abandon ship was obvious, and they made quick work of it, releasing life rafts when possible, shucking shoes if they could, and plunging into the sea. The stern sunk, dragging down all of the depth charges that had been set to safe, and one, a three-hundred-pounder in a K-gun, that had not. When that ash can sunk to 100 feet or 150 feet, or to whatever depth they'd set for the explosion, the TNT burst from its shell, doubling down on the carnage.

The concussion brutalized the men in the water. The explosion ruptured pneumatic life belts and hit survivors like kicks to the stomach and pelvis. The blast perforated the membranes of their abdomens, bruised the loops of their intestines, and opened lesions on their lungs. It was hell on the viscera. Those who weren't killed immediately were so traumatized they drifted to death through the small hours of the morning. Fifty men who'd grouped on one life raft after the stern sunk dwindled to thirty by dawn. It rained in the morning, and when the sun came, it blinded them. They'd seen planes all over the area the previous day, but nothing today until late in the morning.

With Anderson now on board *Plunkett*, the lookouts spotted a group of objects that proved to be three more survivors, clung together. One of the three came aboard with a broken ankle, another with pain in the abdomen, and a third, a pharmacist's mate, wiped out from holding up his two shipmates through the night. When the lookouts heard shouts off the port bow, Jack Simpson scrambled back into the whaleboat to retrieve five more men from the sea. Each of them was smeared black with oil, and it was a slippery, frustrating business hauling them into the boat, and even onto *Plunkett*'s deck. The men who could talk wanted to talk, and they did in the wardroom as oil drained from their ears and noses and buttocks.

A man named Lukasiewski had had the phones on just before general quarters sounded. Last word he heard was this: "Surface contact seventeen hundred yards." Zuick had just relieved the watch in the after engine room. "Ship was hit just as she got up to speed." Wieder had been asleep when general quarters sounded, and he hustled up to his battle station at the 40mm director. After the torpedo hit, he saw the "radar antenna down on the deck by the loading machine." He couldn't see the mast, stack, or bridge, but he could hear several voices shouting for the depth charges to be set on safe. One man didn't say anything. He was black, a steward's mate named Goodson, and he was cut up bad.

After they brought these five men on board, they resumed listening for the shouts, and wondering that the men in the water didn't have whistles, a simple piece of equipment that now seemed so obviously essential.

Plunkett crept along at one-third, cutting a wake that muffled the ability of anyone to hear much of anything. The lookouts were yanked repeatedly to look in one direction or another as they thought they heard the cries of survivors.

Burke nudged the ship into thick fog and watched his lookouts for signals, but none heard the same thing. There were men in the water and they couldn't be heard for the depth of the fog and the churn of *Plunkett*'s propellers. Burke had no choice. "All stop," he said.

The helmsman rang the engine room, and a moment later, *Plunkett*'s bow settled as its screws whined down. The reassuring thrum of the ship underway gave way to a silence made all the more deep by the muffling fog, and that was dreadful to every sailor topside and below deck. They may as well have heard the ticking of a bomb. You might lie to inside a submarine net, but you wouldn't want to in contested waters, and you especially did not want to in the vicinity of a torpedoed ship. A U-boat liked nothing so much as a return to the scene of a crime, where the pickings might be good.

They were still two hours shy of midnight. It was October 9, "OCT 9" from the Ouija board, and Jim Feltz was on deck when the engines went still and the searchlight cut into the fog, lighting the departures of the ship's two whaleboats until the fog consumed them. He could hear, or thought he could, the ping of the ship's sonar sounding for a sub. The sonar signal bounded away from the ship, and with each dispatch Jim found himself listening for a corresponding beep echoing back from contact.

After the action off Gela, in Palermo, and at Salerno, he marveled at how little fear he'd actually felt in those places, in that action, so much so that he sometimes wondered whether he was immune to it, that he might be one of those guys to come out the other side of the war sure of his courage, that it would always be there, himself phlegmatic. Except that it was flapping now. He was afraid. His heart was telling him so, racing ahead of every ping of the sonar to still, poised and vigilant, anticipating the corresponding beep of contact with a sub. The energy bottled up within him required some sort of action, and so there was nothing to do but reach a hand to the back of the neck and rub it vigorously, to drop into a squat like an athlete to loosen the stiffness before a race, to inspect the handy billy pumps in the lockers, anything to quell the onset of nerves that might embarrass him if he didn't camouflage the energy with other measures.

In the dark, he could just make out the gun crew in the no. 2 tub, the gunner leaned back casually in his harness, the loader and the handler pitched forward over the apron like boys on a bridge, a lazy summer day flowing beneath them. They were just as vulnerable as he was. That was the thing about being on a ship at sea: Everyone was equally at peril, no man more so than another, every officer as susceptible as the grimiest snipe. In the infantry, one bullet might find one man, but it didn't work that way in the kind of combat Jim was engaged in. What might get him was a torpedo or a glide bomb, and if it got him, it was going to get a boatload of them. If the Ouija board had it in for him it had it in for all of them. He listened to the soft chatter of men topside, a sound you never heard at sea because casual talk was always embedded in the baseline of noise emanating from the engine. This sudden recognition of communion calmed him. He wasn't out there on his own alone. They were with him.

The whaleboat's faint, distant motor strengthened, and soon one of the gigs resolved out of the darkness, with men standing but silent. The deck force went to the davits and cranked up the boat. Two *Plunkett* sailors were engaged in artificial respiration bent over two lifeless men. The third man, like his two lifeless shipmates, was smeared with oil. He retched as they negotiated him out of the whaleboat, and then doubled over on the deck. They got him to the wardroom, the man calling for help for his stomach. *Plunkett*'s new doctor, Wesley Knaup, administered morphine that did little good.

Jack Simpson went down into the whaleboat again, and a short time later returned with a torpedo man, a cook, and a water tender, all complaining of stomach pain. "We thought we got them all," torpedo man Chester Smith said of the depth charges after they'd brought him aboard.

In the mess hall, Jack went to the black steward they'd pulled from the sea earlier, Goodson. The man was in and out of consciousness, and when he came to, Jack raised the man's upper body and helped him to a spoonful of chicken soup. The man took the first spoonful, and for the next two hours Jack remained vigilant and managed to get down three more servings. There wouldn't be a fifth spoon. Goodson died while Jack held him.

Plunkett had fifteen men from *Buck* aboard now. Burke started the ship's engines, and they resumed their search in a new area. It was near midnight, and Jim was with the men they'd brought on board. William Loggie from New Haven, Connecticut, was hanging in there, but they gave up on Howard Hill after forty-five minutes, and a machinist's mate named Smith after an hour. They carried Smith and Hill to the fantail and laid out the men beside the ash cans, then covered them with canvas. Dutch returned to the wardroom, but Jim stayed on the fantail. It was just after midnight, October 10.

Later that morning, they brought four more men onto *Plunkett*, Charles Rupp and Jack Robinson and Jean Sumner and one man they weren't ever going to identify because all there was to the trunk were the two legs and one arm. Ken Brown watched them hoist the gig and remove the men, and then parts of men. Their work was largely done by then, and the cook had sent sandwiches up onto the deck for men who'd labored through the night.

One of the young deckhands was eating a sandwich as they

emptied this last gig, when Dutch Heissler, who was still in the gig, called for him to lend a hand. The sailor hopped to and waited for Dutch, who lifted from the belly of the whaleboat a last severed limb, this one with the bone exposed. He extended it to the unwitting young sailor. Ken Brown remembered that the kid stiffened, as if catatonic, and stayed that way while Dutch continued to hold the arm out, a gesture that took on the coloring of black humor and that was, if anything, one way to deal with the horrible consequences of a torpedo.

Jack Simpson went into a whaleboat once more that morning to investigate "a large floating object" they could not identify from the bridge, perhaps because the bow of a destroyer is never supposed to assume such an angle. The bow was intact as far as the second sound dome, which sent out the sound waves that "listened" for subs. Ken had the gunners on his 1.1-inch put twenty-two rounds in the bow, and the wreckage went down.

They arrived back in Palermo late in the afternoon, sidling up next to Pier 5, where ambulances were waiting to transfer the survivors and the dead to an Army hospital. In his diary, Jim noted they'd picked up 20 men from *Buck*. Gebhart had the number right at 19. There'd been 260 men in her originally. Ninety-seven survived, 163 had not. Reckoning the numbers mattered to the men on *Plunkett*. They'd tallied the dead on *Buck* and *Newfoundland* and *Savannah* and *Rowan* and *Maddox* and noted as well the numbers of men who survived. They reckoned the number of decks a radio-guided bomb could pierce when it hit a ship, and how many dead men floating they found. They recorded the number of times they were summoned to general quarters, and how many shells they exhausted, and they erred on the side of hope when they noted how many planes they'd knocked out of the sky. They didn't write how any of it made them feel; the math would have to do. Three days after a U-boat got the *Buck*, another U-boat got another Gleaves-class destroyer, *Bristol*, and the men had a new number of dead for their diaries—fifty-two.

That was the same day Burke finally let Jack Simpson go. The orders for Jack's transfer had come in from the Bureau of Navy Personnel in August, but it wasn't until the team had come in from another night patrol in October that Burke signed off on Jack's departure.

He'd been aboard *Plunkett* for nearly two years, and he was getting the thing he'd wanted since he'd emerged from midshipman's school—the Pacific. He didn't know it then, but he was on his way back onto a "happy ship," where the food would be good, as it was on *Plunkett*, and where the captain also cultivated bonhomie, from the wardroom to the bridge. Burke didn't do that. But he was, Jack said, "totally fearless" and a "beautiful ship handler."

Before leaving, he made his rounds on the ship to say goodbye, to his Dead End Kids, to the officers in the wardroom, and then down to the chief's quarters. Ken trailed him down there, understanding he was on the verge of losing touch with his first roommate, though he suspected they'd never lose grip.

One of the chiefs stood to shake Jack's hand. "You were the best chief boatswain's mate we ever had," he told the first lieutenant.

A boatswain's mate was an enlisted man's rating, but the demotion was an honor conferred. "He was that," Ken said later. "All of that."

At an airfield in Sicily, Jack boarded an Army air transport and lifted off in a plane he remembered chiefly for the skirt around a hole in the floor they used as a latrine. Though Jack would dodge the bombs and torpedoes that were coming for *Plunkett*, he was going to see more than his fair share off Okinawa on the USS *Morrison* (DD-560).

Some days after *Buck*'s sinking, and *Bristol*'s three days later, Dr. Wesley Knaup doled out cotton and adhesive tape for every man to carry at GQ. Whatever the protocol, few men bothered paying attention to the doctor's actual instructions if there were any; scuttlebutt had instead repurposed the adhesive and cotton as the butt of a joke. The idea was this: If *Plunkett* started to go down and the crew had a question about whether they'd set all their ash cans to safe, then what they had to do, while treading oil in the wreckage, what they had to do was shove a piece of cotton up their ass, then grab the adhesive tape and secure the cotton with the tape. Every time they explained their version of the procedure to one another in the wake of this directive, they laughed and laughed.

Through the rest of that month, they operated mostly out of Palermo. The Catholics went to Mass on *Brooklyn* and, like the tourists they wished they were, visited the "prettiest little church in the world" and Palermo's catacombs. They shifted their base to Mers el-Kebir on November 1, and some of the crew went to a beer party in Oran that wasn't very good. One of the crew came back drunk and started harassing Jim. "We had an argument," Jim wrote in his journal that night. "Finished it in a fight." They had turkey on Thanksgiving, which was good, and watched Betty Grable in *Coney Island* the day after. She was always very good, both on-screen and when you needed a little company in the afterglow. The ship's black gang played a game of baseball with a team off the destroyer *Edison*. Their roster included one of the ship's stewards who was such a good pitcher, *Edison* sometimes parked its center fielder on a chair in the midst of the game. *Plunkett* nearly gave as good as they got, losing 12–10.

The fun they cooked up with each other gave way to reminiscence about the fun they had at home, and the friends they'd left behind. "They were always a good bunch of guys down the corner," Gallagher wrote shortly after the disappointing beer party. "I will always like them all and never forget them. Boy, we all had swell times together, didn't we? We have a lot of fun too but it's nothing like the old gang."

At the beginning of his service, he declared in letters home that "I am not much for writing letters to anyone," but by that fall, he was corresponding with thirty different friends and family. When he was laid low and put on the sick list one day, whacked by a virus that also got Jim Feltz and 41 other crew, he'd bang out a dozen letters at a time. "I am writing this letter in my bunk, but don't think I would do any better if I had an office of my own."

They idled for days on end in Mers el-Kebir, roused every now and then for a run up to Bizerte or to Naples. But mostly they stayed in the Algerian port town late that fall, basking in the North African sun and even a little bit of adulation. On November 1, three officers from the *Buck* penned a letter to Burke to express their gratitude for what the men on *Plunkett* had done.

"The opinion of the survivors, who were rescued by the PLUN-KETT, is that the prompt and efficient work of her officers and men was a positive factor in saving the lives of many of the BUCK's crew . . . all possible aid was rendered to them and this letter is an expression of their gratitude."

One day in the middle of December, after taking on more than one hundred thousand gallons of fuel oil, *Plunkett* steamed over a buoy chain that ripped a six- by twelve-inch gash in the hull, something they didn't realize right away. But the next day, a shipfitter found water in one of the magazines, flooding five-inch and 20mm shells. Even with a gash in the hull, there shouldn't have been water in that magazine. Pretty soon, it was found out that the gunner's mate responsible for cleaning that magazine was John "Annie" Oakley, who'd recently moved into McManus's gun turret. When Mac had showed Oakley how to manage the magazines, where he'd turned to for two years, he cocked a wrench at him and said you had to dog down each of the six nuts on each hatch when securing the compartments. That, Mac told him, was how you ensured a watertight seal.

That, according to Annie, "was a bunch of bull." He wasn't about to dog down each and every time.

"Do it any way you want," Mac said. "I'm just 'going by the book.'"

Running over a chain and opening a seam in the hull and having the sound dome carried away was one thing. Burke wasn't going to can anyone for bungling that. But this about the flooded magazine was something else.

Who's in charge of the magazines? is what Burke asked the gun boss when he learned of the flood.

"Oakley, gunner's mate second class," Ken said.

"You mean Oakley, gunner's mate third class."

The Allies hadn't made much progress on the ground since the Salerno landings in September. The Germans' Gustav Line stretched across Italy from sea to sea south of Rome, and its linchpin on the flanks of Monte Cassino was to blame. The Allies couldn't break through. "We'd got as high as Naples, and then a little higher, but we couldn't get around Monte Cassino," Frank Gallagher said. "There was the Volturno River and the Rapido River, and we had to keep crossing them. Then we had to go up a mountain. The Germans were always on top of the mountain. Down and up, down and up. That son of a bitch [American General] Mark Clark was a butcher."

It was then that Churchill hatched a plan to conduct an end run around the Gustav Line. The Americans were already fixated on Operation Overlord, the D-Day landings at Normandy scheduled for the spring of 1944, but at the end of December in 1943, Roosevelt acceded to Churchill's request to maintain a fleet of landing craft in the Mediterranean for "the big Rome amphibious operation."

Jim Feltz got word that week that his battle station at general quarters would no longer be amidships with the repair party. *Plunkett*'s engineering officer was about to elevate Jim's rating from fireman first class to water tender third class, which was a petty officer's rating, and they'd determined his highest and best use was down in the hole.

Now that he'd be weathering action in the bowels of the ship, Jim surveyed the aft fire room in the light of pending darkness. He'd managed to shut down the plant after the gland on the auxiliary pump blew, but there'd been too much luck to the success he'd had then. He could do better, and George Gainey could help him get there. With *Plunkett* since its commissioning, George was a plank owner and a prank player. On Jim's first watch in the fire room a year earlier, George and another snipe, Bob Cavany, had put Jim on the top-watch long before Jim thought he was ready. At eleven o'clock

that night, with Jim on the upper grate, the fire room's exhaust ports started backing up and throwing steam. Jim yelled for the burner man to go get Bob; he had no idea what was happening. What was happening was that George was shutting down the return exhaust lines for a look at Jim under pressure.

Underway and on watch, Jim knotted a rag at the back of his head and called for George to simulate a hit on the ship. George feigned an explosion, noting they'd been hit forward. Jim consulted the schematic of the fire room that had taken root in his head and started toward the first valve, one of his fellow firemen hovering at his side lest he make a misstep. Hit forward, he moved aft to open his oil lines. First things first, you couldn't have water in the oil. That would cause the boilers to start panting, and you wouldn't want that.

Scenario after scenario, Jim groped his way about the fire room, reaching for valves he saw in his mind's eye until he got to them as fast as he wanted. The Navy didn't require this kind of intimacy of its engineers, but Jim had a hunch this kind of knowledge would serve him, that it would pay to be able to function a little like Helen Keller, albeit in a war zone.

Gallagher was likewise on the verge of promotion to water tender, but his battle station at general quarters would remain the same— in the gun tub. In letters home, he refrained from reference to his work at general quarters, partly because that kind of detail would be censored by the ship's engineering officer but moreover because he would just as soon keep his family from worrying. Still, two years to the day after the Japanese struck Pearl Harbor and John decided to enlist, he sounded a note of weariness. "I was glad to get in, but boy will I be much gladder to get out after the war. This is alright for a kid about seventeen, to do a few years, but I'm getting older

every day and better get out soon. I am twenty-seven now, but this life makes me feel around fifty-seven."

At Christmas, the men of the *Plunkett* feasted on their own ship, and then went to a party whose sailors included only those who came off the cans. They'd enjoyed a great, recuperative stretch in Mers el-Kebir after skirting disasters that struck so many of their sister ships—the *Maddox, Rowan, Shubrick, Buck, Bristol*, a list that kept lengthening and was bound to stretch further. The Germans still commanded the high ground at Monte Cassino. The Allies were months away from their cross-channel invasion. There was so much more war to be fought, and they all knew it. In the meantime, and for as long as could be had, there was rest. They played more baseball, and had their teeth fixed and ate ice cream and went to Mass. They'd trimmed a tree topside at Christmas and had a "swell dinner" that made Jim Feltz, for one, "very happy." A girl friend from home sent John a pair of silk panties for the holiday. "They're a little small but if I keep eating the way I do now, I'm sure they will fit," John wrote in gratitude. A few days after Christmas, following a morning patrol in which they'd practiced firing their five-inch and their 20mm, they watched Mickey Rooney and Judy Garland in *Girl Crazy*.

As they rung in the New Year in Mers el-Kebir, Russ Wright watched the men come back to the ship from celebrations in their North African backwater and noted their situation this way: "Moored starboard side to in Mers El Kebir / From Ye Olde Berth One we start the New Year / Boiler #4 is lit off and so is the crew."

They'd been lighting it up at the Destroyer Club in Mers el-Kebir. More and more, they understood themselves to be a breed apart,

as men who didn't deign to mix with other species of sailors. They were destroyer men. Other men in the Navy didn't have it so good. GIs loathed sailors off the troop transports that deposited them in battle and retreated, the bastards, and would just as soon fight them as drink with them, but the same GIs celebrated the men on the tin cans, as several of *Plunkett*'s crew learned at a bar soon after the Salerno invasion. "You guys are not leaving till you're falling down drunk," one GI said to men off *Plunkett*. "You guys saved our ass with your gunfire."

This evening, McManus had shore patrol duty, which meant he was carrying a sidearm and a cartridge belt. At the Destroyer Club, the chief petty officer on duty put Mac at the door with his .45-caliber pistol and a nightstick, and orders to shoo away the Arab kids, and anyone else Mac deemed undesirable. You had to be off a can to get in the club, but Mac decided to let in one sailor who worked in the motor pool, who only wanted to play a bit of craps and who promised Mac gasoline anytime he needed any.

Settled into the Destroyer Club, the crew was looking forward to their return to Italy, partly because a signorina was better than a mademoiselle any day of the week. The French, they had a habit of lording it over you. Even after they had collapsed like a house of cards when the Germans knocked on their door, they still thought they were something. The guineas, though, were not holier than thou.

It made no difference to Jim Feltz. After learning from Betty that she didn't know whether he was still hers or not, he knew now that he had to declare what was what, and not with mush, but something even better. And so prior to Christmas, he sent home money to his brother Charlie and asked him to buy an engagement ring for Betty that Christmas. That New Year's Day, he'd be getting a petty officer's rating and a sizable jump in pay, as well as an upgrade on his left sleeve. Where previously he'd only sported the red branch of a fireman, he and Gallagher would now be entitled to flaunt an eagle, a propeller, and one red chevron.

Jim McManus bided most of the evening at the door. The man who relieved him did not have a gun, so Mac loaned him his and wandered over to the craps game to see how it was going for the kid he'd let in and for Dutch, who was having a grand time. Dutch was on his hands and knees, readying another throw, when the kid called out the chief as a cheat. Which was a true enough thing. But Jesus.

Dutch landed a punch on the kid, who responded with a knife, a jerk, and a swipe that drew blood on the Dutch-man's face. Dutch went after him, but Mac got to him first and yanked him away. Mac in the middle was no deterrent to Dutch, who swung for the kid and missed. Mac let him go, and pushed the nightstick in Dutch's gut, folding him up like a pretzel, as Mac would remember it.

Then Mac allowed the other chiefs to restrain Dutch while he went to the door for his gun. The kid still had his knife. He wasn't off a can, but he was in a Destroyer Club, where he'd just wounded one of their own.

"Hand over the knife," Mac said.

The kid wouldn't.

Mac pumped a round into the gun's chamber, like a character in one of the movies they played on the ship's forecastle. "Either hand over that knife or I'll blow your legs away," Mac said.

The kid turned over the knife.

Mac then took charge of Dutch's situation and, not for the last time in his life, shepherded the wounded chief petty officer down to the pier, where the Medical Guard were flying a Mike flag from their ship, meaning the vessel was stopped and making no way. The doctor had been watching a movie and was none too pleased about having to deal with Dutch, who informed a doctor that *Plunkett* was winning the war.

Back on *Plunkett*, Mac decided to call on Ken Brown. It was a fiasco, all that business at the Destroyer Club, and the other chiefs in the club had berated him for how he'd handled the situation, for having let the kid in in the first place and for surrendering his weapon.

"You did the right thing," the gun boss told Mac. To hell with what those chiefs thought.

By four o'clock in the morning on New Year's Day, Russ Wright had the ending for the year-end reflection he'd put in *Plunkett*'s deck logs. There were 265 enlisted men serving on *Plunkett* as they steamed into 1944, and 20 officers, for a total complement of 285. Thirteen of the ship's officers were attached to the USS *Plunkett*, and seven others were attached to Destroyer Squadron 7, of which *Plunkett* was the flagship. Ninety-five of the enlisted men had advanced in rating over the previous quarter, and two of them, including Oakley, had lost ground on their rating. The ship had lost sixty-four man-days to men who'd been sick during the quarter. Only six men had been late getting back to the ship after liberty, and just three men dared to go on liberty without a pass. *Plunkett* was a well-run ship.

"Our gang's set to go now—44's just arrived," Russ wrote in the small hours of January 1. "Let's hope there'll be Peace before '45."

15: ANZIO

JANUARY 16-25, 1944

Frank Gallagher always said he'd climbed up onto the *Plunkett* the day before the task force moved out of the Bay of Naples for the invasion of Anzio. That wasn't true, and Frank's own logbook of the places he'd moved through during the war revealed as much. Beside the entry for Naples in that book, he wrote this: "Last meeting with John—Jan. 17th." Neither Jim Feltz nor Ken Brown, nor any of the *Plunkett* crew I'd talked to, remembered Frank's visit, and the story does smack of something more legendary and maybe even apocryphal than actual. But Frank's logbook is hard evidence, if any more should be wanted to confirm the truth of the story he told for decades. "Go down and bunk with your brother [until] we figure out what we're going to do with you," Frank said Burke told him. That would have been on the evening of January 16. Frank always said it was a "red alert" that prompted his removal from the ship, but the ship's deck logs don't note any red alerts that evening. More plausibly, it was after midnight, it had become January 17, and they had to get Frank off the ship.

Up from the engineers' compartment, Frank and John climbed into a whaleboat helmed by one of the deckhands and flipped on kapok life vests. Two more hands on each of two cranks lowered them from the davits. John threw off the lines, and they motored away from *Plunkett*. The deckhand steered past destroyers *Woolsey*, *Mayo*, *Edison*, and *Ludlow*, all of them darkened, the dim shapes of deckhands in foul-weather gear moving about topside like phantoms. Naples was battened down for the night, and discernible only as a darker shade of stain under a sky thickening with clouds.

The brothers were sunk in silence then, neither quite capable of giving voice to the nostalgia and dread that strained against the superficial composure they'd mustered for the ferry in. Platitudes might have tried out for a shot on the stage of John's tongue— "Keep your head down," "Don't stand out in a crowd"—but the gunner who'd been baptized at Gela, and hardened at Palermo and Salerno, and who knew what it was to watch a ballooned man deflate when punctured with the tip of a knife, that man vetoed worthless talk.

The helmsman steered around a small crescent of breakwater rocks, harboring a jostled mass of bumboats, and inched up to a stone terrace lapping out from a high shoreline banked with massive boulders. Frank ducked out of the life jacket, the buzz he'd brought onto his brother's destroyer settled now. There were things he might have said then, about how the captain owed him half a can of guinea red, about how their mother wasn't looking for any medals, about the Pickwick Ale he was looking forward to lifting with John at Callahan's back in Dorchester. Whatever was said, that's lost now. He put out his hand for a gesture, a handshake, that hardly seemed equal to the gravitas of the moment but that channeled all they had.

At 7:30 a.m., *Plunkett* was underway on Operation Webfoot, a practice run for the actual invasion, Operation Shingle. Webfoot was a bad foot forward. The weather turned bad. Forty "duck" boats sunk. "Not a single unit landed on the proper beach, not a single unit landed in the proper order, not a single unit was less than an hour and a half late," one American general wrote in his diary. "I stood on the beach in an evil frame of mind."

After the Webfoot fiasco, *Plunkett* steamed back to Naples and its anchorage between the Castle and the Fort and the breakwater light. Their ultimate destination was no longer any secret. The scuttlebutt on shore had nailed it, and buoyant Italian vendors were hawking postcards that pictured the beaches of Anzio and Nettuno. Jeeps and trucks clogged the tiny streets of shoreside neighborhoods, and business was brisk in fruit and wine. At any moment, all passes would be revoked, and the boatswain's whistle would preface the commotion of getting underway.

The American command didn't think much of Operation Shingle. This operation was Churchill's doing—"his baby," as naval historian Samuel Eliot Morison put it. As he had with Gallipoli, the British prime minister had imposed his will on the generals and assumed tactical command for this end run around the German lines, and the plunge up the peninsula to Rome. "Whoever holds Rome holds the title deeds to Italy," Churchill declared. But the title deeds to Italy weren't all that imperative as 1944 got underway. Indeed, before the

Allies debarked Naples for the 110-mile run up the coast to Anzio, Eisenhower had debarked from the Mediterranean for England to plan for the D-Day landings in Normandy that spring.

Two days after Webfoot, *Plunkett* steamed away from Naples to neighboring Pozzuoli, the principal staging area for the Shingle convoys. They were part of an armada of 240 ships, including destroyers, cruisers, minesweepers, and 170 landing craft, all jockeying for berths at four different staging sites around the bay, waiting on an initial haul of thirty-five thousand infantrymen. Some of the Christians among them knew the apostle Paul had come ashore at Pozzuoli on a packet boat in the first century. Some of them knew the Flavian Amphitheatre in town was one of the largest colosseums to survive from ancient Rome. None of these men knew that one of the nine-year-old girls then living in Pozzuoli, so skinny her friends called her the Toothpick, would grow up to become known to the wider world as the legendary movie star Sophia Loren. There were LSTs drawn up on the beach, bow doors down, and still more nudged up against the town's stone piers, gangplanks stretched for troops.

At one o'clock on the afternoon of the 21st, Captain Burke was at the conn when *Plunkett* got underway, trailing the vanguard of the task force. The Army's Rangers would land first, followed by more than sixty landing craft bound for Red Beach and several dozen more landing craft for Green Beach on the sandy swaths of Nettuno, just east of Anzio. Then, *Plunkett*'s bunch would go in, emptying out of thirty-eight landing craft in the first follow-up group. Frank Gallagher's transport, an LST, was in this group.

Plunkett steamed at six knots on its no. 1 and no. 3 boilers, and while underway fired up the no. 2 and no. 4 boilers, boosting them just in case the ship needed more speed. The lead elements of the task force feinted for Corsica, before making a hard right for Anzio, but the follow-up group made straight for the beaches. If the Italian postcard hawkers knew where they were going, it was hard to believe German intelligence hadn't sussed them out by now as well.

Right after they darkened the ship at dusk, the ping jockeys in the sonar room picked up a sound contact. Burke developed it, steering for more and more signal until he had a grip on something. He dropped a pattern of nine depth charges and took a cursory look around to see if they'd turned up anything. He didn't think so and *Plunkett* reported as much in the deck logs. The topside crews saw something else, what looked like cork and black oil, brought to the surface in the wake of that pattern. They had silhouettes of downed German bombers in the bridge now, and they were anxious to paste up one of a submarine, too.

At two o'clock in the morning on January 22 the bridge rang general quarters for H hour. Gallagher reported to his gun tub under an auspicious sky, the waning moon not yet up, the seas relatively calm now. He listened through that first hour for the telltale sounds of invasion, expecting the sights and sounds to echo Salerno. But the night passed without incident, as if in a sudden windless calm, and they deposited their crews onto Nettuno's shores at dawn. The headlands and shorefront "looked as quiet as scenery in a painting."

Through the morning, a series of red alerts brought them to attention, but friendly fighters intercepted the threat before *Plunkett*'s gunners had a glimpse of the enemy aircraft. Interdiction was happening for a change. They patrolled the rendezvous area, twelve miles offshore, all day long, hustling to station for red alerts that downgraded to condition white (all clear, no enemy aircraft) every time.

By late evening on D-day, the Shingle ships had deposited more than thirty-six thousand men and more than three thousand vehicles on the beachhead. Casualties were light, with thirteen men killed, ninety-seven wounded, and another forty-four missing.

They had more of the same the next day as reports of enemy planes winged in, notification sounding over the ship's voice circuit, "Red Anzio! Red Anzio!" German bombers did penetrate the dome conjured over the beachhead and transport area by American and British air forces and paid particular attention to the cruiser *Brooklyn* and destroyer *Mayo*, but heavy anti-aircraft fire rebuffed the attack. *Plunkett* made funnel smoke that evening to screen the ships at dusk, and Captain Burke promised action—a scheduled bombardment— on D-day plus two.

"We'll have some fun and shooting tomorrow," Burke informed the crew.

Fun and shooting, as if on a lark. Burke needed a bit of levity now and then, if only as an antidote to the anguish that attended certain parts of his job. Two weeks earlier, he'd had to call one of the enlisted men, Lyle Hollister, out of the radio shack for some unpleasant business. Lyle's kid brothers, the twins William and Richard, had both been killed in the Pacific after a torpedo struck their escort carrier, *Liscome Bay*, in the Gilberts. The eighteen-year-old twins were Lyle's only siblings and had been so thrilled by what they'd read in Lyle's letters from *Plunkett* that they'd enlisted the previous year at the age of seventeen.

In the morning, *Plunkett* followed orders calling for the rendezvous area (farther out) and the transport area (farther in) to be consolidated. While the crew waited on a move toward the beaches for the fun Burke had promised, the ship instead patrolled the seaward side of the consolidated area at five knots. Plans for the bombardment were upended by more of the same yo-yo action to general quarters for red alerts that didn't amount to anything but a jump in the ship's speed to fifteen knots. The klaxon yanked them to battle stations again just before lunch, and then again just after the last lunch mess, and then again just a few minutes after they'd been secured once again. The destroyer escort *Frederick C. Davis* was keeping them all on their toes, monitoring the Luftwaffe fighters, and doing a "splendid" job. It was all too much for Jim McManus's new gunner's mate, a hot case man, who started grousing about how quiet everything was in this backwater. The weather was turning foul now, and a stiff westerly wind was rippling Mac's canvas ragtop. Like everyone else's, Mac's nerves were starting to rattle from all of *Davis*'s splendid work, and his new hot case man was a pain in the ass.

"I'm tired of this," the kid said. "I'm going to put in for the Pacific where I can see some action."

"Sooner or later," Dooley told the kid, "you're going to eat those words."

All of this day's calls to battle stations made standing watch in the fire room a rather tenuous proposition. Gallagher had been in and out of his gun tub five times that day already. Sure enough, twenty minutes after the first dog watch started, a red alert set them hopping, and Gallagher hastened to his gun tub for yet another rendezvous with his loader Tom Garner and their gun's handler.

The seas were heavier now, and *Plunkett* was moving tentatively through them at five knots. On the beach, anti-aircraft fire ripped into the sky after targets none of them could see. They secured a little after five o'clock and shuffled back among one another like a deck of cards, awaiting the next hand.

In the after fire room, the blowers at 9,000 rpm laid down a foundation of whining white noise from each of two corners on the upper level, and the fuel pump clicked like a metronome. What was cacophonous when Gallagher had first come down into it was now a navigable landscape of sound. His ears, like those of a blind man, could detect the slightest anomalies. He wasn't blindfolding himself like Jimmy Feltz, but then again, he knew he'd never find himself in the fire room when things got really hot.

It was January 24, and he'd come aboard *Plunkett* two years earlier to the day, almost to the hour. So had Dutchie Gebhart from Delaware, who was in the aft engine room filling in for one of the other machinists, and Garner from Camden, who was with him in the gun tub, and Hugh Geraghty, down in the engine room, and Ski from Southie and Bill Alverson, a machinist's mate from Arkansas who was gunner in the tub just ahead of him on the the starboard side of the ship. Two years to the day, but all of them so much older now, wanting no more of anything but the end. It will be a happy day for all of us when this is over, John thought.

Coming into the forward fire room again at general quarters, Jim Feltz clamped on a set of sound-powered telephones and hung the transmitter around his neck. He was a water tender now, a big shot, a man capable of drying out steam and boosting it, superheating it, to 750 degrees.

The *forward* fire room, he liked to say, in a go at Gallagher now, is *the* fire room that really puts out the steam that turns the turbines that spin the screws that drive the ship. We put out more steam, John would counter, and everyone on this ship knows it. Snipes, they called themselves, maybe for all the sniping.

Jim was still getting used to being down in the hole at general quarters. He didn't fancy it as much as he liked being topside when there was action, especially when they were rolling six-hundred-pound ash cans off the fantail and lofting three-hundred-pounders with the K-guns. Not being able to see what was coming down on you added another dimension to the trepidation. It was what you couldn't see coming, like the prophecy of that Ouija board, that was the real bogeyman and more unnerving than the silhouette of a Messerschmitt or Junkers Ju.

Instead now he was left to wonder what was happening upstairs, and as often as not, without anything else to look at, what was happening at home. In Overland at Christmas, Betty's brother Bob had got a punching bag. Some of the boys were coming home for a few days here and there on leave, before the black hole of war inexorably sucked them back. The Army had drafted the boss at the dollar store, surprising Betty. "They sure aren't particular as to what they take, are they?" And they'd tried to draft another local boy but failed because he didn't have a palate in his mouth. Betty was just as glad because this boy was a "momma's boy," and she didn't reckon he'd do well outside Overland. Still, she wished Jim didn't have a palate, either, and wrote as much in a letter, but then regretted giving voice to the wish and said so right away. She was glad he had his palate. It had been a year now since she'd seen him, and she was resigned to the fact that it wasn't likely she'd see him "for the duration," if at all.

In the director this late afternoon, Ken Brown settled into his knucklehead seat and pressed his knees against the instrument panel. It was funny how much of a home the director had become to him, this little box roosting on the highest part of the ship, with its myriad circular screens, indicators, dials, cylinders, bronze knobs and wheels, the space for him and five other men ancillary to what was needed for the equipment. Everything inside was Navy gray, but for the bronze and the odd red box, like the one around a button that compelled the battery to cease firing. It was remarkable that such a place could engender a homey feeling in a man, but home he was. It helped that he was only five-nine and had a knack for sleeping while sitting.

The ship lapsed to condition white at 5:05 p.m., and they darkened ten minutes later, just as the sun was setting. They had now come into what they called "happy hour," when the crepuscular light to the west and the darkening sky to the east signaled the advent of the most exuberant part of any day.

Ken had a last look at the day from the director's hatch. He could make out hospital ships in the near distance, and all of the other ships of his destroyer squadron refining their screen around the bigger boys in the roadstead. The light cruiser *Brooklyn* hunkered among them, looking itself like an inflated destroyer with its twin stacks, superstructure, and armament.

They'd all been disappointed that plans to lob a few at shore targets had been scuttled. Enough was enough on the patrol lines. Let them heave a few. They knew what they were doing. Let them do it.

Below Ken on the main deck aft of the bridge, Dr. Wesley Knaup was milling about his battle station with the midship repair party when he spotted two Dornier bombers in the waning light, high in the sky. These aircraft carried the glide bombs they'd first seen at Salerno, and they'd been prowling about the roadstead the night before.

"Looks like a little business coming up," Dr. Knaup said to no one in particular. "I think I'll go down to the wardroom."

The wardroom on *Plunkett* was the ship's battle dressing station.

The klaxon sounded then, and the ship's intercom crackled with additional detail, "enemy planes," and the summons that uncorked the adrenaline no matter how many times they'd heard it. "General quarters. General quarters. All hands man your battle stations." The voice tremored through the ship's sound system in a way that sometimes made you wonder whether it was Donald Duck bawling on the other end.

On the starboard wing of the bridge, Jack Collingwood stood with Burke, looking up at the Dorniers coming in on the port beam and bereft, all of a sudden, of two glide bombs they could now see. The bombs themselves looked like mini-aircraft, pale green and lethal. Their trajectories were clear. They were headed straight for the ship.

At the same time they sighted the glide bombs, a brace of Junkers Ju 88 bombers in dark green camouflage swept in, one on the starboard bow and one to port. At least four, and perhaps as many as six, additional bombers swarmed on the periphery of this dome that now clamped down on the ship.

What they couldn't understand on *Plunkett* as those radio-controlled bombs made for them, and for no one else, because they were all alone on this picket line, was why this much fuss for a destroyer. A light cruiser, the *Brooklyn*, was in the vicinity, though shrouded now in funnel smoke made by *Niblack*. The only thing that made sense to the men on the bridge was that the Germans thought *Plunkett* was *Brooklyn*.

Burke called for the helmsman H. R. "Skunky" Kline to turn in to the bombs. Skunky was from Tewksbury, Massachusetts, and not all that happy about having forfeited a couple of showers that warranted this nickname, but he'd grown not to mind it. Right at them, Burke told him. Better to give them the bow than the beam.

Burke wanted the ship at full steam now and told the officer of the deck, Lieutenant (jg) Evan Thomas, who rang a bell in the engineering department. Jim Feltz heard the annunciator sound down by the boiler and listened to a voice he couldn't identify by name crackling through the phones on his ears.

"Get on the burners," the voice shouted. "We've got dive bombers on our ass."

The ship leaned into the call for more speed, pitching into the sea like a racehorse digging for traction. An awesome wake bloomed suddenly off the fantail, and the ship surged to twenty-seven knots as the skipper turned tight into the glide bombs' flight path. All of this speed was a double-edged sword, because a wake drew a nice aiming line for a bomber pilot and seemed to emit a phosphorescent light all its own, even when the moon and stars were dark. But speed to dodge those glide bombs was his priority now. The Ju 88s he'd leave to the gunnery officer.

Before the lunge to full steam, *Plunkett* had enjoyed relative proximity to *Gleaves* and *Niblack*, each about four miles distant. Full steam at a bearing ordained by the trajectory of the glide bombs meant *Plunkett* was distancing herself from other vessels that might lend support, or that might distract and divert one or another bomber. That didn't happen. The dome moved with them.

Burke was cognizant of the odds against a ship at sea dogged by aircraft, especially one that was out alone. The ship usually lost. What were the odds of a ship on its own against a swarm of aircraft that were numbering up, from eight to ten, and then a dozen, maybe fourteen? On a single ship.

One of the war correspondents who'd come onto the ship at Naples shook his head over their straits. Every ship I've been on has been hit, he said out loud. Burke turned to the man and looked straight at him, wondering whether he had the right to throw a man overboard.

At the klaxon, Gallagher hurried up the ladder, following one of the guys on watch who'd been on the upper grate. He timed his exit from the hatch and hit the main deck, turned right, scrambled up one more ladder, and hauled into his gun tub. He swiveled a look up into the fast-darkening sky, meanwhile shooting his arms through a kapok life jacket. Helmet on, he shoved his shoulders into C-shaped braces and strapped himself in. He bounced his feet on the deck, testing the heft of his gun, and then, fulcrum that he was, swung to the left.

Tom Garner snapped a canister into the breech as a plane winged in, low and slow, from starboard to port at an altitude of fifty feet. Gallagher straightened in his harness to lower the barrel. He found the plane in the new sights they'd put on the 20mm guns as replacements for the older iron sights. These sights were so technologically sophisticated, they'd been instructed to remove them and drop them into the sea if they ever had to scuttle the ship. The barrel didn't line up exactly with the sights, but pointed slightly to the side, anticipating where a bomber flying at 150 miles per hour would be when the shells arrived on target. Every fifth round was a tracer, blazing white, all of them streaming low under the fuselage. Gallagher compensated by leaning back slightly. He found the plane in his sights again and loosed another burst on the plane, missing again. That was mostly what happened. You missed.

On one wing of the bridge, Burke faced the glide bombs, bearing down on the ship at an angle that looked perilous. The operators in the high-level bombers still had a clutch on their charges, and all Burke could hope was that his move to full steam would foil their calculations. Just above the ship, the glide bombs spurted with a final burst of rocket propulsion and slammed into the ship's wake, two hundred yards astern.

The blasts joggled the phones on Jim's headset, and he braced himself for a moment, free-falling into a sudden well of silence that might burst with a repercussion any minute. The silence deepened by the second, and Jim remembered the dread he'd felt as a kid during a thunderstorm, how the space between the blasts was more difficult to bear than the flash and crackle itself. Hearing a bomb burst, as with hearing thunder in a storm, meant you were spared for the time being. Until the next burst, there was nothing to do but dread that the next crack was going to be right on top of you. Topside, at least, he could deploy his eyesight. In the hole, he could only wonder. The noise was incredible. He'd never heard anything like it. *Plunkett* was really giving them hell.

With the glide bomb's geysers not yet settled, Ken shot up out of the hatch into a space swarmed with bombers, all of them angling for favorable position on *Plunkett*. How did *Plunkett* rate this much attention from this many Junkers bombers? What the hell did those guys up there think they had? When he dropped back down into the director, his men didn't have to wait for him to say anything. They'd seen the same planes on their fire control radar. There were targets everywhere.

Gallagher registered a glimpse of the Ju 88s—their underslung engines, their bulbous, glazed noses and long, slim fuselages—before he opened on one of them again. The entire battery was in action now, the five-inch guns, the 1.1-inch, all six of the 20mms. The concussion from that much fire clenched and released their stomachs and bladders in waves and crosscurrents of waves. One canister spent, Gallagher waited a moment while Garner yanked off the drum and snapped in another. The smoke from the barrage streamed to stern as the ship dashed forward into a netherworld of smoke and chaos, where nobody's sweat smelled the same. Over his right shoulder, the four barrels of the 1.1-inch pom-pom gun kept up a relentless barrage.

=====

Burke addressed the angling planes with one rudder change after another. His ship was throwing up as much as she could, but all of that offense made for a bad defense. He could run, but he couldn't hide, not with the perimeter of the ship clearly delineated by tracers spewing from each of his 20mm guns, with the flash of his five-inch guns, pumping shells from bow to stern down the middle of the ship, and with that water-cooled 1.1-inch gun whose efficient loaders ensured a steady torrent of fire.

Moments after the explosion of the glide bombs, the men in the forward 20mm gun tubs watched something drop from the underbelly of a plane at eight hundred yards to the stern of the ship and relayed the news: torpedo. As the offending plane swept by, five times faster than its torpedo, some of the men on *Plunkett* could literally see the pilot in his cockpit.

Burke noted the track of the menace and had Skunky jerk the ship into a bearing that paralleled the path of the torpedo, whirring up on them at a speed only slightly faster than *Plunkett*. Russ Wright bounded onto the wing of the bridge to root around in the low light for a read on the torpedo's vector.

He latched onto the telltale phosphorescent track, a sight that had, from *Plunkett*'s topside, always resolved itself as a porpoise or some other innocuous thing. But not this time. Complicating that fear now was the still-raw memory of what happened to the men on *Buck* in the wake of their torpedo.

The ship's five-inchers pounded targets in great concussive booms, and the 20mms were ripping up the night, drowning out the mechanical whir of the lethal fish. Watch it, Burke had told Russ, until it clears the bow.

Russ watched the torpedo streak up on them, until it was yards from the ship's hull but parallel. Skunky maintained the ship's bearing, and the torpedo slipped by to an unexplosive end.

Glide bombs and torpedoes dodged, Burke turned on the low-flying planes, presenting as much of his five-inch battery as he could to the paths of the Junkers Jus. A bomb burst suddenly twenty yards from the ship, a threat no one saw coming. The conundrum now was clear. They were set upon by low-level and high-level bombers. Coordinated or not, they were working the ship in tandem, the low-level torpedo bombers zipping past like bait. *Plunkett*'s battery lunged at them with an enthusiasm of fire. That fire resolved itself as a bull's-eye to the high-flying dive-bombers. The Germans were doing what Jim Feltz had feared: concentrating on a single ship.

Ken Brown had the battery on full automatic, and they were making adjustments based on what they were seeing: Bonnie Baker's eyes were that good. The targets were presenting in a way that let Ken know Burke knew what he was doing. He was teeing them up, and it was now Ken's job to hit them as hard as he could.

With the gun barrels swung to port, the five-inch guns uncorked a salvo that found a mark off the port beam. The plane flashed once with the eruption of the Mark 32 ammunition, and then again as its torpedoes blew. The plane disintegrated in a streak, sprinkling by fragments into the sea a thousand yards off the ship's port bow. It was 5:50 p.m.

The ship's five-inch guns were judicious in their dispatch of shells, firing a salvo every fifteen to twenty seconds. The 1.1-inch and 20mms kept up a steady barrage. This bothered Jim Shipp, a third-class shipfitter who'd been shunted from work as a trainer in the no. 1 gun mount to the mid-ship repair party after they'd sent Jim Feltz into the hole for general quarters. At least in the gun turret, there was the illusion of some cover. But here now as one of ten men in the repair party, on the torpedo deck hard by the searchlight, Shipp felt exposed and vulnerable, poised on the edge of a bull's-eye drawn by the nonstop fire of the 1.1-inch.

Eddie Webber, known as Skinzo, was thinking the same thing up on the searchlight. But he was used to it. Every time he lit his light in the dark, he knew he was just asking for it. There wouldn't be any need for illumination in this battle, but Christ, that 1.1-inch. Sometimes the thing jammed, and it took a couple of guys with hammers and wrenches underneath to get the gun back in operation. But it was operating just fine this evening. Just fine.

The barrel in the no. 3 gun tub was hot and smoking after they'd exhausted yet another drum. While Garner cranked off the canister, and went for another, the gun's second handler grabbed the barrel with asbestos gloves and twisted it free with a quarter turn. He placed the barrel on deck outside the tub and retrieved a replacement from the cooling tank welded alongside.

Gallagher looked to shore where the infantry on the beachhead were dealing with several dozen of their own problems. The skies were streaked with a "mighty bedlam of ack-ack" that crushed "all thought on shore and far out to sea as the ships themselves let go at the groan and grind of German motors in the sky." The ship jerked over the surface of the sea without regard to a base course, or in accordance with any plan.

With a new barrel and a new drum, Gallagher took another

plane in his sights. His two handlers huddled on the gun, both to brace themselves against the radical maneuvering of the ship and to help stabilize the gun. Gallagher controlled their speed and the angle of fire, and they moved with him, anticipating what needed to be done. They moved in concert, the three of them all bent to the same end, all thought banished but for this: Get it. The mount sputtered under fire, the three men shuddering with the machine, moving to the right as Gallagher poured fire at and then into one of the Junkerses. Bill Alverson in the neighboring tub had the same plane in his sights and drew the same line into the plane's fuselage. On the starboard wing of the bridge, Squadron Commander Clay watched the German bomber absorb fire from the ship's 20mm guns and peel away trailing smoke.

The focus on a single ship in the Mediterranean had always been fleeting. The Germans were always more interested in the panorama of the roadstead than in any one target. That was the way it had been around Sicily and at Salerno. After the radio-controlled bombs blew in *Plunkett*'s wake, someone else was supposed to take the heat. Instead, the *Charley P.* fielded a torpedo.

After five minutes, the focus had been twice as long as was typical. After ten minutes, they were in uncharted territory.

Eddie Burke had parried two glide bombs, one torpedo, and now the bomb drops were on him like hail, falling between twenty yards and two hundred.

Ken Brown brought down the first plane at the twelve-minute mark. Gallagher and Alverson had nailed theirs shortly thereafter.

Burke needed help. There'd been a change in German strategy.

They were not going to relent until this one ship went down. Burke told Russ Wright to go into the chart room and get on the fighter plane circuit. Try to scramble some P-38s out of Naples.

In Jim McManus's gun turret, they'd been coping with shells from the lower handling room with their protective nose caps still on. It wasn't an ideal situation but necessary because their hoist, for some reason, was damaging the fuse on the projectiles. Each time a new shell showed up, the fuse setter would spin the cap off and drop it in a canvas bag hung inside the mount.

But now, shortly after the five-inch brought down the ship's first plane, and with the gun boss calling for another salvo, the hoist quit working.

"Oakley!" McManus yelled.

Oakley was outside the mount. He stuck his head through the hatch.

"Go down to the handling room and check the hoist."

Oakley's head jerked out of the hatch.

It didn't make sense to Mac that the trouble was downstairs. His mind flailed about for what else might be the problem, and he dropped off his platform on a hunch. He fished in the dark, feeling for the trouble, and found it under the foot pedal—a nose cap. The hoist started working properly again.

Matched and trained, firing in salvo, Brown's battery pumped projectiles at another low-flying torpedo bomber until one of the shells exploded close enough. The plane lit with fire and streaked for the sea off the starboard bow eighteen minutes after the action had got underway.

The speed changes and rudder changes coming in from the bridge seemed as arbitrary as child's play, except that Jim Feltz knew each was a response to a lethal threat—a threat confirmed as one bomb after another exploded hard by the hull. He'd counted seven near misses so far, some so close he wondered whether the seams in *Plunkett's* hull could handle it, whether the seams in his skivvies could handle it. They did, and each time, he felt his love for this little ship deepen in a way he'd not thought possible. It was as if she'd come alive in the combat, was herself vested in getting them through this. She was completely on their side. He prayed for the guns to stop firing, for the planes to peel away, but the roar had been continuous for nearly twenty minutes now.

Burke was upstairs rolling his gunnels for the waves with every turn, unflappable, issuing commands in a volume that was just talking, a little louder than normal—it had to be, given the ceaseless fire from the ship's battery—but otherwise conversational volume.

"Right rudder," he was telling Skunky. "Left rudder."

Again and again. Each new move precipitated by intelligence coming from the lookouts. "Here's another on the port bow."

"Right rudder. Left rudder. Steadd-dy right rudder."

Turn it to the right. Turn it to the left. A defensive move that went all the way back to Hector at Troy.

Up in the director, Ken knew they were capable of more. He hadn't known they'd splashed anything at the moment they got one, and though he was sure they'd had some success, he was also aware of all they'd missed.

Gallagher didn't have time to trail the plane he and Alverson dug into, couldn't track what they'd accomplished the way he'd just seen what the five-inch battery did to that one Ju 88. All in good time. He ceased firing a moment as Garner popped out another canister. He glanced over his shoulder at the 1.1-inch, firing from its mount on top of the after deckhouse, not forty feet from his tub.

The 1.1-inch was pouring out as much fire as any three of the machine guns. Because it was water-cooled, not air-cooled like the 20mm, the fire flowed like a stream of light as the gun's half-a-dozen loaders inserted the flat cartridges into the breech. Since the action began, the dozen men in the mount had been getting out nearly one hundred rounds per minute.

From seventeen thousand feet, the tracers spewing from the perimeter of the target winked out intermittently. But the bull's-eye never dimmed. Looking through a little window in the floor of his Junkers Ju 88, a Luftwaffe pilot maneuvered *Plunkett* into position, then pulled his dive brakes with the 1.1-inch gun firmly anchored in his bombsight. The plane's nose dipped through forty-five degrees. Its speed accelerated for 350 mph.

At five thousand feet, a warning horn sounded as tracers flowed past the cockpit. Moments later, the horn stopped and the pilot released his payload. A stick of five bombs, each weighing 550 pounds, dropped from the bay. The first tumbled into the sea, as did the second, and then the third, though they'd walked a path right up on the ship's stern. The fourth exploded twenty yards off the starboard stern, blowing off the ship's port screw.

At 5:58 p.m., the fifth bomb in this stick fell directly on the 1.1-inch gun mount, at frame 134, as the area was known on a diagram of the ship's anatomy, and exploded with a flash that illuminated the vessel in a stark, apocalyptic snapshot, a moment that would cleave time for the crew between everything that happened before Anzio and everything to happen after. In the forward fire room, the lights blanked out with the blast, and Jim felt the ship going down, straight down, a preternatural feeling as if the hand of Neptune had clutched *Plunkett* by the hull and was pulling for bottom. The explosions rattled the men on the bridge like "dice in a cup," and Skunky grabbed the wheel, sure the ship was going down. In the director, the explosion registered as a thump, more felt than heard, that wasn't obvious to Ken Brown as a landed bomb. He had no idea what it felt like to have a 550-pound bomb hit and then explode in the bowels of your ship.

When Neptune released *Plunkett*, the ship rose reluctantly toward its normal draft. The emergency lights in the forward fire room flickered on. The chief petty officer's voice sounded in Jim's phones: "Go see what happened."

He yanked off the phones and unslung the transmitter, scrambled up the ladder, and spun the dogs on the hatch. Poked from his hole like a periscope, he leveled his gaze on a wall of fire that cut the ship in two, from starboard to port. From his vantage at the no. 1 stack, he couldn't see beyond the no. 2 stack for all of the flame.

Gasoline, Jim thought, remembering the five hundred gallons they stored for the whaleboats in tanks between the deckhouse and the after deckhouse he couldn't see.

"We been hit," he shouted down into the hole.

Someone called up a question, but he couldn't make it out.

Jim looked for the shapes of men at the fire with hoses. This was the mid-ship repair party's territory, his old stomping grounds, and there were ten men in that crew, but he saw no one at work. The wreckage he could see meant there might not be anyone. The flames walled off the stern and were trending in that direction by the forward motion of the ship, toward the depth charges.

Ever since he'd come aboard *Plunkett*—before that even, from the very first time the Navy had versed him in its protocols—he'd understood one thing above all others to be true about what to do at general quarters. Until ordered, you did not move off your battle station. You did not make your own decisions. With the ship blazing, and its after magazines and depth charges on the fantail capable of explosion at any moment, and utter ruin for *Plunkett* now as possible as it had been for those other ships in the fleeting moments before *Maddox* and *Rowan* and *Buck* went down, Jim did what he knew he wasn't supposed to do under any circumstances. He made his own decision.

"I'm going out!" he shouted down into the hole.

In the after engine room, Irvin Gebhart had been climbing for the main deck when the bomb hit. The noise was like nothing he'd ever heard before and complemented by gushers of steam spewing from ruptured lines, the roar of flames, and the hysteria of men subject to it all. Irv consumed the rungs of the ladder in a heartbeat, spun the dogs on the door, glanced down into smoke and wreckage, and popped his head onto a deck that looked like a torture chamber out of hell.

No one else below had access to the ladder Gebhart had scrambled up; mangled metal made sure of that. Wreckage blocked the escape hatch, too.

Below, machinist's mate Warren Zingler from Bethlehem, Pennsylvania, was down on the deck plates, and badly burned from head to toe, scalded by a burst of high-pressure steam.

Hugh Geraghty watched as men started working the wreckage at the base of Gebhart's ladder, mantled by thickening steam. He couldn't see escape that way. Geraghty was a big guy, and more prone than anyone else on *Plunkett* to letting his liberties stretch farther than they should. Gebhart's ladder wouldn't enable that.

The flames jerked and stabbed the men in the engine room, eliciting sudden cries that, in and of themselves, were a deterrent to throwing in with that lot. Over all of that was the horrible hiss of superheated steam spewing from ruptured pipes at seven hundred degrees.

Below an escape hatch so tiny, he had to wonder whether he was capable of fitting through under normal circumstances, Geraghty scrambled up the chute as far as the hatch, where he spun the dogs. The wheel turned for him and the hatch should have lifted, but the lid wouldn't give. Something was on it. The little it did give promised more, and he roared into it with a herculean effort, again and again, pounding so hard he would later need a plate installed in his skull. One last burst and he had the hatch open far enough for egress. Steam funneled out of the engine room in a white column, and Geraghty might have streamed out with it. Instead, he dropped back down into the space where he'd left two living shipmates. He let another man, known to the crew as Skidshoes, up the ladder first. Then he picked up Warren Zingler in an artless embrace and jostled him through the escape hatch into the relative safety of a main deck blazing with fire.

The explosion had obliterated the 1.1-inch mount, and every man on it, among them Irving Diamond, who kept the ship's store, and Alfred Gelinas, who'd wanted a topside station at general quarters and, with some lobbying by Jim McManus, had just been moved to the 1.1. There was Bob Winger, John Giardi, Royce Sipes, Arthur Eckert, and Johannes Thorsten, men gone, so thoroughly gone they'd have to be listed forever after as missing in action. Likewise, the no. 5 gun mount for one of the ship's 20mms: gone.

The bomb cratered through the main deck by the no. 6 gun and marooned the nearby 20mm gun mount above the rent. The explosion tore the arms and legs off the trunk of the strapped-in gunner, as well as his head, though the straps held, leaving what remained in the embrace of his harness.

Gallagher's gun tub was fifteen yards from the 1.1-inch mount but was spared the full thrust of the explosion by the back of the deckhouse. Still, the upper reaches of the blast downed Garner and the gun's handler and drove Gallagher into his shoulder braces. Shrapnel flailed his backside like a whip with a dozen tips. He'd have fallen to the deck, but he was held aloft by his harness and draped, suddenly, in a web of buoyed float netting. The heat of the fire was all over him, and there was a wild fusillade of 20mm and 1.1-inch shells, punctuating the roar of flame and the cries of downed men.

In McManus's turret, the concussion was extraordinary. It gripped each man in a vise of air that perforated eardrums and threatened to implode the cavities of their chests. But then it exhausted most of its surge out the canvas top of the mount. The force blew Mac's trainer off his seat and dragged his leg over a jagged end of pipe from hip to heel, gouging an inch-wide channel. Shrapnel raked each of them. The concussion sprang flecks of paint from the inside of the mount and embedded them in exposed skin. Flames flared everywhere.

At the searchlight, the blast blew every shred of clothing off Eddie Webber, blowing out the seams of his jacket, shirt, and trousers, even his underwear, but left him his shoes and the pneumatic life belt clipped around his waist. The integrity of his body was intact, however, unlike men around him who lost limbs to flying shards of ship—limbs that would have no fidelity to where they'd come from and that would scatter about topside like obscene clues to a guessing game that would have to be played later.

Together the searchlight and the men on it were blown forward off the mount, onto men from the mid-ship repair party and toward the ship's second stack. Flames scorched Webber's stomach en route, and the collapsing mount broke the bones in his legs. Shrapnel pummeled his head and torso. One piece shot through his biceps, and another his thigh, and a large swatch of metal lodged in his stomach. The searchlight crashed against the superstructure, tangling Eddie and three shipmates in a heap.

Some of the same superstructure caught Jim Shipp at the waist. Splinters of metal lashed his face as he was brought down to the deck, and just before he blacked out, he said to himself, "Well, this is the end."

In the wake of the explosion, for a spell of time no one measured, *Plunkett* was down. Neptune's hand was on the ship, Vulcan's, too, as if men were but the playthings of gods after all. Like the men on *Maddox*, *Rowan*, *Buck*, and *Bristol*, no one knew in that brief span of time between the hit and the next audible factor that would determine their fate, whether this was the end. The lights were out. Most of the communications were dead. Ken Brown was shouting for his gun captains aft and hearing nothing. But then there was Richardson's voice sounding in his phones from the no. 2 gun "We're okay, boss," and the same thing coming in from Wikstrom in the other forward gun.

By then, the gun boss was already slewing the director through 90° of arc because there were targets still lighting on the range finder. Whatever else was going to happen to *Plunkett*, Ken Brown knew what he had to do. And he did it, blasting a sound that was as heartening to the men in the lower handling rooms, in the forward fire room, in the wardroom and on the bridge, as a bugle call in the distance—the boom of the forward five-inch guns, the ship still fighting.

Now the dread of something sympathetic was on every survivor's mind—the magazines, and their payload of shells, itching for an opportunity to burst, as well as the ash cans in racks on a fantail in flames, each of them combustible, all of them set to safe should the ship go down, though no one knew for sure if that was the case: Were they set to safe? They had to be. They hadn't been chasing a sub. But.

Captain Burke barged from bridge to wing, assessed the extent of the fire, and started calculating how much time they had, if any. He dispatched his junior officers one by one: Oliver to bring the forward repair party to the root of the fire; Thomas to make sure the five-inch magazines were flooded; and Ensign Wayne Fitzpatrick to fight fire on the fantail, where the depth charges might explode at any time.

Burke called Wright out of the chart room. Forget the fighter planes. Get as far aft as you can, Burke told him, and check our condition. Wright started aft, and as soon as he hit the main deck, he passed a man who'd served him as a telephone talker, down and dead with a huge hole through his chest.

Topside now, Jim Feltz saw the shapes of men he knew down all over, and parts of men everywhere. He was no mathematician, but he knew enough calculus to understand that the properties of the derivatives would be no good, that what he was seeing was but a fraction of what was there. A horrible tally was to come, but first things first. Do your job, he thought. That was paramount. Do what you've been trained to do. It was a simple mandate. Even though he knew his "job" was now down in the fire room, it had been here until two weeks ago, with nine other men who were nowhere to be seen. Unless they got the flames that wanted the ship's magazines, and the ash cans, the carnage he'd seen would be but prelude. The blaze of that thought went down deep inside him and cauterized any inclination to assess the situation more deeply. He shut his mind down to everything but what he had to do next. His job. Check that. His old job.

There was wreckage all over the locker on the main deck, where there would be one handy billy pump—wreckage of ship and wreckage of body. Jim cleared the locker and got the door open. Someone was beside him—who that was he'd never remember afterward—but someone helped him drag a one-hundred-pound single-cylinder handy billy pump out of the locker. They rigged a 1.5-inch hose, and then Jim took the rip cord and fired the engine. They picked up the handy billy on either end and hustled it up to the burning wreckage and set it down yards away. The other firefighter dropped a suction hose over the side of the ship. A moment later, Jim had water trained on the burning ship at sixty gallons per minute.

An officer whipped past, running for the fantail and straight for the wall of a flame like a man on a suicide mission. The fire abated momentarily, maybe even miraculously, while the officer plunged through to the other side, if there was another side. There had to be another side, Jim thought, or he wouldn't have had the luxury of wondering.

Still, the only men with water on flames at the moment were he and this other man, and they were but a drop in a bucket needed to put out this fire, unless the fire got to the magazines first.

Junior officers scattered, and the executive officer Collingwood with them to fight the fire, Squadron Commander Clay was on the TBS, calling for *Ludlow* or *Niblack* to approach the ship and shroud it in smoke. The planes would not relent. They needed cover. *Ludlow* was closer and ran for *Plunkett* with all she had.

All of Burke's maneuverings had moved the destroyer to a position roughly fifteen miles due south of Cape Anzio, but not so far from shore that Frank Gallagher hadn't seen what had happened. His unit had yet to move off the beach, and they were hunkered down against their own Luftwaffe assault when he looked offshore and saw the burst of light that was the *Plunkett* hit.

With its after deckhouse in flames, the ship was even more alluring now than she'd been when the bombers had used the 1.1-inch as their bull's-eye. Now the whole ship was an excellent target. The bomber pilots weren't intent on a Parthian shot; they wanted a coup de grâce.

Lieutenant Thomas was aft of the ship now, opening valves that were supposed to flood magazines, except that the five-inch fire-main pipes that tapped ocean water in emergency situations would not produce. Thomas thought he was getting the magazines flooded, but they would all find out later that that had not happened.

John Oliver was intent on the same water line, but he'd found out what Thomas had not: that the fire mains were down. And moreover, that the forward momentum of the ship was carrying the flames aft. He dispatched a runner to the bridge with that intelligence.

Burke was turning the ship into another approach by the Ju 88s, and then, with the runner's news, he called for a full stop. The men in the forward engine room complied. The men in the after engine room did not. Except for the three who'd escaped, they were all dead.

Meanwhile, Oliver was putting additional handy billy pumps into action, and wondering what to do about the impotent plugs on his fire main. One of the chiefs in the repair party, a thirty-seven-year-old electrician named Edwin H. Baechtold, had an idea.

McManus and his stunned crew climbed down from their mount onto the fantail, where the scene was chaotic. The repair parties were fighting the fire with handy billy pumps, and word was getting around that the fire main aft was down, and something else: that the magazines at the rear of the ship were not flooding. Cognizant of that grim fact, and that they were as combustible as a bomb with those magazines intact and that fire flaring, men burst from the no. 3 lower handling room carrying ready five-inch ammunition and threw it over the side. McManus could do nothing. His arms were burned and ridden with shrapnel, and he couldn't raise them.

Like Jim Feltz, two other men thought an independent decision was in order and communicated as much to McManus. Unlike Feltz, who'd flouted protocol to try and help save the ship, these two men had plans to abandon the ship. As a gun captain, McManus was a figure of some authority, and it might have been they'd turned to him as a means of sanctioning a desperate move.

Mac heard them out and called one of the men who'd mixed it up with Burke on the fantail, a fighter from Providence who could do what McManus could not.

"Clobber those guys," Mac told him.

The man did, staunching any more immediate plans to abandon ship.

On the fantail, some of the depth charges had been ripped open and some were rolling around the deck. One of the depth charges was on fire, and Lieutenant Fitzpatrick had a stream of hosed water from a handy billy on it, racing to douse the flames before the fire kindled the TNT.

Russ Wright addressed each of the depth charges in turn, assuring that the depth dials had been wrenched two clicks to safe. He had no light but for that cast by the flames, and the only confirmation he had—that he'd set them to safe—were the clicks he might hear.

McManus watched Russ Wright move off one can in the dark, and rushed to his side, asking if he'd set all the ash cans to safe.

"Yes," Wright answered him.

McManus gave him his flashlight and told Wright he'd better recheck them.

Wright said nothing to McManus's order, but he took the light and went back to the dials.

Mac caught himself in the wake of his command to Wright: Slow down, McManus. You just ordered an officer to do a job.

One by one, Wright and his deckhands literally threw the depth charges over the side. One of the other splashes was Jack Collingwood, who'd tripped overboard while fighting the fire. His shipmates fished him out.

Baechtold knew the fire main was sectionalized, and he had a rough diagram of the ship's chase lines in his head, not only of the wiring but of the piping, too. That water wasn't flowing from one plug didn't necessarily mean the whole system had to be robbed of pressure. Isolate the rupture in one loop by getting to the right *cut-out valves* at the watertight bulkheads, and you might just enable pressure at some of the other plugs. The chief hazarded his best guess on valves he knew to be on the fire main proper, and its cross sections, and he went to them, shutting down some, opening others. And then, all of a sudden, Oliver got water, flowing from one of the plugs through a four-inch line, and now they really had the means to fight fire.

Jim Shipp came back into consciousness under a mass of jagged metal. He could feel the heat all around. He turned his head to one side, and not a foot from him was Jack Heines, known as Goosegut because he could eat so much.

Jim asked Goosegut if he could get loose, but the man didn't seem to hear him. He was writhing against the clutch of metal. His efforts inspired something in Jim, and he tried pulling his feet, but couldn't feel anything below his waist. The recognition of that fact stunned him a moment. It was quite possible the legs were gone, or beyond repair.

When he looked back to Goosegut, the man was gone. Left alone but for the crackling of fire that now seemed closer, Jim felt a surge of adrenaline that got him moving. His legs were with him still and pushing against metal. He dragged himself to clear space on the torpedo deck, but still couldn't stand. A firefighter leapt over him, dragging a hose that trailed over Jim's chest. Around his waist, his life belt had inflated. Because the snaps had not come loose as designed, the belt worked on him like a vise. He was having trouble breathing, and he couldn't stand.

Only one firefighter had passed him, and that one man hardly seemed consequential when Jim Shipp thought about the magazines under guns no. 3 and 4 in the after part of the ship. It was only a matter of time, he thought, and started crawling over the torpedo deck for the front of the ship.

At 6:03 p.m., the Luftwaffe planes slanted away at last. *Plunkett* had exhausted fifteen hundred rounds of the 1.1-inch, two hundred shells out the five-inch barrels, and twenty-five hundred rounds of 20mm ammunition. What the 20mm guns put up in those twenty-five minutes of live ammunition was 27 percent of all the 20mm ammunition that *Plunkett* would expend during the war.

Not twenty feet from Gallagher, Jim Shipp was pulling himself toward the bow of the ship. Shell casings littered the deck, and he plowed through them as far as the door to the bridge. The chief radioman opened the door and stepped out.

Who are you? he asked.

Shipp. Repair division. Can you get this life belt off? I can't breathe.

The radioman released the belt. He squatted beside the downed sailor, tilted him onto his shoulder, and started for the crew mess, where he'd hoped to find a fellow radioman, Lyle Hollister.

In the ten minutes he'd spent on the handy billy, Jim had moved among flames and deranged metal, and mangled men and parts of men, and detritus from other parts of the ship that didn't have any business topside. Sensing there was sufficient manpower to fight the fire now and gnawed by the fact he was supposed to be at his battle station, Jim surrendered the nozzle to one of the topside crew. It was 6:10 p.m., the bomb had hit twelve minutes earlier, and the fire was coming under control.

At the hatch to the forward fire room, he turned and looked once more at the chaos of sprung seams, punctured plates, warped pipe, and gaping holes, most of it now smoldering. At Gela, he'd remembered that first day in action as the one "everybody had been waiting for." It was a threshold they'd been anxious to cross. He'd never look forward to another threshold in this war. He'd seen all he needed to see.

The chief engineering officer, when Jim came back down into the fire room, laid into him for leaving his battle station. Jim told the chief he'd sprung from the hole because the midship repair party wasn't fighting the fire. In fact, there was no midship repair party. He hadn't thought he had a choice. The chief didn't disagree. He'd said what he was supposed to say.

In Gallagher's gun tub, Garner emerged from the shock of the explosion intact, raked with shrapnel and bleeding. He looked to his mount and saw Gallagher at his gun, not manning it, not with the aplomb that was usual, but fused to it in macabre fashion. The blast had driven him deep into the shoulder braces, and his back was a riddled mess. The blast had thrown a shawl of buoyed netting over the tub.

They found Gallagher alive, someone did, and he was extracted from the shoulder braces and carried along the torpedo deck, past the davits that still cradled a motor whaleboat, onto the forecastle deck, and then down into the wardroom on the main deck. They were moving wounded men into the mess and into the wardroom, where Knaup had too little to do much of anything for anybody.

Gallagher's backside was riddled with shrapnel, porous and draining blood. He was conscious. He needed blood. How much? More than they had.

In the director, Ken rose out of the hatch after the planes were gone, keen for a blast of fresh air that was not available. The ship was lying to, but largely hidden now, ensconced in a fog of smoke pouring from *Ludlow*'s stacks. He could still feel the residuals of the action within him, as he had when he was a little kid and whirled himself into a dizzy spell that was fun to dilute with awkward, unsteady steps. It was hard to believe it was over. At first, the twenty-five minutes of battle seemed to go by in a flash. It was started and then stopped, but now, popped from the confines of the director, he realized that what had seemed but a flash was likely to endure as the most intense experience of his life.

On a wing of the bridge, Burke was leaning over the skirt to better hear what was being reported. The fire was all out now. The men had attacked that threat with a ferocity and expertise that was as commendable as anything else they'd done while the Germans swarmed overhead. So much had gone wrong, but much had gone right, from the fantail to the bridge.

Ken's was a dim shape on the highest part of the destroyer, popped from a little box that had been strafed and buffeted and that had, in those five critical minutes after the bomb hit, kept up a stream of anti-aircraft fire that prevented a coup de grâce. They'd splashed two bombers for sure, probably got a third, and damaged a fourth. But he knew as well that the toll on *Plunkett* was bound to be great. The fate of his gun captains aft was unknown. What happened to his gunners on their 20mms aft was unknown. He knew he'd accomplished something significant that late afternoon, getting the planes they got and keeping the others at bay. Though he might have allowed himself a clap on the back, he emerged from the action nagged by something else that competed for primacy with the success he'd had: He might have done more, he hadn't done enough.

If Ken had doubted that Burke was in command of the best possible recourse to anything they might come up against, and that might require some input from Ken himself, those doubts were extinguished late that day. The skipper had not merely handled his ship well that late afternoon and into the evening but wielded it, like a man who's become one with his instrument, the swordsman his blade, the rider his mount. So much was streaming in—the ten, twelve, or fourteen enemy aircraft, their dropped bombs, torpedoes, and not only what the enemy was doing, but what they might do. Beyond that, he was factoring the condition of the sea and the speed of his ship, as well as the peculiar strengths and weaknesses of the men in the wheelhouse, on his battery, in his fire rooms and engine rooms. Synthesizing all that—what he saw, what he heard, what he sensed— he issued a succession of orders that rendered his ship like a fighter on the ropes who rises, between each of his opponent's failed hooks and jabs, to counter hard, to splash one plane, and then another, maybe a third, and quite possibly a fourth. "He fought his ship so heroically," the Navy later said of Burke's command performance at Anzio, as if the thing had been in his hand, for a run of twenty-five minutes, with hundreds of lives in the balance. They got him in the end, but not all of him, and no so badly that *Plunkett* wasn't going to come back one day for another round, and then another, before it was all done.

At 6:30 p.m., the bridge rang the bell for getting underway, and the forward engine room dialed up ninety-two turns on the still-operable starboard screw. They shifted steering back to the bridge and followed a heading for Naples. Fifteen minutes later, the night sky brightened with specks of twinkling, yellow light, like fairy dust cast by the hand of a wayward sprite. The ship's superstructure warmed momentarily under the chandelier flares, an illumination that seemed nourishing and helpful but was yet another attempt on the crippled ship by high-level bombers. They could hear twin-engine planes creeping overhead, and braced for a resumption of action, but nothing happened: The pilots had blinded themselves with their own flares.

At eight o'clock *Niblack* caught up to them, and together the ships steamed for Naples. In the near distance, a British hospital ship like *Newfoundland*, this one *St. David*, burned in the wake of a Luftwaffe attack.

In the forward fire room, Jim Feltz listened to the ship's one compromised screw, dialed up from 92 turns to 142 turns for eleven knots. It was a crude sound—*plop, plop, plop*—that never let you forget, not for a second, that this wasn't a thing you could wake up from but something you would have to think about for a long time. They brought cold cut sandwiches down into the fire room, and they ate silently, waiting for a dawn that might never come. How did you wake up from something like this? In the small hours of the morning, near Naples, they could see the flash and hear the thunder of a city under aerial bombardment by the Luftwaffe, and so the stricken ship changed course for Palermo.

Dawn did come, and with it the search for survivors, a reckoning that required the crew to grapple with wreckage, some of which they threw over the side. Amid the ruins were the severed hands and feet of untold men, other parts, and bodies, too. They couldn't do anything right away about the remains of the man on the no. 6 gun. The 20mm tub was not easily reached. And so the shrapnel-ridden trunk of the dismembered man on the gun hung in his harness, swinging aft and forward with a squeak every time the ship rolled into a new bearing.

On the fantail, they found a man who'd lost an arm and his head, and who was unrecognizable to the men who salvaged him. Except that he was wearing a class ring from Durfee High School in Fall River, where Jim McManus was from. Three men on *Plunkett* had come out of Durfee, and the crew figured they'd found Bill Carey, until Mac bent down and saw "1940" on the class ring.

This isn't Bill, Mac told one of the ship's officers. Bill was older than Mac. It had to be Patten.

The officer consulted the crew list and found him, Louis Patten, signalman third class. They never found any trace of Bill Carey.

Dr. Knaup was back and forth between the mess, the wardroom, and the fantail, summoned time and again when they discovered enough of someone else. Had Knaup not decided to ready the wardroom for casualties, expecting major business when he sighted those first two bombers, they'd have been fishing for his remains among these ruins, for his battle station was with the ten-man midship repair party, seven of whom were now dead.

At first light, Burke had one of the crew survey the damage with a camera. He snapped photos from a number of angles and got one anchored by the downed searchlight. After the photo was snapped, they set to the crumpled structure, removing each piece as gingerly as possible, knowing what was mixed up in all this. They heaved several pieces over the side, exposing a cluster of several men, unwitting congregants whose fates had pulled them together in the end. The crew called the doctor again. Knaup found that Richard Burren, who'd been up on the searchlight, was dead, and that Eddie Webber was dead, too. Eddie was twenty years old. He'd been a machinist's helper at the Link Paper Company in Jersey City. He had a girl named Evelyn Martin waiting for him. He'd come onto *Plunkett* six months before Pearl Harbor. He'd fought the fire with Jim Feltz on *Newfoundland*, and he was a machinist's mate on the ship. He was naked except for his shoes and a pneumatic life belt. He was a mess, and they readied a mattress cover for his body until one of the deckhands beckoned Knaup. "Hey, Doc, I saw that guy's finger move."

They carried Webber to the wardroom and put an oxygen mask on his face. One of the guys from the fire room, Phillip Germain, who'd enlisted out of Buffalo a week after Pearl Harbor, sat by Webber's side all day, refusing relief, and held the oxygen mask all the way to Palermo.

More dreadful than what they were finding topside was what they'd find below deck in the after engine room. Dutch Heissler, who'd been deployed as an assistant when they'd cut into Ken Sahlin's abdomen for an appendix, who'd leaned over the gunnels of the ship's gig to retrieve bodies from the *Buck*, went down into the engine room, clearing the way. At the bottom of the ladder, he came into a pile of men scorched by fire and blanched white from the steam, the flesh fallen away in horrible swatches. Bob Ahlberg, otherwise known as Smoothie, was in that pile. Clark Fisher was down there. And John Bellman, one of two officers killed at Anzio, was among the dead at the bottom of a ladder they'd hoped to climb before they'd succumbed. One by one, they were negotiated out of the hole.

The rigor mortis had set in by then, and these distortions made it all the more difficult to bring them up, and all the more difficult to regard. Jim Feltz, en route to Palermo, had gone back to clean up for one stint that morning, and then he didn't want to go back anymore. He'd seen the bereft gunner in the portside gun tub, and he'd seen anatomical evidence of other men he'd known all over. He was still eighteen years old and might have seen a lot more of the world before he had to see this of men he'd joked with, and shared mess with and bunked with and dreamed about home with. There were things he would not think about or talk about for a long time because he was too young that night, and though he'd seen a lot since he'd come aboard *Plunkett* eighteen months earlier, he'd never seen anything like this. We had a problem, he thought that day, and for the rest of his life he wouldn't think of that evening at Anzio as the night a bomb hit his ship but as the night "we had our problem." He was supposed to be working in a five-and-dime, sweeping floors of dirt, not decks of severed limbs. He'd done his part, and now he'd mind his boilers. Except that the smell was everywhere, on them like osmosis, acrid and coppery metallic because when fire consumed men on *Plunkett*, it burned their iron-rich blood, too, and it burned their organs, layering that metallic odor with a musky sweet scent. There was a sulfurous smell, too, not like the sulfurous smell of ammunition, but something more ominous, that's a by-product of scorched hair, and that's as persistent in the nostrils as a curse. Six months later in Normandy, Ernie Pyle would write, "There is nothing worse in war than the foul odor of death. There is no last vestige of dignity in it." For Jim, there was no getting back to his quarters on the fantail, and so he stayed on watch in the fire room, urging the ship to Palermo.

In the late afternoon, Bob Cavany came down into the hole and reported that they'd extracted as many fallen shipmates as they could from the wreckage; that part of all this was over now, and they'd soon be in Palermo. Dutch and a couple others were working on the men, Cavany told them, meaning the dead men, should anyone want to lend a hand. But you could only lend a hand if you also had a stomach, Jim thought, because he'd already heard what Dutch was doing.

On the fantail, Dutch was addressing fallen shipmates who were flexed in the agony of their last moments. A terrible thing to be caught by, and Dutch would not have it. He would not leave them with these distortions. He would not have them come into Palermo in this fashion. And so he knelt before each of them, breaking a bone when he had to with hands more used to dice and cards. He straightened their limbs, smoothing each one, their arms and their legs, after the violence of what had been done to them, until each of *Plunkett*'s retrieved dead carried with him a semblance of the dignity that's owed a man who died the way each of them had died. He was an indispensable man on *Plunkett* at Anzio, rendering compassion with violence, the previous night and that day, too, seemingly everywhere at once, doing what few could bear to do, tending to the wounded and to the dead. With chief pharmacist's mate John Putis dead, Dutch had stepped up beside the ship's doctor. He was, thought Dr. Knaup watching this man do what he did, "magnificent."

They hadn't bothered to call general quarters that morning. Everyone was already at station. Shortly after dawn, *Niblack* detached from escort duty, and *Plunkett* started into a zigzag for Palermo at eleven knots. Ken Brown and his crew had whiled away the night in the director and descended only after the threat of a morning raid was over. Ken went down first to the after deckhouse where the bomb hit, and saw that the ship's store, which he still managed as an adjunct to his work on the director, had been obliterated. But some of Irv Diamond's stores had survived. Scattered about the deck, like strewn seeds though they were anything but, were condoms, everywhere you looked, condoms.

One of the chiefs stopped beside Ken, in contemplation of all those condoms, which was a better thing to focus on than the alternative. The chief talked quietly to Ken about what had happened, and especially what was happening after the bomb hit, and the reinvigorated bombers came down on a ship whose battery was still in action. He believed that *Plunkett*'s anti-aircraft efforts after the attack made all the difference in the world. (Likewise, when Secretary of the Navy James Forrestal formally commended Brown for his work at Anzio, it was his work after the bomb hit that was of particular note—for "maintaining continuous fire against enemy attackers" after the "attack left his ship severely damaged and ablaze.")

The young man with a "yen for kidding" was apt to accept the chief's commendation as fact, but he also knew what Burke had done, and what the men fighting that fire had done, the men in the mounts and the handling rooms, what Baechtold had done, getting that water into the four-inch lines. All of them, together.

Ken, in retrospect, would talk about teamwork on *Plunkett* that night, and Jim Feltz would talk about how they'd all done their job, reaching for metaphors from the world of sport and employment to communicate, as understatedly as possible, that they had not buckled in fear. They fought, and they hadn't stopped fighting when the odds were stacked against them. It was all they could do, and it had been enough.

In the most resonant of the eleven images of the damage classified by the Navy, John Oliver in his garrison cap and a fellow sailor in a steel helmet stare down onto the deck hard by the escape hatch to the after engine room, through which they'd just extracted a number of men from the black gang, many of them indeed scorched by flame this morning, but blanched more horribly and very few of them of a piece. The man in the helmet has just discovered something at the end of a pole he was using to lever wreckage, and the sight of whatever it was has grabbed Oliver's attention. His arms hang from his side, though they've been puffed out slightly like a cartoon character in surprise. He wasn't looking at condoms.

At two-thirty that afternoon, a patrol craft sortied out from Palermo to escort the ship into harbor. Four Allied aircraft minded the airspace, peeling away repeatedly to double back on the little ship making eleven knots below, a gesture that was partly a matter of security but mostly, perhaps, a matter of honor, what they could do instead of salute like the men who'd stood at the rails for *Savannah*.

Plunkett was met dockside by members of the hospital corps with stretchers and ambulances, and by two lieutenants from the chaplain's corps. They carried off their dead, twenty-four in all, and noted twenty-nine more of the crew were missing, which was a euphemism for being dead *and* vanished. That was fifty-three men. Forty-four of the men who survived had been wounded and would have a Purple Heart. Seventeen of those men were wounded so badly they needed hospitalization; eleven of those men were very badly wounded; and countless others were wounded in ways that nobody, not even they, could fathom.

With the dead and wounded removed, the rest of *Plunkett*'s crew repaired to a Liberty ship, where they bunked while *Plunkett* was cleared and moved to dry dock. Vice Admiral Henry K. Hewitt, who commanded amphibious operations in North Africa and Southern Europe throughout World War II, walked the deck of the ship with Captains Clay and Burke, and then he went to visit the men in the hospital.

They'd tried to carry McManus off the ship on a stretcher, but he balked. "There's nothing wrong with my legs," he told the corpsman.

At the hospital, they tried to cut off the sweater his girl, Ellen O'Melia, had made for him, and he balked at that notion, too, and had one of his shipmates help him wriggle out of it.

Burke came in to see the wounded the next day and stopped at Mac's bunk. "You need anything?" he asked.

"Yes, Captain, I want to get back on the ship before you go back to the States."

"Don't worry. All you guys that can walk will come back on the ship."

Several hours after the captain left, some of the men from the ship returned with items the captain had rounded up—toiletries, writing paper, and cigarettes.

The concussion in Mac's gun turret had ruptured the membranes between his outer ear and inner ear. There was nothing to do for that but wait a couple of months. He'd suffered second- and third-degree burns, and his arms were cut up with shrapnel. Every day, one of the hospital nurses bandaged his arms, and every day one of the deck crew off *Plunkett*, a guy named Woodbridge, would redo the bandaging. Woodbridge was from Kentucky, and had worked at a racetrack, bandaging the legs of horses. The problem with the way the nurses had bandaged McManus was a matter of pressure. It had to be even all the way up and down the limb, Woodbridge told him, working deliberately and solicitously. The explosion had brought this thing out in the survivors, who'd all come into a new sense of fidelity for one another. There would always be the fact that they'd served together on the same ship, in the war, but moreover, there would always be this thing that had forged them at Anzio.

There wasn't anything Woodbridge could do for Goosegut in the bunk next to Mac. Goosegut, who'd been pinned under the wreckage with Jim Shipp, had taken shrapnel in his testicles.

After several days, when it was obvious that a lot of the activity in the hospital was coordinating off Mac's bunk, one of the doctors asked him to talk to two guys who were conscious but hadn't said a word since they'd come in. One of the guys was Webber, and the reason he couldn't talk was that he barely had the strength. But his lips were moving, and Mac leaned in to hear, perforated eardrums and all.

"Get me a cup of coffee," Eddie rasped to Mac.

Mac had less luck with the other guy, Tom Garner, who'd also just come into a petty officer's rating as a water tender. Garner had been topside during the attack and was cut up by shrapnel, and something else. Mac sat beside his bed, waiting out Tom's reticence, but as long as he sat there, ripe with jokes about Goosegut's testicles, and what the flames had done to everyone's hair and his eyebrows, Tom stared fixedly at the ceiling, saying nothing.

"He lost his close buddy," Mac wrote years later. "He took it pretty hard."

Patricia Garner Morrone's fondest memories of her father came from her earliest years. They lived in a row house in Camden, a nice middle-class home with a backyard where Tom built a playhouse for his three daughters. Every year on their birthdays, he cut out their age in a big piece of crepe paper and hung it from the wall. When Pat was seven years old, Tom checked into the hospital for the first time, looking for relief from a thing that haunted him and wouldn't ever let him go. The next seven years had Tom in and out of the hospital, where they tried everything, including shock treatments. In 1968, when Pat was fourteen, almost fifteen, and hopeful there'd be crepe on the wall again, her father was home from the hospital. One day, there was a shot in the house, and Tom Garner was dead by his own hand, nearly twenty-five years after the Germans tried to kill him at Anzio.

"I don't know if his problems were related to his injuries," Pat said. "The only thing I know—my mother told us when this happened— someone who was close to him was on some kind of a gun, and this guy kind of melted onto the gun. He was mortally wounded, and it was a terrible scene."

In the wardroom that night they had their problem at Anzio, Galla- gher lay in and out of consciousness while an IV trickled blood into him, though more was spreading on the floor beneath his stretcher. It was good to be in the wardroom, a schmuck like him, though he was a petty officer now, on his way up.

The light was weak, but he could make out the magazines,

drooped in their racks above the transom, the telltale yellow borders of magazines that had stopped showing up in his house after his father died. Oakton Avenue, he was thinking then, his brothers and sisters, his father, his mother.

And then Jim McManus. Jim was there now, standing beside him, with white bandages wrapped up and down his arms, and an idea that Wesley Knaup might have a moment to look at them, a hope that wouldn't come true, not this hectic evening. So Jim, recognizing Gallagher, came to the side of his stretcher.

"John, what the hell are you doing up here?" he asked.

He'd been dizzy when he'd first come into the wardroom, and he'd been sweating. But he was cold now. His heart was pounding, and though that might have been interpreted as a good sign, the reality was that it was looking for blood. There was little left in him, but his mouth worked out some words for McManus. "I'm a tough Irishman. Those Germans can't kill me."

John's gaze fell from Jim to the familiar covers of *National Geographic*. With that last pronouncement, with that bravado, it appeared then that John had started back to Oakton Avenue, back to his boyhood home in Dorchester with all of the fruit trees in bloom, and the broad veranda across the front of the house. Fragments would have been coming to John now. His dog Rex, a good dog, a shepherd. His late father all those years ago, before Saranac, before the TB, before that night he heard his mother sobbing with her sister Nellie in the downstairs kitchen, his father taking him down to Charlie Adams's for ice cream. His brother Charlie, his Irish twin, the bedrooms they shared all through his boyhood, his mother shuffling them together from room to room, God only knows why. That day when he was five years old and

Charlie encouraged him to ride down the kitchen stairway on a dishpan, which he did because Charlie thought it was a good idea. Not a good idea, his chin all cut up, and his forehead, and Doc Littlefield coming up to put in stitches. All the old gang from the corner, and the fellows up at the Baker Chocolate factory, and the streets of Dorchester filled with the scent of chocolate every afternoon when they exhausted their vents, and the money he made for a 1932 Chevy Roadster. What a car. So far away now. And his mother, so far away, his indomitable mother, with her sense of humor, and what this was going to do to her, to all of them, his brothers and sisters, and that beautiful house on Oakton Avenue.

As *Plunkett* struggled for safe harbor on its one screw with the missing blade, and the horrible plopping sound, it was nearing 7 p.m. on Oakton Avenue. At the top of the street, Charlie and Bernice had cleared the dinner dishes and were getting Mary and the Weatherstrip into bed. Helen had been up to her mother's room and removed her dishes and had the radio tuned for Fred Waring, who'd be coming on momentarily with his old-time music and the banter that would set the house ablaze with Martha's laughter. Lowell Thomas had just delivered the news. The Germans were hitting the beaches in Italy, where Frank was and John had been, and the news clutched Martha hard. It always did, and she braced for an unwelcome revelation. The life drained from her face, like seawater from its bed, leaving her momentarily exposed, stark and awful. But it was over in a moment, and here was Fred Waring to "bring out the beauty of the song." Steaming south off the Italian coast, Dr. Knaup was holding John's wrist at that moment. As fast as the transfusions had been going into him, it was all coming out of him. He was King of the Reserves but he was shaping up to be a twenty-year man in the Navy. That was what Irvin Gebhart noted next to John's name in his address book. And then he noted this in his diary: "Gallagher died at 0100." McManus, years later, wrote this: "Old John died during the night. When they rolled him over, his back was pulverized."

16: AFTERMATH

"I cannot even now
Altogether disengage myself
From those men"

GEORGE OPPEN, *OF BEING NUMEROUS*

Jim Feltz started reckoning the losses in his journal right after the battle. "The men killed in the engineering force were . . . ," and then he started a list, with the surname of a man each on his own line below: "Gallagher—on 20mm gun, Alverson—on a 20mm gun." Winger, Giardi, Sipes, Thorsten—each on the 1.1 gun. Smoothie, Fisher, Dedovich, Bellman—all trapped in the engine room. He remembered that Eckert had been on the 1.1 gun and recorded his name. Burren was on the searchlight. Snyder and Anderson were in the no. 2 repair party—his old repair party. They each got a line. He ran the math, and he was right: fifty-three dead and missing, the same number of men Betty Kneemiller feared had been lost on *Plunkett* a year earlier.

That evening when they arrived in Palermo and relocated to the Liberty ship, Jim was lying on his bunk, looking up at the depression in the springs above him, when a man come around with a basket, asking if he wanted some fruit. Jim sat up and looked down into a wicker basket of what looked like oranges, except that one of them was cut open to reveal pulp that was anything but orange. It was as red as blood. They were in Sicily now, and blood oranges were a specialty there.

Jim peeled the orange, and ate it slice by slice, listening to the unfamiliar sounds of this vast compartment, the squeak of beds as the crew shifted for sleep, and the lucky sonorous sound of men already into it. He lay back down on his bunk, looking up again at the depression, until he wasn't sure what he was looking at. He got out of bed and stood up to look at the shape of a man he'd hoped to recognize but didn't, who was off *Plunkett* but not of the black gang.

In Overland that day, Betty Kneemiller stopped at the dollar store after work to buy a small pane of glass. Strangely, when she'd awakened that morning and come out to breakfast, she'd found that the glass in the framed picture she kept of Jim on the family piano had cracked.

While the ship was still in Palermo, a telegram came to Oakton Avenue in the afternoon, its message in all caps: "THE NAVY DEPARTMENT DEEPLY REGRETS TO INFORM YOU THAT YOUR SON JOHN JAMES GALLAGHER WATERTENDER THIRD CLASS USNR DIED OF WOUNDS FOLLOWING ACTION IN THE PERFORMANCE OF HIS DUTY AND IN THE SERVICE OF HIS COUNTRY." It was January 27, 1944, a Thursday.

Bernice was across the street at her mother's that afternoon when the telegram arrived. They'd seen the messenger stop in front of No. 58—Bernice and her mother, and her sister Rita, who was living at home—and they all teared up because they all knew why a messenger stopped at a house with four blue stars in its window.

After a while Bernice did what she knew she must do. She left the kids with her mother and walked through the unlocked door to be with the Gallaghers.

Later that afternoon, she left little Charlie and Mary with her mother and walked back up the street to her three-decker apartment building, timing her arrival to coincide with her husband's return from the shipyard. It was a terrible thing she was carrying, both for herself and her husband. She climbed the stairs to the third floor and let herself in. There was water running in the bathroom. He washed, and he shaved, too, when he came home from work. She could hear the incidental little noises, of the water in the porcelain basin and the banging of his razor as he tapped out the whiskers, little noises uninformed by the weight of what she had to tell. This bad thing was out there in the world, but not known by her husband, and oh, how she wished it might have stayed that way. What a distance there was between where he was now and where he was about to go. John was his sidekick and, moreover, a representative of what was best about all of them. They believed that about him even before they'd lost him.

Charlie had heard her come in, and had said nothing at first, waiting for her or for the sound of the kids, and then he called out, "Bernice."

She went to the partly open bathroom door. She hadn't thought of what she had to say until she said it, not opening the door but standing outside it.

"I have some bad news to tell you, Charlie," she said, adding his name to the end of the sentence, a thing she wouldn't ordinarily do and that cut him to the bone—the invocation of his name.

The water stopped and he waited a beat for her to fill the space with words. "What?" he asked impatiently. He opened the door, and there was Bernice, twenty-four years old.

"Some bad news about your brother John. He was killed."

He gripped her with his eyes for a moment. The magnitude of that word, "killed," rendered him speechless, and he was incapable of language. He stared at his wife long and hard, confirming the truth of what she had said by the glistening in eyes that were red from weeping intermittently all afternoon, and then a wild thing sprang in his chest and in his steps as he made heedlessly for the doorway. He plunged down the stairs of the three-decker. He ran up Oakton Avenue, past the historic old Pierce House, up the front stairs, through the front door, up the grand oak stairway, to the room where his mother lay in bed. His sisters, Helen and Gert, were with her, and they were dealing with this enormous, new thing that had come into their lives. Charlie went to his mother. "I cried like a baby," he said about that night.

Grief consumed them for hours. "I didn't see him again until two-thirty or three o'clock that morning," Bernice said later.

Tom and Joe Gallagher would find out in time, and Frank would, too, in a letter from Helen while he was holed up in Anzio. But Frank already knew part of what had happened. He'd seen the ship hit, and he knew it was *Plunkett*. "I was worried, but I couldn't get any information. Then I heard from Helen, who wrote me a letter."

Later, when Frank landed with the infantry in Southern France, he spotted *Plunkett*'s hull number again, the way he'd spotted it in the Bay of Naples earlier that year. And he went to the ship again. He met some of his brother's shipmates, and they gave him three pictures from Palermo.

═══

Plunkett buried its dead on January 26, the day after they'd arrived in Palermo, in U.S. Military Cemetery No. 4, located on the outskirts of the city, hard by the elevated berm of a railroad line. A barren-topped mountain loomed in the near distance, and a handful of trees shaded a growing congregation of crosses in this temporary graveyard. The dead lay in twenty-six wooden coffins that looked like packing crates, in two rows before a flagpole where the Stars and Stripes flew at half-mast. Why twenty-six, when they'd only been able to account for twenty-four men dead, is not known. Some of the coffins rose only to the height of the knees, some to the thighs, all were draped by a flag. A Navy chaplain named Bordenave spoke over the men while one of *Plunkett*'s officers stood by with a sword. Dozens of men from the ship who were able stood a respectful distance back from the coffins, Burke front and center among them. They stood bareheaded, with their hats clasped against their chests. When the chaplain's remarks were over, a rifle company of nine enlisted men from *Plunkett* raised their rifles and fired a three-shot volley. Someone took three pictures of the service. Prints were made and clutched by the crew for decades afterward in photo albums where they saved images from the war.

Two days after the service, they gathered John's possessions from his footlocker and prepared to send them home. He'd been especially well endowed with light undershirts and socks, with thirteen of the former folded in his locker and eight pair of the latter rolled up. He had four dollars in his wallet, and a small collection of foreign coins. He'd kept a watch, even though it was broken. He had two rosaries, and two catechisms, four notebooks, two writing sets, a passel of personal pictures, the ship's picture with eighty-five signatures of his shipmates on the back, a *World Almanac*, five white hats, three pairs of blue trousers, two pairs of white trousers, and no dungarees. He was wearing the dungarees when he was killed. Lieutenant Thomas, who'd run for the fantail at Burke's orders after the explosion, attested to the inventory, and they inventoried the lot for shipment, at some point, back to Oakton Avenue.

John Gallagher was making $93.60 per month when he died. His base pay was $78 and he got $15.60 per month for sea and foreign service duty, effective from June 16, 1942, which was the same day he had been absent over leave six hours and got into a fistfight on shore. The Navy sent home six months' gratuity pay of $561.60 on April 6, 1944.

One thing they'd forgotten to collect from John's locker, a thing Jim Feltz noticed when he was back in their quarters and steaming for the States, was a little aluminum tag, they'd had made on Sands Street in Brooklyn a lifetime ago and used as a substitute dog tag and as an ID tag for their lockers. They'd removed all of John's stuff to the supply office in the base at Palermo, and so Jim removed the dog tag as a memento that he planned to return to John's family someday. He'd also stashed a fragment of the bomb that hit the ship.

When *Plunkett* came out of dry dock in Palermo and steamed east for home, men tapped secret stores of booze in their compartments, wine mostly, risking what they wouldn't risk when steaming as before, and drank themselves into a state. Burke tolerated this behavior until he could no longer tolerate it. He walked through every compartment of the ship one evening, accompanied by two deckhands carrying a bushel basket, collecting bottles of wine.

"Next guy I see with a bottle, he's going to meet me on the fan-tail," Burke said. "If you don't believe me, try me."

He had to say the same thing in all of the ship's compartments.

They steered for Bermuda first, then changed course on February 17 for the home stretch. They plowed into one storm that slowed them to eight knots, and then got whacked by another with 85 mph winds and swells that rolled the ship in the middle of one night to fifty-two degrees. In Brooklyn, the yard workers were waiting for them, like men in a pit crew, backed by antidotes to *Plunkett*'s problems. They'd already requisitioned a new engine for the one they'd lost, turbines, a stack, a 40mm gun as a replacement for the 1.1-inch, and deckhouses. It was all crated and stored on the pier. They were going to have to cut a lot of the ship away to rebuild her, and the Navy was granting passes, not measly three- or four-day passes as was usual, but seven- and even fifteen-day passes.

The ship's engineering officer gave Jim something he'd never seen before, would never see again, and didn't know of anyone else on *Plunkett* getting: a thirty-day pass. "Maybe he knew something about me I didn't," Jim said.

At the Navy Yard, the paymaster gave Jim McManus $887 in back pay, including eight one-hundred-dollar bills. Mac put $500 in a bank in Brooklyn, then boarded a train for Fall River. Fall River knew three of its sons had been downed on *Plunkett* at Anzio. One had reportedly been killed in action, one was missing in action, and one was wounded in action. Before Jim returned home, the parents of the three had contacted one another, asking for information beyond the confines of the telegram they'd each received, but no one learned anything more until Mac stepped over the threshold of his family home. Some of the crew had written letters home after

Anzio. Mac didn't. He knew he'd be getting leave, and he didn't want to worry anyone. He hadn't known there'd been a telegram and hadn't thought his family would have known what happened to his ship before he told them.

At home, he gave a one-hundred-dollar bill to his mother, who'd never seen one before, then headed to the hospital where his father was recuperating from a heart attack. He stopped at the sign shop on the way, and a bookkeeper advised him to call ahead to the hospital. Don't just show up on your father, she told him. He's just had a heart attack. The last word Mr. McManus had had from the Navy was that Jim had been wounded in action. Full stop.

Mac went into the hospital unannounced. His boyhood friend, Henry O'Melia, who was himself home on leave after being shot down in Sardinia, tagged along for the ride. The elder McManus, when he saw his son walking at the foot of the beds in the ward, raised a ruckus in the bed, shouting and crying at the same time. A nurse came running to his bedside and berated Mac for whatever he'd done to the patient.

"He's my father. Is that a problem?" Mac asked.

She apologized, and Jim's father came to after a moment. When he'd seen Jim come into the ward, he'd thought he was hallucinating. When he saw Henry behind him, he trusted what he was seeing—hallucinations weren't that real—though he still couldn't handle it.

During his leave, Mac dreaded the visits he was obliged to make to the homes of the other two men from Fall River. He preferred drinking with Henry and hanging out in the sign shop. There was one other survivor from Fall River on *Plunkett*, Tom Casey, but Casey wasn't home yet, and so the responsibility of those visits fell to Mac. Still, it took some nudging – "moral support," Jim noted—from the mailman Eddie Monarch one day at the sign shop before he could bring himself to visit Bill Carey's home. The mailman went with him. They walked to Robeson Street in the Ruggles Park neighborhood and sat for a while with Bill's family. Bill was missing in action, which meant he'd been obliterated, not that Jim would say as much. Bill's wife had been a cheerleader in high school. She was blond, of Polish extraction, and had been crying so much since they'd learned of Bill's status that Jim barely recognized her.

"I want you to come and see me before you go back," Bill's mother said to Jim when he was leaving.

Jim said he would.

Eddie Monarch ushered Jim out of the Careys' and shepherded him to Louis Patten's house, in the southern part of town. Louis was an only child, and his father was away in the Merchant Marine when Jim visited.

Was he hurt badly? Mrs. Patten wanted to know.

Jim had dreaded this visit especially. He never knew what happened to Bill Carey and had no picture in his mind of that shipmate's fate. But he had bent over Louis's body, and lifted the hand to read the graduation date on the ring. What he told Mrs. Patten was that everyone on the ship had got "banged up." It all happened so fast, no one knew what hit them. He couldn't tell her what he'd seen when he looked up from Louis's ring to confirm that this was Louis. "How can you tell a guy's mother he had his head blown off?" Mac wrote.

He did stop by the Careys' again before his leave was over. He was in his uniform for the train trip back to Brooklyn. One of Bill's brothers was there, and Bill's wife, and Bill's father. Mrs. Carey told Mac that whenever Bill was returning to the ship, she'd give him a little bag of goodies—some candy and gum, some cigars. She handed Mac a little brown paper bag and smiled at him faintly.

Jim wanted to say something but was incapable of saying anything. Bill's wife then stepped up and gave him $5. "I want you and Tom Casey to go to a bar and order three drinks, one for you, one for Casey, and one for Bill."

Back in Brooklyn, the gun boss was waiting for Mac, and started haranguing him for information beyond Jim's ken.

"Where's the chief gunner's mate?" Ken asked, evidently irked, and persuaded, it seemed to Mac, that Jim McManus ought to be in the know.

"How the hell would I know?" Mac said. He was tired, having stood on the train all the way from Providence.

Ken grinned until Mac got it. "You're the chief now." Ken shook Mac's hand, and then told him to get his men to turn to in the five-inch handling rooms. He wanted them chipped and painted white.

The elation of this sudden promotion, and all that it meant—the new, spacious quarters with the other chiefs, the boost in pay, the bragging rights, and the possibility of a deeper future in the service—all of that was subsumed by the prospect of that much drudgery. Dooley stood up. "You can't chip that paint."

Ken turned and looked at him. "Do it," he said.

Plunkett had come into the Navy Yard in Brooklyn like a cue ball, scattering its crew to barrooms far and wide as the men tried to put more distance between them and Anzio with the intervention of a

bottle. One night shortly after they returned, Ken Brown and Captain Burke were drinking in the same officer's club. They'd never
been out drinking together overseas, and hadn't come out to this
club together, but they found each other nevertheless. Burke had
heard that one of the officers off *Plunkett* was in a fix on the ground
floor of the bar. He went downstairs to where Ken was on the floor,
regarding a puddle of vomit he'd deposited. The "local gentry," as
Ken dubbed them, were coming down on him pretty hard when
Burke "more or less picked me up off the floor." He brought Ken
back to the hotel they'd both checked into for the night and negotiated the junior officer to his room. While Ken retreated at once for
the toilet bowl, Burke lost his own steam and flopped on the other
bed in Ken's room. It was a putrid scene in the morning, each of
the men a miserable casualty of the night before.

They hadn't discussed what had happened to them at Anzio.
They didn't need to. They'd developed a quiet, undiscussed fraternity
they hadn't had before. The Navy was going to award Burke the
Navy Cross for his actions at Anzio. "When his ship was subjected
to the simultaneous heavy attacks of enemy bombers and torpedo
planes, Captain Burke maneuvered his vessel with extreme skill and
directed intense and accurate anti-aircraft fire on the hostile planes,"
the citation read, the language stiff and formal and hardly capable
of carrying the esteem the crew would carry for Burke in the wake
of that action. For all of his complicated feelings for Burke, and no
matter the slighter commendation he'd had for having taken out
those planes, Ken acknowledged that Burke's handling of that ship at
Anzio was a remarkable achievement—the evasive action and bombs
dodged to be sure, but moreover the wherewithal to maneuver the
ship so that Ken's battery could address the fighters. At Pearl Harbor,

90 percent of the damage done was accomplished between 0755 and 0825, a mere thirty minutes. Consider that twelve to fourteen planes bore down on *Plunkett* for twenty-five minutes, and that the ship would live to fight another day, and Burke's accomplishment comes into high relief. Ken recognized as much after he'd emerged from the director at Anzio. With regard to Burke, he was a changed man. If they'd come to some sort of accommodation at Anzio, that didn't necessarily mean they'd forgotten who they'd been. Ken woke first that morning in their hotel room. Burke was a mess, mired in his own effluvium, an image you'd never want to escape the clutch of your own black hole. "Of course," Ken said, "everyone found out." If this hadn't changed in Ken, neither had Burke given up his inclinations. He stirred out of sleep eventually and suggested they head to the gym.

For what? Ken asked.

Some boxing, Burke said.

With thirty days' leave, Jim Feltz took the train home to Overland, and he went to Betty. This was the time, Jim said, when "everything came together." In a melodramatic rendering of Jim's homecoming, they'd have gone out to Tunetown and Jim would have made good on his promise to dance. He'd have taken to the floor like he was born to it, and Betty would have dropped her arms and stood stock-still to gaze in wonder at this metamorphosis. That didn't happen. Jim still couldn't bring himself to the dance floor. And it didn't matter.

At the end of his leave, he flew back to New York. During a layover, when the whole thing came together, he phoned seventeen-year-old Betty Kneemiller and told her to come to New York and marry him. There wasn't any bended knee on his offer, no mush. Indeed, "I never did ask her," Jim said. "I called and told her to come to New York." Her father, the colonel, had a fit, never having resigned himself to her marrying a "stock man," but Betty paid no mind. She came to New York; they took their blood tests, and then got waylaid by bureaucracy and missed getting permission from the Navy and so were married at Madison Baptist Church on 4/5/44, a day after the sequence of numbers they'd wanted, a day that might have been foreordained by a fortune-teller or a Ouija board. Jim paid $1.25 for a room in the Hotel Astoria that night, and then, for their honeymoon, they relocated to the Century, where the room cost 75 cents.

When he'd detached from *Plunkett*, Jack Simpson had been assigned to a new Fletcher-class destroyer in the Pacific, commissioned USS *Morrison* shortly after he met the ship in Seattle. They'd been waiting on him a long time due to Burke's reluctance to part company.

"Where the hell have you been?" his new CO asked.

"Fighting Germans," Jack said.

Where the Army was at center stage in the European theater, the Navy was the keel of the American effort in the Pacific. The things he'd experienced in the Mediterranean found amplification in the Pacific, seemingly in the same way that the Pacific was a bigger body of water than the Med. The most significant fire he'd fought after *Newfoundland* was on *Princeton*, a carrier hit by a five-hundred-pound Japanese bomb in the Battle of Leyte Gulf, the largest naval battle of the Second World War. *Morrison*'s skipper brought his vessel up against the carrier's starboard side, as Burke had closed on *Newfoundland*, and deployed his firefighters. Jack, who was by now the ship's executive officer, volleyed back and forth between the bow and the fantail, directing the firefighting. All the while, the aircraft carrier plunged up and down in heavy swells, grating against the destroyer. The up-and-down abrasion worked on the port side of *Morrison*'s bridge, demolishing its windshield, pelorus stand (mounted compass), torpedo director foundation, flag bag, and lookout seat. The forward stack was bent at its base and loosened. Eight feet of the after stack was sheared off. The rubbing eventually split the superstructure and sprung the main deck. "Cargo lights, search lights, radio signals and other communications were smashed bit by bit as the *Princeton* surged up and down against the smaller ship." *Morrison* managed to pull away several minutes before an explosion ruptured in the bowels of *Princeton* and ripped off a third of the carrier.

After repairs at Pearl Harbor, *Morrison* steamed back into the fray and was off Okinawa on a bright morning in early May. While posted to the first position in a picket line, the ship engaged several dozen enemy planes before one of them penetrated the flak and crashed into the ship's forward stack, just aft of where Jack was working in the ship's combat information center. Three more planes struck the ship with glancing blows, none so severe as the first, but the damage had been done. The ship's communications were cut, but it was clear the ship was going down.

Jack retrieved his life jacket from his stateroom, just across from the combat information center, and started aft to assess the damage. Two of the ship's junior officers told him there would be no getting out in that direction. Another told him the captain was dead. By the time Jack got to the bridge, he could see the ship's fantail in the water. The bow was rising, and the ship was listing, then rolling. "I stepped over the railings, and walked on the bottom of the ship," Jack said. He was right above the ship's sound room, and though everything was happening so fast, he sat down beside the sonar dome and put on his kapok life jacket. It was a curious moment of calm for Jack, before the consequences of all that had happened tallied its toll. He knew then that dozens of men, and probably many more, were trapped in the hull beneath him and would not survive. He'd been on the bridge of *Morrison* when a data report had come in noting *Plunkett*'s fate, and he'd since learned that fifty-three were lost on his first ship. The toll was to be triple that on *Morrison*. In the Pacific, Jack found what he'd wanted, a war where most of its intensity was happening on the Navy's front lines, and more than that its picket lines. He stood on the hull a moment, the last man on *Morrison*. Then "I stepped off as she was sinking, and swam away from the ship, afraid some of the depth charges might not be set." One of the first men he encountered could barely keep his face out of the water. It was the ship's captain, not dead. Jack summoned a nearby swimmer, who was in decent shape, and ordered him to stay with the captain. Then he swam away through the flotsam and oil, pairing wounded with non-wounded as best he could. He encountered another man in a life jacket, one of the ship's ensigns, who was sounding an alarm about sharks, though none had come and there was nothing to be done if they did.

"Don't be ridiculous," Jack told him. "Sharks won't come near oil." He felt for the sheath on his belt where he still had the knife he'd made on *Plunkett*.

"I'm glad you told me that," the man told Jack three hours later after they were plucked from the sea by a landing craft. "I didn't know that."

"I didn't know that, either," Jack told him.

On May 5, 1944, *Plunkett* came out the other side of its repairs in the Brooklyn Navy Yard and got underway for Belfast, though the crew wouldn't know as much until the 11th, when Jim Feltz scribbled in his journal: "Found out where we were going (Bellfast [*sic*] Ireland)."

From Belfast, the rumblings of something major pinballed all over the ship. The invasion of Europe was imminent, they all knew that, but that was all they knew for sure until May 29, when Jim wrote this in his journal: "John Ford Movie producer and chief come aboard to take pictures of invasion we think." They all knew of Ford, the man behind *How Green Was My Valley* and *The Grapes of Wrath* and the documentary short *The Battle of Midway*. He'd had a million dollars' worth of camera equipment hauled aboard *Plunkett* and a handpicked crew of Coast Guard photographers to deploy as much. All that equipment, and the presence of the legendary director, was a catalyst to wild flights of scuttlebutt. If Ford was on board, they were headed into something epic. On June 3, *Plunkett* got underway at two o'clock in the morning with four battleships, four heavy cruisers, and ten destroyers. "Don't know where we're going to hit as yet," Jim wrote.

Ford spent a good deal of time on board *Plunkett* with the chief petty officers and the enlisted men, playing cards. Bill Souza, who'd come aboard *Plunkett* after Anzio, used to talk with Ford while he stood watch on the torpedo deck, and got to know the director well enough to ask for the man's address. Ford complied. "I was thinking when I got out of the Navy I would go to California," Bill said.

One of *Plunkett*'s sailors might have told Ford about the time his grandmother won the lottery and took her family up to Peaks Island in Maine, to Sunnyside, in fact, the cottage where John Ford spent his summers as a boy. Perhaps he remembered that visit? That sailor's grandmother and John Ford's mother were cousins, but Ford wouldn't hear this story from anyone that day, because it was John Gallagher's story.

At seven o'clock in the morning on June 4, underway for Normandy, the men on *Plunkett* learned the invasion had been postponed twenty-four hours to let the worst Channel storm in forty years blow through. The ship, and hundreds of others, turned off course, *Plunkett* to head back the way they'd come. At seven o'clock that evening, they turned back for Normandy, the invasion on again. "All you can see is ship," Jim Feltz wrote, referencing the awesome panorama around him. "Don't know how many." Jim was scribbling it all down in a three-by-five notebook, his third book of the war, squeezing out a hundred words per page, understanding that history was being made around him.

On Monday, June 5, *Plunkett* veered away from the battleships to pick up the attack transports, which they'd screen going to the beaches. Then the klaxon started, with calls to general quarters at 1921, at 1951, at 2030, at 2230. John Ford was up on the bridge at one of those calls, chatting with one of the ship's lookouts, who told the famous movie director that he was scared. "I am, too," Ford told him.

At one o'clock in the morning, *Plunkett* arrived offshore between Le Havre and Cherbourg. Indeed, the ship was off Omaha Beach, though Jim didn't have that name when he was getting it down in his journal. As they bore down on the beach, Ford noted the ship's position at the rear of one convoy, but then after a quick maneuver by the flotilla, he found *Plunkett* in the lead.

"I am told I expressed some surprise at leading the invasion with my cameras," Ford told *The American Legion Magazine* in 1964.

Jim Feltz noted the aerial bombardment of the beaches that morning, and then the naval bombardment, and then at 6:30 a.m. it was H hour, and the GIs streamed for shore in their landing craft. Ford watched the landing craft pass by the ship, the sailors bailing out their boats against the heavy seas.

"I could even hear [the infantrymen] puking over the noise of the motors and waves slapping flat bows all the way to the beach," Ford said.

At the time, *Plunkett* was patrolling a buoyed channel swept by minesweepers, screening the troop transports. No matter the sandy bottom threat to the ship's hull, Ford wanted more proximity to the landing. He "was on the C.O. to get close to the beach so he could get some good pictures," McManus wrote. The exasperated captain "told Ford he was going to put the whaleboat in the water [so] he could get as close to the beach as he wanted."

The battleship *Texas* pounded shore targets with direction from artillery observers already on shore and from recon planes flying overhead. The Talk Between Ships poured a play-by-play account of the battle into *Plunkett*'s wheelhouse, and for a while all looked swell from this one perspective on the invasion. The Germans held their fire, according to Ford, and there was an idea that "they were going to make it without any opposition from the coast."

Then the Nazis opened fire. *Plunkett* was so close to the action that Ford said he watched troops jumping out over the sides of the landing craft rather than risk the streams of incoming machine gun fire when the bow ramps dropped.

"From the *Plunket* [*sic*], I recall vaguely seeing a landing craft off to my right hit a mine and suddenly go up, and another tangled in an underwater obstruction swinging around in crazy, uncontrolled circles. Most of the kids on board got off and waded ashore."

While the infantry emptied out of landing craft onto the beach, *Plunkett* weighed into the fray with its battery. Ken Brown targeted a stone building just behind the beach and started pumping five-inch shells into it. Ford didn't think much of that target.

"I wouldn't think the Germans are stupid enough to stay in there," Ford said to Captain Outerson. "It's too prominent. I bet if you raised your guns and fired at that little house back up there, you might stir up something."

In time, Ken moved his fire off the stone building onto the little house.

With fire from *Plunkett*, said Ford, "the place spewed German troops like a hornets' nest. It erupted."

Ken Brown, who'd been handling targets on shore since they'd come into Gela eleven months earlier, had no recollection of Ford's advice.

What Ford was doing on D-Day has always been a matter of debate. He said Outerson put him and his camera crew into "duck" boats in mid-morning, some four hours after the invasion began, and that he positioned his crew "behind things" so they could expose their film. He recalled seeing the dead in the water and looking back offshore to see the destroyer that brought him there.

"I . . . remember being surprised at how much closer the *Plunket* [*sic*] looked from shore, much closer than the shore had looked a few minutes earlier from the *Plunket* [*sic*]!" he said.

The ship's war diaries make no mention of Ford, or of his anecdotes from D-Day. It's not likely that Ford transferred from *Plunkett* to shore, as he claimed, and more likely Ford was printing another legend with little regard to the facts. More authoritative histories say Ford transferred from *Plunkett* to another ship in the task force later on D-Day and did not go ashore on the first day of the invasion.

In the midst of an air raid near midnight on June 6, *Plunkett* fired on a Ju 88 bomber. The next day, Ken Brown's battery pumped eighty-two rounds of five-inch at a target on shore to no effect. They chased down a sub. On D-Day plus two, they had more success, and took out a target at a road junction on shore. The Army called for *Plunkett* to put more shells on a concentration of German infantry, and Ken dispatched 179 shells. The results, according to the shore fire control party, were "perfect."

The results were less than perfect a week after D-Day when *Plunkett* addressed the German E-boat menace with a number of shells that struck a British cable-laying ship, HMS *Monarch*, killing two men in a friendly fire incident. Mostly, though, *Plunkett* got it right in Normandy. The ship bombarded positions all along the coast and then, at the end of June, worked with several other destroyers and two battleships to bombard Cherbourg and open up that city's harbor to the Allies.

They moved back into the Mediterranean that summer, and shot down another plane, the fifth of *Plunkett*'s five confirmed during the war. In the middle of August, they bombarded the southern coast of France near Nice during the ship's fifth and final invasion during the war. For the rest of the year, they patrolled the Med, bombarding enemy positions, and spent Christmas in Mers el-Kebir, where Jim Feltz was "very homesick" and disappointed with the "Lousey Chow." They got underway for the United States on December 28. Except for one run back to England in May of 1945, *Plunkett* was done with Europe, and with fighting. They patrolled the East Coast all spring, and then headed to the Pacific and Japan, arriving just after the Japanese called it quits.

In a memoir worked up right after the war was over, one of the ship's officers noted that during the war *Plunkett* had fired 9,285 rounds of 20mm, 1,842 rounds of 1.1-inch, 1,248 rounds of 40mm (the gun that replaced the 1.1-inch after Anzio), and 1,480 rounds of five-inch. The ship "participated in every major invasion of Europe, and it is believed to be the only major warship so distinguished."

In February of 1954, the United States transferred *Plunkett* to Taiwan, where she rendered service to that nation's Navy with a new name, *Nan Wang*, and a new hull number, 17. In 1972, the ship was stricken, and in 1975, thirty-five years after its launch in Kearny, New Jersey, *Plunkett* was scrapped, somewhere in Taiwan.

After the war, Jack Simpson stayed in the Reserves, and the Navy called him back for Korea. At the Boston Navy Yard, where he'd boarded *Plunkett* in 1941, he reconnected with Dr. David Bates, and they talked about the day that Bates had extracted the shrapnel from Jack's ankle, without morphine. Bates had been on one of the ships off Iwo Jima during the landings and told Jack he'd needed all of the morphine he had there.

Jack crossed paths with Ken Brown during Korea, too. They'd steamed into the war together on *Plunkett*, and Ken remembered

Jack as a man who'd exhibited a maturity far greater than anything Ken decided that he himself had achieved at that age. Jack was a deliberate thinker, and people liked him. That was what Ken remembered, and he told Jack when they met that he was the kind of man he'd like to have worked with, or have worked for, or have had work for him. "If he stayed in the Navy, he would have gone quite high," Ken said. Neither of the men in their dotage looked back on all of the men they served with in a halcyon light. Being frank and true about this or that person seemed to be as necessary as waxing nostalgic about others. It is true that fine feeling flowed both ways between Jack and Ken. "I was always disappointed that he didn't get into any other kind of work after the Navy," Jack said of Ken. "He was real bright and energetic." For the private sector, Jack said, Ken's decision to play a lot of tennis in retirement was "a loss of talent."

Ken also met Burke once more after the war, at Guantánamo Bay in Cuba, when Burke was in command of the cruiser *Des Moines* and Ken was in command of the destroyer *Cassin Young*. They were both in the midst of refresher training courses. At the officer's club one night, Ken ordered a drink at the bar and noticed Burke at a table with his wife. Drink ordered, he referenced Burke to an officer at his elbow. The man knew of Burke and asked if Ken was off the *Des Moines*. Before Ken had a chance to say anything, the man answered his own question. "You couldn't be. You're smiling."

Ken hadn't seen Burke since *Plunkett* more than ten years earlier, and so he made his way across the bar to say hello. In the wake of a handshake, Burke launched their reunion this way: "How many times did I throw you in the hack?"

"Just once, sir," Ken said.

Burke swilled his drink and gulped a swallow, then steadied a gaze on Ken and said what he'd written in a letter of commendation: "You were the best damn gunnery officer in the fleet."

Long before they had their first reunion, the desire to come together again was brewing in some of the men. In the mid-1950s, a petty officer off a destroyer escort boarded the *Cassin Young* and told the officer of the deck he'd like to pay a call on the ship's captain. A messenger escorted the petty officer to Ken Brown's quarters. The door was ajar, and Jim McManus knocked.

"Yes?" Brown said, without turning from his desk.

McManus knocked again.

"Yes," Brown said.

McManus knocked a third time. Ken spun in his seat, slightly miffed, then sprang from his seat and grabbed McManus by the neck. "Get in here, you Irish bastard," he said.

Ken rang the steward for coffee and proposed that he and Mac summon the men off *Plunkett* for a reunion.

Mac quickly ran the math. "You can't do that as long as you're on active duty," he said. "You won't know where you'll be in six months."

Ken acknowledged this was so, but now that he'd made contact with one of the men off *Plunkett*, he didn't want to lose him. "Here's what I'm going to do. I'll have you transferred aboard and make you chief master of arms, then we'll square this ship away."

Mac liked the idea. He liked Brown. But Mac was married, and he knew *Cassin Young*, unlike his destroyer escort, sortied for long spells away from home. Ken confirmed as much. In ten days, they would be off on an eight-month world cruise.

"Forget it. My wife will divorce me," Mac said.

All of Ken's enthusiasm for getting back together deflated all of a sudden, but he had this, at least, to offer Mac: After the cruise, he was to be stationed in Washington and would be in a position to redress wrongs if anyone gave Mac any crap.

Mac warmed to the affection. Brown had been one helluva man to serve under. Nevertheless, he told the old gun boss, "You know nobody gives McManus any crap."

When *Plunkett* steamed into South Carolina in January of 1946, the Navy detached Jim Feltz, nearly three-and-a-half years after he had boarded *Plunkett* in Brooklyn. He'd known, well before they docked, that the Navy was letting him go, and he was packed and ready to go as the ship tied up. He was a petty officer then. He owned his own fire room. He was making $350 per month, and when they told him he was good to go, "Man, I was gone." He left without fanfare, without any of the routine goodbyes to the men he'd served with, so desperate was he to get home to Betty.

In his blues, he rode a Greyhound that was half filled with men coming home from the war. The bus broke down en route to St. Louis, and he, like all of the other servicemen on board, strung out along the road with his thumb in the air. Each of them was taken, Jim said, immediately. He arrived in St. Louis at 6 a.m. and phoned home to his sister and brother-in-law, asking would they pick him up. He hadn't told anyone he was coming home. They dropped him off at Betty's and he knocked on the door. She opened it. "Surprise, surprise," he said.

They settled in St. Charles on the Missouri River. He and Betty had three sons, and he built a business in truck parts. The colonel got over his reservations about Jim's prospects, and they became friends.

Discharged into an employment field crowded with veterans, Jim had got a job making $225 per month at the truck parts company. He later bought the business from the firm that hired him and built a company that employed a dozen people and thrived for decades. As successful as he was, Jim never thought of himself as anything but a "parts man."

In the late 1960s, with his business well established and Betty's interest in dancing unabated, she persuaded him to take some classes. He learned how to dance to swing music, and how to jitterbug. He became proficient in the rumba and the foxtrot, and he especially liked a variation on the jitterbug that, in St. Louis, they called the imperial style. For the rest of their lives, until Betty succumbed to muscular dystrophy and moved into a wheelchair, they danced all the time.

For decades after the war ended, Jim Feltz didn't talk about his time in the service. But then in 1980, there was a small reunion of *Plunkett* sailors on the East Coast, organized by George Gainey in Charleston, South Carolina, and as coincidence would have it, another small reunion on the West Coast. The men were retiring now, or on the verge of it. They'd made what they could of their chances postwar, and had begun casting back now into their past, at last more intrigued by where they'd been than where they were going.

Those first two efforts at getting together were undertaken by the black gangs. But they knew, after that first get-together, they had tapped something that had been gathering steam within them for decades. At least one man, before they started the reunions, had made it a point to call on any old shipmate whenever he and his wife traveled. Sometime in the 1970s, Jim Shipp phoned Ken Brown one day and told him he was coming to Dago, as they referred to San Diego: Could he stop by and say hello? By all means, Ken said. He couldn't picture Shipp clearly from their time on *Plunkett*, though he knew about the man's crawl from the wreckage of the searchlight to the bridge. Shipp knew Ken, as they all knew the gun boss, as one of the men who'd saved the ship, not merely for having commanded a battery that took out three or maybe four of the twelve to fourteen planes at Anzio, but as the man who'd kept that Luftwaffe squadron at bay while the ship was blazing. When Shipp came into the house, the recognition of this man as a shipmate triggered a response that Ken, at the time, didn't know he was capable of in such circumstances. He started to cry.

"Oh no," said Shipp's wife, Liz, who'd accompanied her husband on several of these visits. "Not you, too."

They came together for the first time in a major way in 1982 at a Falls Church, Virginia, hotel, not far from Washington, gathering in one of the ballrooms that had been set up as a venue for their party. Most of them were seeing each other for the first time since the war. That alone was enough to rouse emotion in any of them, for they'd been sailors once and young. They'd been on the same ship. They'd been through war together. Beyond the wistful contemplation of these shared histories, and how that united them, they were bound by cords that tremored with the memories of the fifty-three men they'd lost. This was a thing that would never be quiescent within any of them.

One man's arrival into the mix was representative of what they were all going through now in their own way. This was Edwin H. Baechtold, who'd plunged into the ship's fire and found the valves that opened the water lines that, according to John Oliver, "saved the ship." Ken Brown remembered Baechtold's arrival this way: "He came through the door to where we already were—more than crying, he was weeping, and he rejoined us."

Once they started, they couldn't stop. They'd spend liberally to fund trips in the wake of Falls Church, to Charleston, Buffalo, and Branson, to Minneapolis and San Diego. They'd hire a photographer to take candid pictures of their dinners and their excursions in these cities, and formal pictures of themselves with their wives, and they'd publish commemorative booklets after the reunions.

In the spring of 1992, with *Plunkett*'s reunions a fixture on his calendar, Ken Brown thought to memorialize those twenty-five minutes at Anzio with a painting. The most dramatic moment of the afternoon occurred as the bomb slammed into the 1.1-inch gun mount. But they wouldn't want that remembered in watercolor. Ken, in consultation with the crew, decided to picture the downing of an enemy plane. He contacted a seasoned nautical painter, Richard Moore, who himself had served as a junior officer on a destroyer after the war, and Ken worked on a prospectus, describing as many details of the ship and the setting and the moment that he and his shipmates could dredge from memory. And then Dick Moore went to work for $1,000.

In his painting, he sought a depiction that would bear "looking at over a long period of time" and that would not "do great violence to the facts," understanding that some concessions would have to be made to "artistic considerations." He emphasized the ship itself in the watercolor, for Gleaves-class destroyers "were good looking ships compared to some of the newer ones." Unlike a carrier, a destroyer was a ship that looked like a ship. He let the ship be lighted by the natural light of dusk, and highlighted portions with muzzle flashes. To bring out the light of the ship, he deepened the darkness of the sky and the sea. Initially, Ken wanted as much of the action in the picture as possible, but a torpedo wake was not possible in Moore's chosen moment. At the angle he'd selected, the torpedo wake would be invisible. The painting comes onto *Plunkett* off the ship's port bow and shows two bomb splashes, at midship and the stern. All of the movement in the picture flows from the ship's battery of four flashing five-inch guns, as well as the Mark 37 director, all trained on a torpedo bomber that's "being splashed" in the upper left corner.

Ken reproduced 431 of the watercolors and sold 72 prints at the next ship's reunion for $60 a piece. Jim Feltz bought one and won another in a raffle. Over the next five years, as more of the prints were sold, Ken produced a series of financial reports and mailed rebates to his shipmates as the cost came down. He sent out small, meaningful checks on a regular basis until, in the end, they'd each paid $11 for this image of their ship at Anzio. "A fine acquisition at a great price, one which will grow in sentimental and dollar value," Ken wrote in his "final report," having watched too much TV in his retirement perhaps.

However triumphant *Plunkett* was in that one moment at Anzio, it was a fleeting gesture by Ken, who, for as long as I knew him, dwelled more on all the things he might have done but didn't. He knew that he'd put John Gallagher on that 20mm gun, and on several occasions he addressed that fact in a way that surprised me. That first time, we were standing in his kitchen, drinking maple-flavored whiskey that his daughter Kerry had brought back from a recent trip to Alaska. The taste was somewhat exotic for him, all that maple, but he liked it and looked at the amber in the glass and thought then of all the times he'd drunk whiskey during the war, and what he might have done instead of that.

"You would be perfectly within your rights, Jim," he said to me then, "as family of one of the men who died on *Plunkett*, to say, 'Brown, why the hell didn't you work your gunners more than you did? Why did you spend time in a gin mill when you might have been training those men? And if I had, Jim, then maybe you'd have got to know that uncle."

For my part, I couldn't admit his criticism as worthy of retrospective consideration, though I believed he himself most certainly believed it was. He was capable of cognitive dissonance. At the same time he took pride in what he'd done in the director, he was haunted by what he'd failed to do. He'd have liked to have thought that what he'd done in the director was heroic, and he let himself believe as much sometimes; other times—more frequently, I think—he rued his liabilities.

The image of Ken Brown at Anzio that endured for me was of a twenty-three-year-old young man, perched in the highest part of a Navy ship, shoved out of his hatch and completely exposed to a swarm of German bombers, slewing his guns to do what he could to keep enemy aircraft from hitting his ship. And doing it well, as good or better than anyone might have hoped. If he read what I've written here, and he never will, he'd probably remind me he wouldn't want to be called out for having done any more than his fair share at Anzio. "Let's not horse around, Jim."

Year after year from 1982 on, they would set a date for the next reunion, cast that appointment into the near future like an anchor, and then haul themselves hand over hand toward one more chance, maybe the last, to float on the most buoyant memories they had.

Dutch Heissler was a man they'd have liked to see again. In retrospect, his name couldn't be mentioned without kindling a chuckle, and a concomitant admission of awe. While the Dutch-man played fast and loose with his dice and his cards and was as liable to precipitate all kinds of alarums and excursions, he'd earned the gratitude of his shipmates for his willingness to do anything and go anywhere to get them fed, to get them fixed, and to save their lives, when the time called for it. At the end of the day, all of the shipmates I talked to who remembered Dutch agreed with Dr. Knaup that the man had been "magnificent."

By 1948, Dutch had amassed twenty years in the regular Navy. He then embarked on ten more in the Reserves. He and his wife, Ginny, divorced after the war, and then remarried. They divorced again, and then remarried. His niece, Carla, believes they were divorced and married four times. There were shenanigans, and rumors circulated among *Plunkett*'s crew that Dutch had been tossed in the brig for a spell, which would have surprised no one if it was a matter of scheming or cards. Eventually, Ginny relocated to Mexico and disappeared from the radar screens of Dutch's family. The man himself settled in Compton, California, and died there in 1972.

Jack Collingwood spent most of his career in the Navy on destroyers, including a two-year stint as captain of the USS *Smalley* in the 1950s. Collingwood was well liked on *Plunkett*, and lived up to the Smiling Jack moniker, but it was a personality trait that might have collided with his ambitions as a naval officer. His son, Jeff, said his father told him he had *not* been well liked by his men in the 1950s. Maybe he'd started cultivating a persona that didn't come naturally, understanding that a more dour regard of the world would send you further up the Navy's ladder. He'd tried to get command of a cruiser in the 1960s, understanding that he wasn't going to make rear admiral unless he did, but the Navy passed him over. He captained a hospital ship in Vietnam, and when he retired after thirty-two years in the Navy, he divorced his wife and married a nurse off that ship. In 2001, dying from prostate cancer he knew he couldn't beat, he "ate the business end of shotgun," as Ken Brown put it, and died in his backyard on his own terms.

John Oliver, who succeeded Jack Simpson as the ship's damage control officer, transitioned from the Navy to the State Department, and then into the CIA, where he worked as an analyst. Oliver had come from a well-established family in Pittsburgh. His father was publisher of the *Gazette* before it was the *Post-Gazette*. And his grandfather had been a U.S. senator. When he retired in 1980, the onetime captain of the squash team at Yale ended up in Vermont. He died in 2010 at the age of 91.

Ken Sahlin, who'd had his appendix removed on the way to Salerno, joined the U.S. Forest Service and died in the early 1960s after his spotting plane crashed in Arizona.

Lyle Hollister, whom Burke called out of the radio shack several weeks before Anzio to relay the news that his twin brothers had been killed on a carrier in the Pacific, was among the missing at Anzio. A year after he went missing, the Navy finally and officially notified Mr. and Mrs. Howard J. Hollister of Robbinsdale, Minnesota, that Lyle had been killed. In the span of three months, they'd lost all three of their sons. Mrs. Hollister was a night worker at an ordnance plant, and Mr. Hollister drove trucks for a living. In a living room that contained bookcases and lamps made by her sons, the forty-two-year-old mother received a visit from a newspaper reporter, who noted the pronounced streak of gray shot through her otherwise dark hair. "Well," she told the reporter just days after getting official notification from the Navy, "that's the last of the Hollister boys." In October of that year, with $230 raised by their neighbors, Mr. and Mrs. Hollister took a train to Seattle, where Mrs. Hollister broke a bottle of champagne against the bow of a new 2,220-ton destroyer that would be commissioned the USS *Hollister*, DD-788.

Jim McNellis, who'd stood with Gallagher, Feltz, Zakrzewski, and Irvin Gebhart in that Casablanca picture, came to the first reunion with a baseball cap that named the ship and its hull number, one of those black hats that were just coming into fashion among vets then. Jim Feltz expressed an admiration for the cap and was surprised when McNellis took it off his head and gave it to him, though McNellis declined to share news about the cancer that would kill him within a year.

Zakrzewski stayed with *Plunkett* all the way to its decommissioning in 1946, where he's pictured on the ship's forecastle with forty-eight of the ship's officers and crew. Ski is squatting at the front of the group photo and grinning while he points a pistol at the head of an unwitting officer just in front of him.

Ski stayed in the Navy Reserves until 1954. He met his wife on a blind date in 1952 and raised his family just south of Boston, in Braintree. He worked for Raytheon, a defense contractor, until retirement in 1983, all the while painting and wallpapering on the side. "His one goal in life was to be a family man," said his daughter Gail Johnson. "He took us everywhere, even just running to the store to get the paper. He never bought a brand-new car and he turned his paycheck over to my mother every week."

Like so many veterans, he buried the stories of his service with the war, which seems like an affected gesture until you remember that service during World War II was the default position of so many young American men. Making much ado about something like that was akin to putting on the high hat when everyone else rated a high hat. His kids pinned his medals to their shirts when they played Army as kids, but they never saw the pictures of his time on *Plunkett* until after he died. He never told them what had happened to the ship at Anzio, and they only learned about it after he died.

The daughters of men on *Plunkett* impressed me as the more fastidious custodians of their fathers' legacies. Such a generalization sounds like bias, except when you think of how we have Daughters of the American Revolution, not Sons, and when I remember how Kerry Haygood and Bonnie Reavis could recount their father's stories about the war note for note, and how I repeatedly tried to get two sons of men on *Plunkett* to call me back and couldn't.

Bonnie Reavis, when talking about that moment her father, Jack Simpson, sat down on the overturned hull of *Morrison* with more than half his crew dead, paused as her father paused. It couldn't have been a long pause for Jack; his ship was on its way down, after all, but there was a glottal stop in his momentum, a moment fraught with weariness and resignation when all of his past might have stirred to rush before him as the old cliché says, with men having lost their lives and about to lose their lives all around him. "And then," Bonnie told me in a voice choked with emotion, "my father put on his life jacket and stepped into the water."

Doris Putis Warren had no memory of her father, John Putis, who was the chief pharmacist's mate on *Plunkett* and who was killed at Anzio. Doris had been born four months before the action at Anzio, and her father had been glad she was a girl. "War is hell," he wrote to his wife. "I'm glad it's another daughter."

Many children of the men lost on *Plunkett* clung to men who survived and who would talk to them of their fathers. Jim McManus became one of those men for Doris, and for others, a surrogate of sorts. She learned from him that her father never went off ship at liberty, that he was always reading, and that he was better at what he did than many ships' doctors.

After Anzio, Doris's mother "never went out with anyone else," Doris said. Even though her husband was not among the missing, Doris's mother still waited for him to come home. When Doris married, she married a man who served on a destroyer in Vietnam.

Seventy-two years after her father's death, she was still yearning for a man she never knew. She'd lived all of her life with a fervent belief in afterlife, and a dream she'll meet him someday. It's plausible, she always figured, but she didn't want that plausibility to be merely an abstraction. She puzzled through the ways and means of how she might one day meet her father. She didn't believe there would be any kind of corporeal meeting, but would it happen? She's hoping.

Irv Gebhart returned to Delaware and to work as a machinist for DuPont. He raised two sons and told them little about his time on *Plunkett*. "We were too scared to ask," his son Steve said. Not that Irvin was a dour man. "He was talkative, he loved to drink a beer, and he always wanted you to stay and have *one more*. He was always the life of the party, and he worked three jobs all his life." When there were major events, family and friends called on Irvin to hire the bands, procure the beef, and make sure there was beer. He lived long enough to attend two *Plunkett* reunions, and died in 1985.

Jim McManus, who'd tried so hard to get into the Navy in the

1930s, stayed there for twenty years. He was retired, or "piped over the side," as a chief gunner's mate in 1961. He returned home to Fall River and worked for the city and then for the state, for a while as the driver of a bookmobile. Which seems just an incredible thing—that a man in a gun mount under a swarm of German aircraft could one day be a man who sits in the driver's seat of a bookmobile. In his spare time, he made lamps from the blocks or pulleys he'd become familiar with during his days at the sign shop—lamps that eventually found their way into the homes of his shipmates on *Plunkett* and their families. Doris Warren had one. Ken Brown had one. Jim Feltz had one. People were getting more block lamps than they needed, but Mac kept on making them. He made more than two hundred block lamps in his lifetime. He died in the late spring of 2008, at eighty-nine.

Not long after we'd started talking, Jim Feltz told me he wanted to send me some things. He'd been scrupulous about finding homes for artifacts he and Betty had collected through the years—leaded glass chandeliers, antique toy planes and helicopters, a 1951 Magnavox television in a console. Knowing they'd be in good hands when he was gone meant something to him, and so one day, I opened a cardboard box on a spent 20mm shell he'd taken from *Plunkett*, an aluminum dog tag inscribed with the name "JOHN JAMES GALLAGHER" in all capital letters, and a fragment of the bomb that had killed the same.

After Ken received the 431 prints of the *Plunkett* watercolor, he sent one to Captain Burke's only child, a daughter, in the fall of 1992. She answered his gift with a letter that told Ken she knew very little about her father's time in the war. "I know my dad brought back a ship that had been severed in half and the men in the other half perished," she wrote. "I remember his anguish at writing letters to their families."

The Navy detached Burke from *Plunkett* as soon as the ship returned to the States. Officially, they transferred him on February 15, but he wouldn't leave the ship until they docked in Brooklyn February 26. He would not command another ship during the war. A week before the end of the conflict in Europe, the Navy promoted Burke to full captain, one rank below rear admiral, and then sent him to Berlin as a naval advisor. He did a brief stint as a college professor, teaching naval science. Then he went back to sea, first as commander of a hydrographic survey group, and then in April of 1954 as commander of the cruiser *Des Moines*. If they gave you a cruiser, they were also going to make you a rear admiral in due course.

Burke wore his stature well. His rank called for participation in diplomatic missions, and he rose to the occasion in his dress whites and blues, like a character from central casting, the personification of American postwar might—powerfully built, no nonsense, capable of a cigar and a cocktail, and of sitting down to affix his name in a ledger when occasion called for it. When he retired in the mid-1960s, they made him a rear admiral.

His one daughter had four children, the oldest of whom she named for her father. Ed Gipple inherited his grandfather's name, but not the carriage. "He's more of a hippie," Gipple's wife, Karen, told me when we met in Annapolis.

In the last year of his grandfather's life, Ed was seven and eight years old, and just coming into an appreciation of a grandfather who was in many ways larger than life. One day in Washington, D.C., Ed

Burke was visiting his daughter when he noticed his grandson outside playing football with the neighborhood kids. He went outside and called for the ball and told them all to "go deep." They did, but it wasn't far enough. He sent them across the street. Then up the hill. Then down the block. And then the onetime all-American tossed a ball that soared over the heads of all those kids.

"The kids on the block talked about that for a long time," Ed said.

He presented each of his two oldest grandsons with boxing gloves, and when he visited, the first order of business was always some training and a bout. Once when they visited him at his retirement home in Sarasota, he taught his two grandsons how to swim by heaving them into the deep-water part of the backyard pool, a commonplace story to be sure, except for the part where Burke's elegant daughter, with a martini glass lifted high in one hand and a cigarette high in the other, jumped in the pool in her dress and with her accouterments to retrieve her sons.

He was a grandfather who flexed muscles that had atrophied as the father of a daughter who would not play football, or box, or go to the Academy. But there was a soft side, too, a man who would take his grandsons on clandestine runs to the toy store and who'd tell stories. When he was dying of emphysema in 1967 and staying with his daughter so he could be near the Naval Hospital in Bethesda, he'd beckon his two grandsons and they'd climb up into bed and listen to his stories. Ed Gipple does not remember his grandfather telling him what he may have most liked to hear, about the time he forced the surrender of an island off the coast of Sicily, or the time he tried to save a burning hospital ship, or picked up sailors off a torpedoed destroyer, and he never told them about those twenty-five minutes off Anzio when he played defense and offense at the same time, the way he had at the Academy all those years ago, and how he'd nearly won the day. That was how he was remembered in his obituaries in August of 1967, for what he'd done for the *Newfoundland* and *Buck* and for *Plunkett*. Before he died, he told his grandsons in one of those bed-top chats that he was going to leave them two things that were really special to him. Ed's brother got that man Burke's graduation ring from the Academy, and Ed got his pocket watch. When Burke was detached from the ship, the crew did come together on a telegram of sorts. On the back of the watch, there was this inscription:

Presented To
Comdr. E.J. Burke
U.S. Navy
From
the Officers and Crew
U.S.S. Plunkett
431

Late on a Friday afternoon in the fall of 2018, my phone rang while I was driving on the highway. Clasped in a holder stuck to the air vents, the phone's screen pulsed a name with the ringtone: Ken Brown. I was struck once again by this weird disconnect between the Ken Brown who'd come alive for me as a twenty-three-year-old junior officer, and this voice on the other end of a cell phone. Knowing where he'd been and what he'd done on *Plunkett*, and then talking to him today, was a little like having a statue give voice to what's put him on a pedestal. I picked up, of course. You didn't send a statue to your voice mail.

Usually, I phoned Ken, or he called me back after receiving documents I'd unearthed and sent to him for elaboration. There was no specific pivot to this call. Instead, he said he hoped all of the time we'd spent together, in my visits to Colorado and on the phone, had been of some value to me. His voice had the same distinctive depth, but there was a weariness in it I'd never heard before.

I knew then he was calling to say goodbye. I told him the time we'd spent talking had been of great value to me, both from a professional standpoint and from a personal one, too. Even if I hadn't been trying to do something about *Plunkett*, the richness of the relationships I'd developed with Ken and with Jim and with Jack was something unexpected, and rare. Many of us sound a desire now and then, to have a beloved relative back for just one day. *What I wouldn't give. No matter how much work it was in the end. Just one hour.* I was getting that with Ken and Jim. I understood that then, and felt bad, understanding that this would be it with Ken, and that soon he'd be one of those people I'd dream of having back for the hour. It was a short, three-minute call. I was driving through New Hampshire on I-95. It was near dusk.

The following Sunday, I got a text message from Kerry. The phone flashed momentarily with a thumbnail of a picture she'd sent me two-and-a-half years earlier, of her father at sea in the 1950s, perhaps when he was captain of the *Cassin Young*. One of his elbows was on the gunnel, and his eyes were narrowed against the light as he gazed ahead. There was only one reason I was seeing this picture now. I pulled over to read the text. "My dad passed away this morning at 11am," Kerry wrote. "He was ready to go. . . ."

I'd asked Ken once whether what happened at Anzio was the defining experience of his life. He mulled this a moment, never having

considered the question, and said it had not been. He went on to say that getting command of his own destroyer escort in 1946, as a twenty-six-year-old, had been the moment he most cherished. Or maybe, he went on, it was getting command of the destroyer *Cassin Young* in the 1950s, or his later work as a squadron commander. But Ken was wrong in the way we can be wrong about ourselves and what most defines us. Or maybe he was not wrong, but the thing that was greatest within him was freighted with something beyond articulation and definition and recognition. Pivots are hard to identify, even in retrospect. But look no further than the marble stone that stands above his grave. There's only one ship noted there, and one phrase to define who he was on that ship: "Gun Boss."

Frank Gallagher hunkered down at Anzio for all of the months of the siege, making the best of a miserable situation. He was the great-uncle who cut into the electricity that supplied a colonel's quarters so he could have light in *his* bunker. He had a little kitchen down there, and a wine cabinet, and he'd found a wineglass, too.

When the Allies finally bombed Monte Cassino, the road to Rome opened. Frank's unit went into the city the day before the Allies landed in Normandy. In Naples, he'd commandeered a bumboat; in Rome, the once and future streetcar driver commandeered a city trolley. "I drove that goddamned thing all over the city," he said. The goddamned harbor, the goddamned trolley. His unit camped on the grounds of the Vatican, where nuns gave him the first milk he'd had in a long while. Pope Pius addressed a huge assembly of troops, including Frank, in St. Peter's Square.

All the while, Frank snapped photos with his Brownie. He took one

of the landing craft on the day of the invasion of southern France. He took another of an American pilot laid out on the wreckage of a plane that had just crashed and was still in flames. At Dachau, his unit was part of the first group in, and he took pictures, of bodies not stacked like cordwood but in a jumble, before the stacking. Another one of his pictures showed a German naked from the waist up, standing with his hands in the air. The man had run among the prisoners when the Americans came into the camp, and he might have made it but for a tattoo of the SS on the underside of his arm. "An American brigadier general, he was so mad at what happened at Dachau, he put him in a little round cement blockhouse and put fifteen bullets in him." The general, Frank said, "had gone off his rocker." Then again, he said, they all had. "We almost died when we saw what we saw."

For the rest of his life, Jewish groups in Boston invited Frank to "their times," as he called them. He would go and tell them what he'd seen. He bristled at nothing in the news so much as people who would deny the Holocaust.

After the war, Frank returned to Boston's streetcar network, the MTA, and parlayed his personality into a leadership position within the carmen's union. He moved into a house four or five doors away from the house he'd grown up in, and he became a regular again at the pub John Gallagher told all the guys on *Plunkett* about—Callahan's. Frank was a regular at Callahan's from the time they pulled the plug on Prohibition in the 1930s, through the bar's expansion into the dry cleaner's next door and its expansion as the Eire Pub. When Frank died in 2012, the year before he was to turn one hundred, the Eire Pub put a plaque on the back of a barstool for Frank Gallagher. He'd told a lot of stories on those stools, and he saw to it that the city of Boston named a square for his brother in the 1990s.

But for the jottings in his logbook about when he'd seen John at Arzew and then again in Naples, Frank never wrote anything about his brother, or tried to make any sense of the loss. He told the same story over and over again, more for himself than for any need to have his listeners comprehend. Because in the telling for Frank, it was always January 22, 1943, and *Plunkett* hadn't gone in yet.

The city of Boston rededicated that square to John Gallagher in the spring of 2018—they were rededicating all of the veterans' squares twenty-five years after the fact—and I phoned the Eire Pub to tell the owner, John Stenson, that a whole bunch of Gallaghers would be coming in after the ceremony. I didn't know Stenson, but with my reference to the Gallaghers, he launched into his own memories of Frank, a man he missed, and then started telling me this one story—did I know it?—about a time in Naples right before the invasion of Anzio when Frank jumped in a little boat.

That first night after Betty died in 2004 was a curious one for Jim Feltz. He'd gone back into their bedroom and lain down on his side of the bed, but he couldn't sleep, not alone in that place where he'd had someone beside him for sixty years. There was in that house a room that Jim had anchored with his memories of *Plunkett*, a room he'd started work on after the reunions started in the early 1980s. There was a print of the Dick Moore watercolor framed and hung above a wooden mantel over a gas fireplace. An American flag that had flown over the Capitol in commemoration of *Plunkett* was folded into a triangle and housed in a wooden box below the painting. There was a black veteran's baseball cap, like the one Jim McNellis gave him, in one of the mantel's cubbies. A framed picture of the Ship's Party at the Hotel St. George hung from the wall, as did reference to all of his commendations. There was a recliner in one corner, facing the mantel. That night, after coming home from Betty's funeral, Jim got up from his bed and went to the easy chair in his den and pulled the lever into a recline and went to sleep. Every night for the past fifteen years, though there is a bed in that house with sheets he keeps clean, he has passed the night in the berth of that easy chair.

In my first call with Jim after I'd caught him at the home show, he told me he'd been troubled by something for years—decades, in fact. Later, when I talked to his daughter-in-law Pat for the first time, she said the same thing, that there was one thing from the war that bothered him a great deal and that he couldn't ever figure out: John Gallagher's family had not brought him home after the war. It was a hard thing for Jim to fathom because John had been such a well-liked fellow. He knew that personalities like that didn't just happen; he suspected John had come from a good place, and from good people. But why hadn't his family brought him home?

At the end of the war, the military exhumed the dead from their temporary graveyard in Palermo and presented a choice to their families. Option no. 1, as the military form phrased it, allowed families to have the remains reinterred in a permanent American military cemetery overseas. Option no. 2 would send the remains home. Martha Gallagher had lost her mother when she was two, and her father when she was four, and then a daughter as an infant, and then her husband when she was a young woman, but none of these losses had rendered her stronger in the broken place. Martha's eldest daughter conferred with the doctor after they learned there had to be a choice, and they talked about what to do next. The doctor told Martha's children he didn't think she would survive John coming home that way. Her blood pressure was a significant problem, and she might not make it through all that would be ceremoniously necessary in bringing him home. And so John's brothers and sisters told their mother they thought it would be better for John to lie with his shipmates. He should remain buried in Italy, they said. Martha agreed to Option no. 1.

That was what I told Jim Feltz. I told him that, and there was that silence on the other end of the phone again as Jim digested all of this. "I sure am glad you told me that," he said.

In Nettuno, Italy, about twelve miles as the crow flies from where a 550-pound bomb hit *Plunkett* in the late afternoon of January 24, 1944, we debarked from the 9:42 a.m. train out of Rome at an unassuming little art deco train station that had been built during the war. There was a sign in front of the station, pointing toward the Sicily-Rome American Military Cemetery, and we walked for it in bright sun through un-touristed streets.

My wife detoured into a fruit shop with my mother and my brother Jeff, to load up on olives, nectarines, peaches, tomatoes, a melon, and half of a big round loaf of white bread. My two kids and I plodded on and came to a roundabout named for 9/11 and waited outside the main gate for the rest of our party to catch up. Across the street on the 9/11 roundabout was a McDonald's.

Inside the gate, though, there were thousands of serried crosses and towering pines groomed like those on Rome's Palatino Hill. In the near distance, flanking a memorial built of travertine, the same

material the Colosseum is made of, two American flags fluttered
from on high.

They'd dedicated the cemetery at Memorial Day in 1945, which
was a thing I didn't know until Ken Brown asked me whether I
knew as much one night at supper. Then he told me. There'd been
thousands of American dead buried in the cemetery by the time the
Germans surrendered in early May of 1945, and more would be
coming from temporary graveyards all over. Several U.S. senators
had come for the Memorial Day ceremony, and there was a great
crowd gathered for this commemoration. General Lucien Truscott
stepped up onto the stage. "And then," Ken said. His voice choked
up and he reached for the hand of his wife at the table beside him.
I was sitting just to his left at a long table anchored on the other end
by his daughter Kerry, and Ken stared for some time in silence. I'd
glanced at him only long enough to notice the sheen in his eyes, and
I looked down into the tumbler of my whiskey as moisture welled
in my own.

"Truscott turned his back on the living," Ken said, the words not
so much spoken as exhausted one by one. "And he addressed the
dead men under the crosses," Ken went on.

The general apologized to the men. He wasn't reading from any
papers, but speaking from a deep place within him, and speaking in
a way that was uncharacteristic of a man who was otherwise taciturn
and hard-boiled. It wasn't like Truscott to engage in theatrics. The
general said he hoped the dead men would forgive him for any mis-
takes he'd made, though he knew that was asking a helluva lot. He
told them he wouldn't refer to them, then or ever, as the "glorious
dead" because he didn't see much glory in getting killed when you
were a teenager or in your twenties. In the future, he promised them,

if people started talking like that around him, about the glorious dead, he would "straighten them out."

Ken had tried to straighten me out by talking at length about all those things he believed he'd done wrong, at Palermo and Anzio, and off the coast of Normandy. And maybe he straightened me out some, but I couldn't ever stop hearing the trumpets of a fanfare in the wake of my calls with him, and Jack Simpson, and Jim Feltz.

In the cemetery at Anzio, we walked toward John's grave, carrying dirt from the backyard of his boyhood home on Oakton Avenue. The first three children that had been born to John's brothers and sisters after the war were named for him. Two of them were girls, and had to make do with Joan, but then Frank had a son and he was named John Gallagher. Before the children came, though, John's things came home. The war was over, and the Weatherstrip was now four years old and he knew that they were on the verge of a big day. John's things were coming home, but in the Weatherstrip's mind, it was to be his uncle. At the house on Oakton Avenue, when the family gathered around the box, little Charlie couldn't believe how small a man his uncle had been.

Unlike other relatives we'd loved and lost, there was always something different in the affection we felt for John Gallagher, for this uncle we'd never known. He didn't have a family of his own; we were all he had, and so he belonged to us. Each of us felt an individual responsibility to the maintenance of his memory, and to the name of his ship. The sounding of those two syllables—*Plunkett*—has always been holy in the halls of my family. There is genuflection in the way we broach Frank's story about that night in Naples, and all of the other fragments we have of John Gallagher. We bring him back as best we can. Resurrection is a powerful thing, the kind of thing that can sustain a people a long while.

My uncle Charlie's wife, Kathy, once pointed out the oddness of his feeling for a man who'd died when her husband was a toddler. "You never knew him," she said, trying to get a handle on this thing.

"But he knew *me*," Charlie told her.

When I told Jim Feltz we were going to Anzio with dirt from John's backyard, he wept some on the phone. Jim didn't break up much. He had lost his wife, and he'd talked to me about having lost all three of his sons, two from cancer, one from emphysema, and he'd been able to recollect those losses with composure. But it was different when he talked about the friends he'd lost when he was young, and they were young, and the futures they'd dreamed about and talked about were extinguished.

Jim had never been to the cemetery at Anzio. He'd once visited a World War II memorial in Missouri where the names of all the dead were inscribed on massive walls of white stone. When he got to the Gs, he walked for the wall with his forefinger pointing and landed his print not four inches from John Gallagher's name. This time, the planchette almost got it all right.

If I got to Anzio, Jim said to me, which seemed an improbable thing to a man who'd lived through that night and that problem more than seventy years ago, the word "Anzio" not so much the name of an actual place anymore as a memory that hadn't ever stopped smoldering, and that could still flare, he wanted me to deliver a message to his old shipmate. It wasn't all that involved, but it struck me, as I carried the dirt from Oakton Avenue, that something hadn't ever died in Jim, that the dead, like his sons who'd "gone to be with their mother," and the shipmates he'd lost at Anzio and in the long run of years afterward, didn't only exist in the past. They were alive in his memory, and accessible, removed to some other place for sure but not vanished. And I said what Jim asked me to say, sprinkling the dirt from Oakton Avenue on the grass, and giving up a message that I guess was as much from me as it was from a man who'd become a proxy for an uncle I'd never met: "Hello, Johnny."

APPENDIX

KILLED IN ACTION AT ANZIO

Robert J. Ahlberg	MM1C
William E. Alverson	MM1C
Lawrence N. Anderson	CMM(PA)
John T. Bellman	D-V(G)
Claude Bourque	TM1C
Richard A. Burren	EM2C
Harold H. Chipps	S2C
Robert M. Crow	RM2C
Clark Fisher, Jr.	MM2C
Robert J. Fritzen	RdM3C
John J. Gallagher	WT3C
Iley L. Gee	S1C
William B. Gilman	S1C
William R. Hampton	TM3C
Charles A. Hood	S1C
Jay V. Johannes	Msmith1C
Burford M. Lynch	SM3C
Walter W. Nasser	TM2C
Louis Patten	SM3C
John A. Putis	CPhM(PA)
John W. Richmond	RM2C
Sherwood S. Snyder	MM2C
Thomas A. Will	TM3C

MISSING IN ACTION AT ANZIO

Charles d'Autremont	LTJG
John S. Bennington	S1C
William T. Carey	RM3C
Virgelio Carrolo	S2C
Joseph W. Cave, Jr.	S2C
Raymond Charlesworth	SoM3C
Demko Chomiak	S2C
James D. Cliff	TM3C
Newell S. Dedcovich, Jr.	MM2C
Irving F. Diamond	SK1C
Arthur C. Eckert	MM2C
Bronislaw J. Feduk	GM3C
Alfred O. Gelinas	SoM3C
Carlisle S. Gentile	RM3C
John J. Giardi	MM3C
Lyle E. Hollister	RM2C
Gilson R. Jones	S2C
George A. Kramer	S1C
John E. Larkin	TM3C
Patrick R. McGaffigan	Y3C
Henry A. McMahon	TM2C
Timothy R. McNamara	S2C
Michael J. Mizopalko	SC1C
Lacy B. Pyle	S1C
Royce A. Sipes	F1C
Christopher P. Tambe	RM3C
Johannes G. Thorsten	WT3C
Jessie R. Wilson	S2C
Robert H. Winger	MoMM1C
Stanley W. Wojtyto	SM3C

ACKNOWLEDGMENTS

This book was born of the desire to *know more* that's common to many who research family history. Before the research became the grist of this book, it was an exercise in genealogy and, ultimately, a record of something I wanted my kids to know. But then, things got out of hand.

My brother Jeff posted Frank Gallagher's story about Naples on social media, and a young man from Delaware named James Gebhart messaged him to say his grandfather wrote frequently about John Gallagher in his wartime diaries. In the spring of the following year, in the midst of planning a family trip to Italy, the floodgates opened after I began talking to the likes of Jim Feltz, Ken Brown, and Jack Simpson. By the end of summer, after we'd come back from Italy, it became clear to me there was a book in all this.

Ken's daughters Kerry Haygood and Karen Fratantaro helped jump-start the project by setting up conference calls with their father. Kerry and her husband, Jerry, opened the door of their home to me as a place to stay on two weekends I spent with Ken in 2017 and 2018.

The families of so many on the *Plunkett* have bent over backward to aid in the effort to get the ship's story told. When Jim

McManus's daughter, Alice Gipe, sent me her father's unpublished memoir in the spring of 2017, I struck the kind of gold any writer of history hopes to find. I struck the same kind of gold on a visit to Jim Feltz's home when he opened an old cardboard box and showed me literally hundreds of letters he and Betty had exchanged during the war.

Ed Burke's grandson, Ed Gipple, sent me dozens of photos that helped bring the ship's captain back to life. And then he worked with me on a number of attempts (that ultimately proved successful) to obtain his grandfather's records from the National Archives.

Likewise, Jack Simpson's daughters Bonnie Reavis and Sunny Barr spent as much time as I needed, before and after Jack's death, supplementing what Jack told me about his time in the Navy.

So many other family members were instrumental. They submitted to interviews and sent me what they could. I'm thinking in particular of Ed Spagnolo, Barbara Geraghty, Fran Poulin and Carla Polzin (nieces of Dutch Heissler), Doris Putis Warren and Laurie Pierce, Christine Mott, Steve and Dave Gebhart, Sally Carthell, Charles d'Autremont, David Bates, Pat Morrone, Cindy Zingler, Marjorie Kaffenbarger, Peter Oliver, Jeff Collingwood, Gail Zakrzewski Johnson, Barb Mueller, and Cliff Dornburg. I spoke with Edwin Baechtold's sister one day. She was 104 years old, and her mind was as crisp as can be.

Other sailors who'd been on *Plunkett* at Anzio remembered for me what they could—H. R. "Skunky" Kline, John Capito, and Russell von Glahn. More *Plunkett* sailors who'd come aboard after Anzio also spent time answering my questions. There was Ted Mueller, John McMahon, Russell Baxter, Frank Hughes, William Sousa, Pat Corriero, and Alex Shimkonis.

At the destroyer *Cassin Young*, once under the command of Ken Brown and now a museum ship at the old Boston Navy Yard, Steve Briand and Sam Goodwin opened many a dogged-down door so I could familiarize myself with the inner workings of WWII-era destroyers.

While all of these noted above helped fill the coffers of this story, I had friends and family along the way, providing enthusiastic boosts as I talked some of this out loud—Scott Canfield, Mike Moran, Kara and Jim Woolverton, and Kristin and Bob Leonard. I'm grateful to Ed Hellenbeck, who listened to so many set pieces of this story (after our weekly squash match) with interest that was genuine and more encouraging than he can know.

My old pal, Don Snyder, read an early run at this story and gave a pat on the back that propelled me a long way. I'm grateful to Tom Barbash for more of the same midway through the writing, and to Jack Beaudoin, who read the first half of this book and wrote a long email that carried me all the way to the end.

It was a revelation to me halfway through reading Jim Hornfischer's monumental books on the Navy in World War II that he was also a literary agent. I sent him a chunk of this book by email one day, and I heard back from him like this: "I dare say, you've queried the right guy." He was right about that.

And he was right about getting this to Colin Harrison at Scribner. I can still recall trying to find a place on an island in the Rangeley Lakes of Maine where I could get cell phone reception. I spoke with Colin for fifty-one minutes and knew in the wake of the call that I would have exactly the right editor for this book.

In my own family, I owe so much to so many for keeping me going on this story, my brother Jeff, first of all, for lighting this story up on all our radar screens again. Patrick Gallagher carried a torch for John Gallagher at family gatherings for a long time and gladly handed it to me when I started down this road. All of the Gallaghers have been enthusiasts from the start: Tommy, Kristen, and Katie. Their parents, Nancy and Tom Gallagher, accompanied my family on a second trip to Italy that was partly holiday but mostly (in my mind and perhaps theirs, too) research.

So much of the family turns out for this sort of thing. When John J. Gallagher Square in Dorchester was rededicated after twenty-five years, there was Joe Robichaud and his sister Renee Robichaud, Chuck Gallagher, as well as so much of the extended family all the way out to Lois Huss Breignan, who remembered John Gallagher from when she was a girl. Frank Gallagher's daughter, Carol Keneally, was likewise a great source of information, and documentation, over the past several years.

This story has always had special meaning for my uncle Joe Robichaud, because he served on a Navy aircraft carrier in the 1960s, and for my aunt Mary Robichaud, because John Gallagher carried her when she was a baby. Likewise, there's a lot of relevance here for my uncle Charlie Gallagher, the Weatherstrip, who shared a lot of memories that informed this book.

My parents have been a big part of this journey. My father, James B. Sullivan, was a radioman on a destroyer escort, the USS *Price* (DE-332) in the 1950s and was a great sounding board on all things Navy. My mother, Joan Gallagher, who was one of three nieces and nephews named for John, has been my greatest booster all the way along, and was with us every step of the way on both trips to Italy.

Closer to home today, my wife, Thuy, has obliged me with patience and love, and has put a foundation under our home that I've been able to write from every day. My college-aged children, Cullen and Vivian, have listened to much of this story with so much eagerness it's as if *Plunkett* is but another sibling on the way.

And of course, there's Jim Feltz, Ken Brown, and Jack Simpson. Had they been lesser men, I never could have written this story. My contact with them has been inspiring, sustaining and, indeed, resurrecting. Ken and Jack are off to the big reunion now, but Jim's holding steady. And here's to hoping he does a good long while. One hundred, Jim.

NOTES

PART I: THE DAWN

1: THE GODDAMNED HARBOR

5   *the war thus far*: These details about the *Plunkett*'s position, here and throughout the book, are drawn from the ship's deck logs. When I note where the ship was anywhere in the book, the reference has been drawn from records.

5   *"that was the shit"*: This was Frank's phrasing exactly, pulled from an audio recording I made with Frank in the summer of 1998 about this incident in Naples.

5   *the American assault*: In that audio recording, Frank said the "Germans had tanks right in the water."

6   *"the goddamned harbor"*: This was the dialogue as Frank remembered it and how he always told the story.

9   *"do with you"*: Burke's language, as Frank remembered it.

11   *old sailor just laughed*: This sailor was Alex Shimkonis. I got him by phone on May 22, 2016.

11   *"all the time"*: Jim Feltz, phone interview, June 30, 2019.

11   *what* Plunkett *had*: The squadron commander stated as much in a classified report to the Commander U.S. Naval Task Forces, Northwest African Waters, 4 February 1944: "It is believed there have been few more savage attacks on a single destroyer by aircraft than in this action."

13   *Rome was burning*: Norman Lewis wrote in *Naples '44* that the object of the invasion was generally well known and talked about at dinner parties. In *The Day of Battle* (New York: Henry Holt, 2007) Rick Atkinson writes about the hawkers selling postcards of Anzio.

2: BOSTON

16   *"ignore a harmless sandblower"*: *The Lucky Bag*, Naval Academy yearbook, Class of 1942. At the U.S. Naval Academy, "sandblower" was slang for short men whose breaths exhausted so close to the ground they might stir up the sand. See www.serviceacademyforums.com.

16   *wanted that day*: Ken talked about the coding work and his arrival in Boston in an interview on February 16, 2018.

17   *equipment onto the ship*: Specifics of sounds and scent on a destroyer in a navy yard from Joseph A. Donahue, *Tin Cans and Other Ships* (Quincy, MA: Christopher Publishing House, 1979), p. 58.

17   *yard free of explosives*: Deck logs, January 23, 1941.

17   *the ship's transatlantic crossing*: Ken Brown on his first memory of *Plunkett*: "It was in total disarray, wet deck and wet carpet. It wasn't quite the welcoming sight that I might have had in mind." Interview, October 21, 2017.

18   *opinion as Charles P. Plunkett*: Richard Shafter sketches a portrait of Charles P. Plunkett in his chapter on *Plunkett* in *Destroyers in Action*, published in 1945.

18   *clean this place?*: This was Ken's exclamation exactly. He recollected his first impression of *Plunkett* in a phone interview January 27, 2017.

18   *Hap was concerned*: Reference to the source of Hap's worries in the *Lucky Bag*, the Naval Academy yearbook.

19   *person too soon*: In an in-person interview on October 21, 2017, Ken said they'd decided to make Reed the assistant gunnery officer because he was on the ship temporarily, and the assistant's position was one in which "they didn't have anything for him to do."

19   *military indoctrination*: Jack Simpson's daughter, Bonnie Reavis, provided

the description of her father, noting his posture, baldness, eyes, and grippers. Interview, January 29, 2019.

20   *grim as their guns*: The phrase "grim as his guns" was borrowed from James D. Hornfischer's description of an officer in *Neptune's Inferno* (New York: Bantam, 2011).

20   *pacific in January*: Background on Jack Simpson compiled from multiple interviews from 2016 to 2019.

21   *ship into mutiny*: Reference to the XO's prescription of a "black-and-white" to hungover sailors comes from James "Jim" Patrick McManus's unpublished memoir, *My Journal*, p. 67. Mac wrote that the XO got his "jollies" over watching men run to the head. Jack Simpson told the story about Goo Goo's haircuts and how the ship was "close to mutiny" in an interview on March 27, 2017.

22   *"He screwed up"*: Ken couldn't remember who it was that communicated Standley's respect for his grasp of the torpedo manual, but he did remember the language of his own irreverent comment in an interview, October 21, 2017.

22   *This is stupid*: In an interview on December 16, 2016, Ken remembered the language Flanagan and Standley used. He also remembered that incident as evidence of the stupidity that sometimes reigned among certain officers.

23   *restrict them to the ship*: Jack talked about the required correspondence courses in a phone interview on March 27, 2017.

23   *you purchased one*: This is Ken's language from an interview on September 25, 2016: "If my Dad said you needed a typewriter, you may as well buy one. He wouldn't leave you alone until you did."

23   *"along for the ride"*: Ken's recollection of his father's enthusiasm for the Academy came in a phone interview November 7, 2016.

25   *"my substantiating exams"*: Here's a little of the language Ken used one time to describe his trip home from the racetrack at Elgin, Illinois, when he told me the story in a phone interview on November 9, 2016: "I do recall when I got home [from Champaign], I sat down to make a phone call. . . . [I was] sitting in the stairway, asleep, and my

dad found me there and carried me into bed and never woke me. . . . They [the cops] said your dad is looking for you, get home. At the gas station, Wally said you better get home. Your dad is looking for you. I still remember coming down the drive. My dad standing in the drive with the letter in his hand." I'd had him tell me this story several times, and each time realized a new detail.

25 *officers on the attack*: Midshipman Franklyn E. Dailey remembered as much in his book, *Joining the War at Sea* (Alpharetta, GA: Daily International Publishers, 2009), on p. 27.

26 *had to be reassigned*: Disposition of the Class of 1942 noted in *Time* magazine, December 29, 1941, "June in December."

27 *attacked German submarines*: Germany's Declaration of War Against the United States: Hitler's Reichstag Speech of December 11, 1941.

27 *"the world has ever seen—trained"*: From the text of Secretary Knox's speech as published in the *New York Times*, December 20, 1941.

27 *something to Secretary Knox*: Ken remembered that whispered gesture in his recollection of graduation. Interview, October 21, 2017.

30 *those clothes home*: All the surrounding detail about life at Newport comes from Joseph Donahue's memoir (*Tin Cans and Other Ships*) and Gallagher's service jacket, which is a collection of nearly all of the documents the navy produced on him during the tenure of his service.

32 *"for the duration"*: *Boston Globe*, January 24, 1942.

3: UNDERWAY

35 *her seventy-five years*: The *New York Times* on March 10, 1940, ran pictures and an article about *Plunkett*'s launch.

36 *according to General John J. Pershing*: From a *Time* magazine obituary, April 6, 1931: "His most famed exploit was to silence Germany's 'Big Berthas' in 1918 by mounting a battery of long-range 14-in. naval guns on special carriages, moving them to the Allied front lines. This work, said General Pershing, left the enemy 'nothing but surrender or an armistice.'"

37 *fifty-eight seconds*: The *New York Times*, March 10, 1940, "2 New Destroy-ers Launched in New Jersey."

37 Plunkett *in service*: Account of *Plunkett*'s commissioning in the *Brooklyn Daily Eagle*, July 17, 1940.

38 *"destroyer-man" at heart*: John Wukovits, *Tin Can Titans* (Cambridge, MA: Da Capo Press, 2017), p. 4.

39 *"stragglers into line"*: Richard Shafter, *Destroyers in Action*, chapter 1, "A Lovely Ship."

40 *as well as itself*: Eric Larson, *Dead Wake* (New York: Broadway Books, 2016), p. 56.

41 *"the armored fleet from attack"*: Norman Friedman, *U.S. Destroyers: An Illustrated Design History* (Annapolis, MD: Naval Institute Press, 2004), p. 28.

42 *"useful destroyer weapon"*: Ibid., p. 28.

42 *have a subclassification*: Guy Derdahl and Tony DiGiulian, "History and Technology: USN Ship Designations," http://www.navweaps.com/.

43 *cessation of hostilities*: Theodore Roscoe, *Destroyer Operations in World War II* (Annapolis, MD: Naval Institute Press, 1953), p. 10.

43 *"fought the last war"*: Robert Sherrod, *Reporting World War II, Part I* (New York: Library of America, 1995), "The Marines at Tarawa: November 1943," p. 684.

44 *back in the day*: Nestor: "None of the men who walk the earth these days / could battle with those fighters." *The Iliad*, Book I, pp. 317–318 (translated by Robert Fagles, London: Penguin Books, 1990).

44 *"a thing to do now"*: William Manchester and Paul Reid, *The Last Lion* (New York: Little Brown, 2012), p. 155.

45 *predicament that fall*: Winston Churchill, *Memoirs of the Second World War* (New York: Houghton Mifflin, 1959), pp. 384–385.

45 *"all over the world"*: Doris Kearns Goodwin, *No Ordinary Time* (New York: Simon & Schuster, 1994) p. 210.

45 *"another step closer to war"*: Ibid., p. 212.

45 *"throughout the American Union"*: Ibid., p. 213.

46   *one of its pamphlets*: Wayne Cole, *America First: The Battle Against Inter-
      vention 1940–1941* (Madison: The University of Wisconsin Press,
      1953), chapter 9.

46   *"sea cabin by the chart house"*: Herman Wouk, *The Winds of War* (New
      York: Little Brown, 1971), p. 563.

47   *Navy with his temper*: McManus, *My Journal*, p. 1.

47   *the next five years*: Ibid., p. 4.

48   *"left on that ship"*: Ibid., pp. 3–6.

49   *41 percent approved*: Goodwin, *No Ordinary Time*, pp. 233–234.

49   *in hostile waters*: Roscoe, *Destroyer Operations*, p. 34.

50   *compartments as ballast*: *Plunkett* deck logs, December 7, 1941.

50   *several months earlier*: Ibid.

51   *"Pearl Harbor is being attacked"*: This was the radioman's language, as
      McManus remembered it in his memoir, *My Journal*.

51   *action on the Atlantic*: Ibid., p. 8.

51   *Where the hell was Pearl Harbor?*: The question McManus asks in his
      memoir defies credulity today, so ingrained is Pearl Harbor in the
      collective consciousness. But the "man in the street" in December
      of 1941, wrote S. E. Smith, who edited a history of the Navy in
      World War II, "had never heard of Pearl Harbor." S. E. Smith,
      The United States Navy in World War II (New York: Morrow, 1966),
      p. 25.

4: OVERLAND

53   *you bought something?*: The Overland Historical Society has in its archives
      an image of the Overland Dollar Store at Christmas.

55   *"They've bombed Pearl Harbor!"*: Jim's recollection of December 7,
      1941, from an interview on October 2, 2016.

55   *money into war bonds*: Robert E. Parkin, *Overland: Trails and Trials* (City
      of Overland Inc., 1956), pp. 96–98.

55   *Nazis in Germany*: Jim talked about the refugees in his grade school
      in an interview on December 11, 2016.

57   *Red Rock and Woodson*: Jim talked about his father's accident in an interview on October 2, 2016.

58   *"Betty to go, too"*: Mickey's language and the memory of that first date from an interview with Jim on October 2, 2016.

58   *still being there*: Betty confirmed her attitude in their first few meetings in a letter she sent to Jim. She remembers that when they started going out, "I didn't like you hardly at all." She was "distant" and "mean," and wished she could start all over again.

61   *wait him out*: Jim discussed his early-on relationship with Archibald Kneemiller in a phone interview on October 2, 2016.

62   *decision to enlist*: Jim remembered this conversation with his mother in an interview on December 11, 2016.

62   *six pairs of socks*: Letter from Jim Feltz to Betty Kneemiller, June 12, 1942.

63   *"Write every night"*: Letter from Jim Feltz to Betty Kneemiller, June 12, 1942.

63   *penmanship "isn't bad at all"*: Letter from Jim Feltz to Betty Kneemiller, June 21, 1942.

63   *wrote his name twice*: Letter from Betty Kneemiller to Jim Feltz, June 16, 1942.

63   *"walked straight"*: Letter from Jim Feltz to Betty Kneemiller, June 17, 1942.

64   *4 years signed*: Poem written into letter from Jim Feltz to Betty Kneemiller, June 17, 1942.

64   *"worry about that"*: Letter from Jim Feltz to Betty Kneemiller, June 17, 1942.

64   *"with any Italian fellow"*: Letter from Betty Kneemiller to Jim Feltz, June 22, 1942.

64   *"mothers are right"*: Letter from Jim Feltz to Betty Kneemiller, June 24, 1942.

65   *"concentration camp"*: Additional detail about Pier 92 from Stanley Morrison's *Letters Home* (Willow Grove, PA: King of Patagonia Press, 2014), pp. 14–15.

66   *assignment on the USS* Plunkett: Jim described his time on Pier 92 in an interview on October 18, 2017.

66   *"three quarts of tootie-fruitie"*: Ken Brown, in an interview on September 25, 2016, said the ship had been painted pink at once. That precipitated the message from the skipper, which is Ken Brown's language.

66   *his new romance*: In an interview on October 2, 2016, Jim said there were two songs he remembered playing from the Navy Yard speakers when they shoved off—"String of Pearls" and "Kalamazoo."

5: CASABLANCA

69   *in a single day*: Goodwin, *No Ordinary Time*, p. 345.

70   *the second wave*: Description and feelings for 35th Street Pier in Donahue, *Tin Cans and Other Ships*, pp. 59–60. The author sailed on *Niblack*.

70   *a torpedoed troopship*: Details on the DesRon 7 from the Destroyer History Foundation: http://destroyerhistory.org/benson-gleavesclass/desron7/.

71   *"as to quantity and quality"*: Specifics of *Plunkett* provisioning pulled from the ship's deck logs.

71   *gained 30 pounds*: Letter from Jim Feltz to Betty Kneemiller, October 27, 1942.

72   *eat bread anymore*: Jim told the story of his interaction with George Schwartz and his first seasick experience in an interview on December 23, 2016.

73   *strangely to a drawl*: Jim never called it a record player; it was always a Victrola.

73   *a freaky resemblance*: Jim relayed the story of the broom handle in an interview on December 23, 2016.

74   *first and always*: Jim told me about what they talked about in an interview on December 23, 2016, noting that home was front and center as the subject du jour. Legendary correspondent Ernie Pyle confirmed the same thing about talk among sailors at war.

75   *stayed in formation*: Ken's "horror," as he describes that moment at the conn, was detailed in an interview on May 27, 2017.

76   *backbone of the Navy*: Background on Miller from Naval Academy yearbook, *The Lucky Bag*, 1926.

76   *Brooklyn Navy Yard*: Jack Simpson recalled the Hudson River cruise with his wife, Peggy, in an interview July 1, 2017. He said Peggy never forgot how small *Plunkett* looked beside *Queen Mary*, or the one-hour cruise upriver.

76   *"I'll get it"*: In an interview on July 1, 2017, Jack Simpson noted Miller's directive to Heissler.

76   *something that happened*: A review of Jack Dempsey's record doesn't show any bout against Heissler.

77   *shipmates had pilfered those*: Letter from Ken Heissler to his sister, December 29, 1942.

77   *sterns of the vessels*: Samuel Eliot Morison described escort screens as a "loose-jointed necklace" in *The Two-Ocean War* (Boston: Little Brown, 1963) p. 106.

78   *account of the operation*: Samuel Eliot Morison, *The Battle of the Atlantic* (New York: Little Brown, 1947), p. 18.

78   *the war at last*: Note the mood of the ship when news of the invasion sounded in Donahue's *Tin Cans and Other Ships*, p. 61.

78   *"the end of the beginning"*: *The War Speeches of the Rt. Hon. Winston S. Churchill* (New York: Houghton Mifflin, 1953), p. 343.

79   *relative near neighbor*: *National Geographic*, July 1943, p. 1.

79   *"And don't get me in trouble"*: Jack Simpson told me this story about the motorcycle in our first talk, on May 22, 2016. The Army officer's language is as Jack remembered it.

80   *French North Africa to explore*: Jack Simpson: "Every time I would go over there, he had a motorcycle for me." December 20, 2016.

81   *lonely cliff in Morocco*: Jack talked to me about his motorbike escapades in several different interviews, each time not quite sure he'd told me as much before and each time finding some new detail to share. But they always ended the same way, with him on that cliff: "I hollered

like I used to holler at my hound dogs, and I could hear the echo coming back," he told me.

81 *the thick of it*: In my first interview with Jim, he talked about how he hadn't been one for liberty. "Guys would pay you one dollar to stand watch," he said, April 9, 2016.

82 *scented with charcoal*: Franklyn Dailey in *Joining the War at Sea* notes that whenever they were ashore in North Africa there was the scent of charcoal.

83 *they could prove it*: The several pictures of this series from the studio come from family photo albums that belong to Gail Johnson, James Gebhart, Jim Feltz, and James Sullivan.

83 *"the same as I am"*: Letter from Betty Kneemiller to Jim Feltz, July 4, 1942.

83 *"sparkle for you either"*: Letter from Betty Kneemiller to Jim Feltz, November 6, 1942.

85 *"exciting and moving tale"*: As described by the *New York Times* in a review by Bosley Crowther, "*Casablanca*, with Humphrey Bogart and Ingrid Bergman, at Hollywood—*White Cargo* and *Ravaged Earth* Open," published November 27, 1942.

6: STEAMING AS BEFORE

89 *the ship for 6 a.m.*: In 2016 and 2017, James Gebhart transcribed his grandfather's wartime diaries as *The War Journals of Machinist's Mate 2nd Class Irvin J. Gebhart*. This journal was the source for details about the dentist, Goodman, and Rogers Corner.

90 *indicating a hit*: Ken Brown notes from *Plunkett* deck logs on sound contact.

90 *fruit mostly, it seemed*: Description of Norfolk during the war from *Tin Can Man* by E. J. Jernigan (Annapolis, MD: Naval Institute Press, 2010), p. 16.

91 *"bedsprings in town tonight"*: Jack Simpson remembered Miller's language as they came into New York Harbor, "the symphony of bedsprings," in a phone interview on December 20, 2016.

92 Plunkett *to berth*: Details of the bungled docking at the Brooklyn Navy Yard from *Plunkett*'s deck logs, December 13, 1942.

92 *memento of a menu*: Jack Simpson repeatedly noted that Miller cultivated a "happy" ship.

92 *largest in the world*: History of the St. George noted here: https://stgeorgetower.com/history/.

93 *take on a pilot*: Jack Simpson was insistent that Miller's termination was a direct result of the demurral in Norfolk, not the accident in the Brooklyn Navy Yard, and the ship's deck logs seem to bear this out. They do not reference a pilot for Norfolk, but they do reference the fact that *Plunkett* had called for a pilot in New York.

93 *Franklin Delano Roosevelt*: Jim McManus writes about the telegram and the messenger boy on p. 69 of his memoir, *My Journal*. He says that a number of the men each gave the kid $5 and he made out like a bandit. Jack Simpson told the story about the telegram in a phone interview on October 1, 2016. Jack contributed the part about how the mixers ran out and it was the drinking straight that caused all the trouble.

94 *see the place*: In his unpublished 1996 recollections, *The Ball*, Charlie Gallagher talks about the *Plunkett* crew at Callahan's at Christmas 1942.

95 *the degradation*—Petit: An S. R. Clark is featured in a book about the Naval Academy's team in 1920. Inference suggests it's the same man.

95 *had put them up to it*: McManus, in *My Journal*, noted that the commander's overarching concern was whether or not Miller put them up to the telegram.

96 *he'd been warned*: Clark's language is lifted from Jack Simpson's recollection, in an interview on October 1, 2016, of his appointment with the squad dog.

96 *war in North Africa*: Cargo noted for several ships of the UGS convoy at Uboat.net.

96 *"signals and insolent comebacks"*: Morison, *The Two-Ocean War*, p. 107.

97 *Burke at the Naval Academy*: On December 7, 1941, Burke had assumed

command of the USS *Simpson* (DD-221), a four-piper that had been launched in 1920. The ship was so old that twenty-two commanding officers had preceded him. Source on his command is Navy Source archives: http://www.navsource.org/archives/05/221.htm.

97   *to Army at the Polo Grounds*: Ken said that as long as he'd served on *Plunkett*, and since the very beginning of Burke's time on *Plunkett*, it was understood that he'd played on a Navy team that had its worst season ever. Interview, October 30, 2016.

97   *"never say die"*: Grantland, Rice, *Baltimore Sun*, October 11, 1928.

98   *knock a junior man*: In an interview with Jack Simpson, October 1, 2016: "On the bridge, if he [Burke] wanted to go somewhere, he would knock you aside. He was not popular from a personal point of view. [But] you couldn't have had somebody with more courage."

99   *four-day leave, not liberty*: Gebhart's journal makes note of the card game and locker cleaning on March 1, 1943.

100 *five-hour run to Boston*: Exact dates of Gallagher's "leave of absence" to be found in a memo signed by *Plunkett*'s engineering officer, J. G. Spangler. The four days' leave expired at 0800 on March 17, 1943.

100 *off to the war*: Details about fruit trees from the first chapter of Charlie Gallagher's 1996 recollections, *The Ball*. Frank talked all his life about the numbers of cars he buried in the yard at Oakton Avenue. Even the owners of the house at No. 58 in 2016 knew there was a veritable junkyard of scrapped cars under their turf.

100 *evening in March of 1943:* Roscoe, *Destroyer Operations*, p. 274.

100 *Joe and Frank*: Lois Huss Breignan remembered seeing the blue stars on the banner in the Gallaghers' window. She lived across the street and was the niece of John's sister-in-law, Bernice.

101 *baked on Friday*: Description of food in the Gallagher household from Charlie Gallagher's recollections, *The Ball*, p. 5.

101 *game of* Scrabble*: F-A-R-T*: Charlie Gallagher recollections, *The Ball*, p. 10.

101 *hedge against bad behavior*: Charlie Gallagher unpublished recollections, *The Ball*, chapter 1.

103 *melancholy over all of them*: This song was a staple in Tom Gallagher's repertoire.

104 *"Give me the baby"*: Whenever Bernice told the story of her last meeting with John, as she did when the author was taking notes on August 20, 2004, she always said John called for the baby this insistently: "Give me the baby."

106 *jitterbugged the dance floor*: Description of date from picture of Ship's Party.

106 *"So he could write shorthand"*: Letter from Betty Kneemiller to Jim Feltz, January 28, 1943.

106 *"I'll give you a ring"*: Letter from Betty Kneemiller to Jim Feltz, January 24, 1943.

107 *"sorta mean" to him even*: Letter from Betty Kneemiller to Jim Feltz, March 27, 1943.

107 *shut it off*: "To begin the mush" from a letter by Betty Kneemiller to Jim Feltz, February 8, 1943. Record that played ten times from Irvin Gebhart's journal.

107 *"nearly passed out"*: Letter from Betty Kneemiller to Jim Feltz, March 18, 1943.

108 *"I just gave up"*: Letter from Betty Kneemiller to Jim Feltz, March 18, 1943.

108 *"he will take care of you"*: Letter from Betty Kneemiller to Jim Feltz, January 31, 1943.

109 *the other two passengers*: In his journal entry for March 19, 1943, Gebhart reported that he and Gallagher had got in a fight in a taxi with two other sailors.

109 *the wholesome pretensions*: "As vivacious as a country fair." Carson McCullers, *The Mortgaged Heart* (1955).

109 *worse for wear*: Jim talked about getting that Mauser out of the Navy Yard in an interview on April 30, 2017.

109 *what the hell could he tell Gebhart?*: In a phone interview on February 12, 2017, Jim credited his authority in the fire room as the primary reason some of the guys talked to him as if he were an "old man,"

believing that the authority he exhibited on the boilers extended to matters of the heart as well.

110   *the no. 2 stack*: Brown said he'd assigned Gallagher to that gun because at twenty-six years old, Gallagher was older than many of the crew and thus more likely to be able to handle the work.

PART II: THE MED

7: THORNTON, COLORADO

124   *"vilified him for it"*: Shafter, *Destroyers in Action*, *Plunkett* chapter.

8: SICILY

128   *It never happened again*: McManus memoir, *My Journal*, p. 68.

128   *code-named Operation Husky*: Irvin Gebhart's journal notes Mr. Jolly's communication to the crew in the mess on July 6.

128   *"No matter what"*: Donahue, *Tin Cans and Other Ships*, p. 104. Donahue notes contents of Liberty ships.

129   *sixty miles long*: Roscoe notes breadth and length of column in *Destroyer Operations*, p. 318.

129   *a sea itself*: Conditions of the sea noted by a sailor named Frank Krall, who was on another destroyer headed for Sicily. Krall's comments are in a diary posted at www.shubrick.com.

129   *sky over the ship*: Gebhart wrote in his journal on July 10: "Paratroopers went over our head this morning. About 250 planes." Frank Krall made reference to the same skytrain of what he'd understood to be 225 planes. Frank's comments are in a diary posted at www.shubrick .com.

129   *hit them with spuds*: In *With Utmost Spirit* (Lexington: University Press of Kentucky, 2004) Barbara Tomblin reports that there were 222 C-47s, carrying 3,405 paratroopers on a three-hour flight from Tunisia to Sicily, pp. 174–175. One destroyer captain said these transports

slid by so close, there was a question about whether they were close enough to be hit by spuds (Roscoe, *Destroyer Operations*, p. 318).

130 *light gray paint*: This photograph hung in the hallway of Oakton Avenue for decades after the war. My uncle Charlie Gallagher remembered the picture from his childhood and didn't know where the picture had gone after the house was sold in the early 1990s. One of John's nephews, Mark Gallagher, had taken the photo. It was hanging in his son's bedroom when I called one day and asked if he had it.

130 *fire control director*: Wirt Williams referenced the call to general quarters this way in his book *The Enemy: A Novel of Life Aboard a U.S. Navy Destroyer in World War II* (New York: Houghton Mifflin Company, 1951).

131 *mishap the day before*: Reference to derelict whaleboat in *Plunkett*'s deck logs for July 11. *Swanson* and *Roe* accident detailed in Samuel Eliot Morison's *Sicily-Salerno-Anzio: January 1943 –June 1944* (New York: Little Brown/Castle Books, 1954/2001), pp. 78–79, hereafter SSA.

131 *chalk-gray but imposing*: "Little," "chalk-gray," and "imposing" is how Morison described Gela in *SSA*.

132 *the roadstead, off Gela*: Morison in *SSA*, p. 109: "As at Tarawa, 'the issue was in doubt' until well on into D-day plus 1."

132 *one target after another*: Morison details the shells lobbed by Navy ships and why in *SSA*, p. 113.

132 *a magician's trick*: Whenever Ken Brown mentioned Bonnie Baker, and he did in multiple interviews, he'd remember again just how amazing his eyesight was.

134 *a sickly yellow light*: The ship's deck logs report magnesium flares and firing at 9:50 p.m. and *Plunkett*'s first shots in combat at 9:57 p.m.

134 *for hours on end*: The *Handbook of Damage Control*, NAVPERS 16191, 1945, notes this fact in its Introduction.

135 *to hold his fire*: About Gela, Ken said the "instruction to not fire came in after the lighter guns had already started to fire." Interview, August 28, 2017.

136 *out of the water*: Roscoe writes that destroyer *McLanahan* had her stern bounced out of the water at Gela. *Destroyer Operations*, p. 323.

136 *happened to* Maddox: Roscoe noted that destroyer gunners were "mind-ful of the doom" that had taken down the *Maddox*, and that was why the "sky-searing aerial barrage." *Destroyer Operations*, p. 323.

136 *clearing the ship by ten feet*: Donahue wrote about this ten-foot pass by a German bomber in *Tin Cans and Other Ships*, p. 106.

136 *its radar, to boot*: Roscoe, *Destroyer Operations*, p. 323.

136 *all over the harbor*: Benson's action report blamed friendly fire from 20mm guns for "injuries to personnel and material." Roscoe, *Destroyer Operations*, p. 323.

136 *charged with securing*: See Morison in *SSA* (p. 121), Tomblin in *With Utmost Spirit* (p. 198), and Carlos Este in *Bitter Victory* (Harper Perennial, 2008, p. 308) for more detail on a circumstance that Morison called "the saddest event of the day."

137 *he hated it*: In an audio recording made September 20, 2017, Ken talked about the uncontrollable trembling in his legs at Gela in a conversation about fear.

137 *to be American*: With understatement that doesn't adequately convey the magnitude of the loss, Morison called this friendly fire incident "the saddest event of the day." *SSA*, p. 120.

138 *stern pointing to the moon*: That phrase exactly taken from ship's deck logs.

138 *burning one red light*: Reference to U.S. Army plane from deck logs.

138 *holocaust of friendly fire*: Morison noted that twenty-three of the para-troop transports were brought down.

9: PALERMO

139 *not knowing what to do*: Ken parsed the difference between whether he was afflicted by fear or uncertainty in a recorded audio interview on October 20, 2017: "I won't say that I was scared, but I was uncertain as to what to do."

140 *they'd never forget*: Both Feltz and Gebhart noted in journal entries for July 12, 1943, that they'd been at GQ for thirty-two straight hours.

The ship's deck logs report that they were secured (released from general quarters) intermittently through the day. Gebhart wrote in his journal that it was "a day I will never forget."

140 *the architecture familiar*: More than half the people who lived in Algiers in 1942 were European. *National Geographic*, July 1943, "Americans on the Barbary Coast," p. 14.

140 *pansy by comparison*: Anecdotal analysis of the ship's deck logs shows that Burke was doling out court-martials and revoking liberties at a far higher rate than Miller.

140 *"Don't hold back"*: Jack Simpson, Ken Brown, and Jim Feltz all remembered Burke's sparring matches on the fantail. Burke's grandson, Ed Gipple, said his mother had received a number of phone calls from enlisted men after her father's death—men who told her that Captain Burke would invite men into the ring, and that there'd be no repercussions if they did well. The language of Eddie Burke ripping off his shirt is a paraphrase of what Ed Gipple told me.

141 *ship should be run*: Brown said that he'd become "sufficiently alert" and knew better than to ever get too close to Burke when the conversation turned to boxing. Interview, April 22, 2017. He said on a number of occasions that Burke was always trying to get him back on the fantail.

141 *materiel as they could*: Captain Franklyn E. Dailey, Jr., USN (Ret.), *Joining the War at Sea*, p. 181.

141 *the island's defense*: Frank Krall reported that they'd actually learned as much from the BBC while they were still on ship at Gela.

142 *looked like a gang fight*: Gebhart likened the fight to a "gang fight" in his journal on July 23, 1943. Jim Feltz reported the same fight in his journal.

142 *trooping to his chair*: Details about John B. Stango's haircutting from Jim McManus's memoir, *My Journal*, p. 16.

143 *"I can do that"*: McManus tells this story, with the language in quotes, in his memoir, *My Journal*, on p. 64.

143 *as much as he needed*: Jack talked about the paint trip in an interview February 3, 2019. This was the last *Plunkett* story Jack told me before he died. He'd told me many stories, but not this one, until after I had talked to his daughter and she told me the story of how the Dead End Kids procured paint in North Africa.

144 *Suitcase Simpson*: Jack didn't know the enlisted men had bestowed him with this nickname; Jim McManus noted the nickname in his memoir, *My Journal*.

144 *help might be needed*: Martha Gallagher was for twenty years brought from a second-floor bedroom every spring and returned to her winter quarters after Christmas and New Year's, according to her grandson, Charlie Gallagher, aka the Weatherstrip.

146 *the Fifth Army*: Details about Frank's journey to work as a medic from an article in the *Dorchester Reporter*, August 16, 2001, and from an interview recorded by the author in the summer of 1998.

146 *"gaunt and pitiful" people*: Ernie Pyle's description of the people of Italy in *Ernie's War*, edited by David Nichols (New York: Random House, 1986), p. 355.

147 *abet them than stifle them*: Ken Brown noted this rumor in a phone call on October 30, 2016. All the while he served on *Plunkett* and afterward, he said, they all believed Burke had played on a Navy team that had its worst season ever.

147 *harbor in the darkness*: Directional finger of fire noted in war diaries of cruiser USS *Philadelphia*, August 1, 1943.

147 *happened at Pearl Harbor*: Morison (*SSA*, p. 192) likened this attack on Palermo to the Japanese attack on Pearl Harbor.

148 *shrapnel at the calf*: *Plunkett*'s deck logs note that Simpson, Frederikson, and Lewellen were all hit at 4:30 p.m., which was the same time that the war diaries say the ship started to make smoke.

149 *the weirdest thing*: More than any of the other planes *Plunkett* took down in the war, this was the one Ken remembered most vividly. He described this action in an interview recorded on October 20, 2017.

149 *parse in low light*: Dailey described an incident off Sicily where he'd identified a C-47 and passed the word down the picket line to the next ship. Turned out the supposed C-47 dropped a bomb on the American ship and was actually a Ju 88. *Joining the War at Sea*, p. 172.

149 *perspective in battle*: Morison describes this "strange state of affairs" in *SSA*, p. 192.

149 *"There wasn't any mailing address on it"*: Jack told me the story of his wounding several times, and always referenced the fact that there wasn't any "mailing address" on what hit him. He never knew whether the fire that hit him was enemy or friendly.

150 *shot down by other ships*: Reference to the two planes shot down in Destroyer Squadron 7's war diary for August 1.

150 *the only explanation*: All of the language after the colon is Ken Brown's from a recorded interview on October 20, 2017.

150 *"One of ours"*: Ken's recollection of what the Brits said from the same interview, October 20, 2017. The dialogue is what he said the Brits said to *Plunkett*'s crew.

10: THE BOOT

151 *"We gave them a run for their money"*: Gebhart's *War Journal*, August 4, 1943.

152 *spurting from ruptured lines*: Accounts of *Mayrant* and *Shubrick* from Roscoe, *Destroyer Operations*, pp. 324–326.

153 *CO from the ship in a straitjacket*: Frank Krall, in his account of the bomb hit on *Shubrick*, mentions that several men went into shell shock and describes the remains of the torpedo officer, Mar Adams. McManus wrote on p. 60 in his memoir, *My Journal*, about the commander who tried to get a Purple Heart for an infected pimple.

153 *stacks of the ship*: McManus wrote on p. 67 of his memoir about the "snow job" he'd give guys from the fire rooms, asking after a battle, and he later claimed that a near miss had sailed between *Plunkett*'s stacks.

153 *"military force there stationed"*: Orders dispatched from Combined Task Force 88 to *Plunkett* August 1943.

155 *tables in the wheelhouse*: Ken Brown remembered Bill Maner's report of the squadron commander's behavior on the ride in (interview, August 28, 2017), and Jack Simpson remembered seeing the squad dog under a table during enemy attack (Interview, July 1, 2017).

155 *signalmen for a translation*: Account of the surrender included in the squadron's commander's war diaries.

155 *we just took a island*: This phrase is how Jim put the surrender in his diary.

156 *troops on schedule*: Patton had claimed that "never in history" had the Navy landed an army at the prescribed time and place. S. E. Smith, *The United States Navy in World War II*, p. 160.

157 *Germans on Sicily*: Gebhart journal, August 9, 1943.

157 *"Thank God for that"*: Jim Feltz journal, August 12, 1943. Jim said they were going out after a 90mm, but that was an American gun. The Germans would have deployed an 88mm.

157 *by a single man, a German*: Details of this recovery in *Plunkett*'s deck logs, in interviews with Jack Simpson, and in the McManus memoir, *My Journal*.

158 *tried to kill you first*: Jim McManus later wrote his account of the captured airman for the *Tin Can Sailors Quarterly*'s July 1995 issue. His and Jack Simpson's accounts of the episode are the only first-person reports available. Jack's version of the events seems more credible. The logs of the ship and squadron do not say the captured pilot offered any resistance.

160 *knew it at the time*: After the war was over, McManus met Oakley in the Philippines, and "Annie" admitted he'd pilfered the pistol. McManus didn't let anyone know as much until decades later, after Oakley went to that "big destroyer in the sky" and he wrote a story about the incident for the *Tin Can Sailors*. "Now, all you old *Plunkett* sailors, do you believe me when I tell you McManus didn't steal the old man's pistol?" McManus memoir, *My Journal*, p. 18.

160   *learned Sicily had fallen*: Gebhart notes movie and news in his journal.

161   *"the early fall of Messina"*: Letter from Admiral L. A. Davidson to Burke, November 26, 1943.

161   *any and all circumstances*: In an evaluation of all of Burke's fitness reports between 1929 and 1943, he most frequently received the highest possible rating in "Endurance."

161   *"during war conditions"*: Burke's commanding officer, L. S. Parks, wrote as much on a fitness report filed March 31, 1936.

162   *"Don't try to tell me how to do this"*: Burke's order to Ken Brown remembered by Brown in an interview on April 16, 2018.

162   *a gondolier's moon*: Roscoe describes the moonlight this way in his description of the operation on p. 328 of *Destroyer Operations*.

163   *bombed Continental Europe*: Roscoe, *Destroyer Operations*, p. 329.

163   *How many shells?*: In his recollection, Ken Brown pumped his thumb on an imaginary clicker, resurrecting the moment. He told me this story several times, the first time during a visit to his home on September 24, 2017.

164   *back on the squawk box*: Jack Simpson said Ken's flippant reply to the captain sounded "on the intercom of the ship" and that the flippancy was obvious. "Nobody could get away with that." Interview, November 13, 2016.

165   *"For the next five days"*: Burke's sentence comes from Brown's remembrance of the incident in the September 2017 interview referenced just above.

II: READYING

167   *Mac was Dooley to many*: *Plunkett* nicknames from Jim McManus's *My Journal*, p. 46.

168   *Jailbird Brown*: Ken Brown told this anecdote during an in-person interview on September 24, 2016.

168   *jettison the ship's trash*: Jim Feltz: "I made a habit of not eating on liberty. I'd never eat when I went on shore leave. I figured they had so little

food, I figured they didn't need to feed people like us." Interview on July 30, 2018.

168 *let men come calling*: Tomblin, *With Utmost Spirit* (University Press of Kentucky, 2004), p. 213.

169 *there'd be "fornication"*: "If ye touch at the islands, Mr. Flask, beware of fornication." Herman Melville, *Moby-Dick*, chapter 22, "Merry Christmas."

170 *married the other girl*: Betty's account of her visit to the fortune-teller in a letter to Jim Feltz, June 25, 1943.

171 *survive the war*: In a phone interview on August 28, 2018, here's how Jim phrased this encounter: "I asked the question in my mind, 'Will I live through the war?' and it came up to no. That worried me. I then asked what date."

171 *he was feeling now*: Jim said that Ouija board accounted for the scariest experience he had during the war. About being scared in battle, he said, "You don't have time to think about that. You're so busy. The only time I was really leery, was when me and Cliff Dornburg went to a Red Cross Club and they had a Ouija board, and I asked the question in my mind."

172 *threw it all back up*: Franklyn E. Dailey, Jr., on the destroyer *Shubrick* writes about the prohibition against raw fruit and vegetables and the sickness in Palermo in August 1943 on p. 183 of his book *Joining the War at Sea*.

172 *pointed out the weevils*: Jim Feltz talked about the weevils one night at dinner in the Lewis & Clark in St. Charles, Missouri, November 15, 2019.

172 *It was both*: Jack Simpson remembered Dutch staying up all night to bake, and Jim Feltz remembered that Dutch always stocked up on more butter than they needed, for trading purposes.

173 *thought they could*: Jack Simpson: "We heard them singing a long time before we saw them."

173 *"I'm down here"*: Jack Simpson said the Italians treated *Plunkett*'s men as liberators. His daughter, Bonnie Reavis, who'd heard her father tell this story her whole life, remembered the detail about the man who fell overboard.

174 *most to part company*: Franklyn Dailey makes this observation in *Joining the War at Sea*, on p. 69.

174 *being a torpedo*: Ken Brown noted that these tacks at night were one of the most unnerving things about standing watch.

174 *"I can't let you go"*: Simpson and Burke's exchange recounted by John Simpson in interviews, October 1, 2016, and July 1, 2017.

174 *"hopelessly romantic"*: Samuel Eliot Morison, *SSA*, p. 231.

176 *"the best present she got"*: Details of the Gebharts' reunion in Irvin's journal, and in newspaper stories published in September 1943.

177 *on the Algerian border*: Frank Gallagher detailed all of the names of every place he'd been during the war in a souvenir book he picked up in France in late 1944. The place names run chronologically beginning with his trip to Casablanca on the *Mariposa*.

179 *the dock at Mers el-Kebir*: Gebhart notes the Masses on *Benson* and on the dock in his wartime journal.

12: SALERNO

181 *Tunisia on the way*: Jim Feltz recorded Hap Jolly's communication in his journal on September 5, 1943.

181 *righted their radar*: Reference to *Delta* in Gebhart's journal and to radar trouble in war diaries of ComDesRon7.

182 *called for extraction*: *Plunkett*'s deck logs note that an "emergency appendectomy" was done on September 7. Jack Simpson had not been able to pinpoint the date, but knew they were en route to Salerno, that the seas were rough, and that they were at general quarters.

182 *spoons from the mess*: Account of a World War II appendectomy found on Naval History Blog, article published September 2, 2010, "World War II Submarine Appendectomy." A *New York Times* reporter named George Weller won a Pulitzer Prize for his telling. The sub used spoons for retractors.

182 *Bates dug in*: Jim Feltz noted that one of the men read the directions

out loud. Jim confirmed as well what Jack said about both the patient and the doctor being strapped in. Jim thought the operation happened in the mess, but Jack said it was the wardroom, which would be the more likely venue.

183   *save the man's life*: Bates's son, also David Bates, didn't know his father had conducted an emergency appendectomy on *Plunkett*, and knew little about the details of his father's service. He recalled the open-heart cardiac massage in a phone interview on September 26, 2017.

183   *deposit fifty-five thousand men*: Atkinson, *The Day of Battle*, p. 199.

184   *a milk run*: Morison writes about the confusion and complacency in the wake of Eisenhower's announcement on p. 253 of *SSA*.

184   *"we were on our way"*: Line lifted verbatim from Gebhart's journal.

184   *"our guys land on the beach?"*: Donahue asks that question on p. 124 of his memoir, *Tin Cans and Other Ships*. Atkinson reports the reaction on *Mayo* on p. 200 of *The Day of Battle*.

184   *dreams of another world*: Franklyn E. Dailey quotes a fellow officer, Ensign M. T. Jacobs, who described the stars and clarity of the night in *Joining the War at Sea*, p. 213.

185   *beaches of Salerno*: Morison wrote, "any [German] Officer with a pair of dividers could figure out that the Gulf of Salerno was the northernmost practicable landing place for the Allies." *SSA*, p. 249.

186   *trouble getting water*: In a notebook that he penned in France near the end of the war, Frank Gallagher wrote that he went into Salerno on the *Durbin Castle* [*sic*], but there's no record of the *DC* going in until September 15. An officer on one of the landing craft, Hugh Michael Irwin, said in a 1987 oral history that the *DC* had trouble getting water and was detained at Mers el-Kebir.

186   *"quiet breathing of untroubled sleep"*: Description of the gentle inshore waters from Roscoe, *Destroyer Operations*, p. 331.

186   *Tarawa two months later*: Morison makes the comparison to Tarawa on p. 260 of *SSA*.

186   *"We have you covered!"*: Morison notes the loudspeaker trash talk on p. 265 of *SSA*.

186 *for that day, at least*: In an after-action report, Vice Admiral Henry
     K. Hewitt noted the number of targets engaged by Navy gunners
     on D-Day and wrote "the Army could not have remained on shore
     without the support of naval guns." Roscoe, *Destroyer Operations*, p. 332.

187 *eighty-three men had survived*: Gebhart and Feltz each recorded these
     numbers of dead in his journal.

188 *same war as the Navy*: In his chapter on the Salerno landings, Dailey
     notes that both the U.S. and British air forces were " 'out of the loop'
     pursuing their own war." *Joining the War at Sea*, p. 198.

188 *lower handling room*: Irvin Gebhart made reference to the five decks
     that night in his journal.

188 *"they made quite an impression"*: *Plunkett* deck logs, January 1, 1944.

188 *Second World War*: Atkinson, *The Day of Battle*, p. 217.

189 *"the blue Salernian bay"*: From "Amalfi" by Henry Wadsworth Long-
     fellow.

190 *already climbed past two hundred*: Atkinson, *The Day of Battle*, p. 218, notes
     how sailors across the Salerno anchorage "braced the rail, saluting."

191 *into a transport area*: "We hated to see those hospital ships come in,"
     McManus wrote in his memoir, *My Journal*.

191 *the European mainland*: General Mark Clark promised these nurses they'd
     be first on the Italian mainland. Evelyn Monahan and Rosemary
     Neidel-Greenlee, *And If I Perish* (New York: Anchor, 2004), p. 195.

191 *"sure to sink"*: Account of the German's pilot's language detailed at
     http://www.qaranc.co.uk/, a website that surveys the history of
     Queen Alexandra's Royal Army Nursing Corp.

192 Newfoundland*'s port quarter*: Reference to *Mayo* and four nearby
     hospital ships in *Plunkett*'s war diaries, September 13, 1943.

193 Plunkett *was going in*: Burke's conflict with the squadron commander
     detailed in Jim McManus's memoir, *My Journal*, p. 13.

193 *nozzle of a fire hose*: Jim's diary entry for September 13, 1943, notes
     he was first man onto the *Newfoundland*.

195 *save the ship*: The squadron commander's war diaries note the return
     of *Newfoundland*'s master to *Plunkett* at 0900.

195 *"We have never done this"*: Atkinson, *The Day of Battle*, p. 228.

196 *he'd admit as much*: "I deserved it," Ken said of Brown's putting him in hack (April 16, 2018). "That was all my fault. I should not have been such a smart mouth." Jack Simpson later told me that Ken, when he told the story at reunions, always owned up to the misstep. It plagued him for years.

197 *redress with a song*: Ken first told me about how much singing they did in an interview on April 16, 2018. He said they sang up there frequently, and that the songs would be the simple ones they all knew. "Someone would start something, and we would hum along."

199 *"he's dropped something"*: The dialogue here is as Ken remembered it in an interview on June 12, 2017.

199 *"Take cover"*: Ken described this scene again in a phone interview on August 6, 2018.

199 *flashed all over topside*: Ken Brown, whenever he told this story, referenced the fact that he'd seen men airborne: "I can still in my mind see bodies flying from the explosion before I ducked down into the cover of the director." Interview, June 12, 2017.

200 *presume it was sunk*: Only three landing craft were sunk in Operation Avalanche, and only LCT-241 in the way Jim Feltz describes.

201 *shy of its mark*: *Plunkett*'s action report notes that the ship was at flank speed when Burke put the "helm over hard to port."

201 *no mistake about it*: Details of *Plunkett*'s gunnery on September 15, 1943, in Captain Burke's action report.

201 *"Near dead by dive bombers"*: Cliff Dornburg, like Jim Feltz, wrote in tiny books that seemed to be popular at the time, perhaps as a way to keep private matters hidden. The diaries are in his son Cliff's possession.

202 *went out to investigate*: Retrieval of bodies noted in *Plunkett*'s deck logs, September 15, 1943, by Jack Simpson and Jim Feltz in recollection, and in the diaries kept by Feltz and Gebhart.

202 *survey of Able sector*: "*Plunkett*'s deck logs noted this at 1640 on September 15, 1943: "Seven male bodies in advanced state of decomposition

picked up by MWB [motor whaleboat] examined for marks of identification by medical officer and results negative."

203 *the destroyer* Rowan: In his journal for September 17, 1943, Jim Feltz
notes that the bodies were off the USS *Rowan*.

203 *nobody wanted to do it*: Jack Simpson's language from an interview,
October 7, 2017.

204 *fifty-two-pound shells per canvas*: Jack Simpson described his role in the
administration of the bodies and his subsequent speech in a phone
interview on October 7, 2017.

204 *"depths of the sea"*: Jack remembered the words he'd said in an interview on October 7, 2017.

205 *4:40 in the afternoon*: Coordinates and time noted in *Plunkett*'s deck
logs, September 15, 1943.

205 *machine guns opened fire*: *Plunkett*'s deck logs note that the ship's 20mm
opened fire at 0137.

205 *the ship's gun tubs*: Ken Brown ceded oversight of the machine guns
to the assistant gunnery officer, but he was nevertheless plagued by
how little training he'd initiated in the gun crews.

205 *and they listened. To nothing*: In all, the 20mm expended 190 rounds,
and the five-inch but four shells. The action commenced at 0137 and
was over by 0142, according to deck logs. The details on how things
played out in the director are to the best of Ken Brown's recollection
in an interview on October 20, 2017.

206 *coming in from the east*: Deck logs report the time for GQ, the red alert,
and direction of enemy planes.

206 *1,550 pounds of pressure again*: McManus wrote that they exercised
their mounts every morning and notes the work he and Richardson
did in *My Journal*, p. 19.

206 *called general quarters*: Deck logs note bomb hit fifteen hundred yards
to *Plunkett*'s stern at 1331.

207 *high and fast*: Details about lookouts sighting them in binoculars and
"high and fast" from action report for September 16, 1943.

208 *too much to do*: Some accounts of destroyers at war have the men on

board cheering when they down enemy aircraft. No one on *Plunkett* remembered much of that, particularly because the ship was maneuvering radically and there was not the luxury of rallying a cheer. The men were too busy.

208 *Disappeared. Vanished*: Particulars noted in action report for September 17, 1943.

209 *"They're guessing, by golly"*: When Jim and I discussed the *Our Navy* reference to how the Germans changed their bombing strategy, he used this phrase to talk about how he'd thought about it. Interview, February 16, 2020.

PART III: THE DUSK

14: THE FALL

221 *"Jack for a Jerk"*: Betty Kneemiller wrote as much in a letter to Jim Feltz on October 4, 1943, and she wrote "I still call you mine" from a letter on August 31, 1943.

222 *"You're a luggage-saver"*: Though Jim saved all sorts of material from the war, he hadn't saved this letter and could only remember that this was the import of what the nurse had written.

223 *They'd been neighbors for a year*: In my first interview with Jim Feltz on April 9, 2016, he described John this way: "John was a happy-go-lucky guy. He always had a smile on his face and was real sharp. Everyone liked him. I don't think he had an enemy aboard that ship."

225 *"You blew up my fire room"*: Gallagher's language from a May 14, 2016, interview with Jim Feltz about incident in aft fire room.

226 *"in support of the invasion forces"*: Language taken from a citation drawn up by Secretary of the Navy Frank Knox on April 1, 1944, and a commendation by Admiral L. A. Davidson on December 1, 1943.

226 *"alertness of Com'd'r Burke"*: Clay's language pulled from a "Report on the Fitness of Officers," November 2, 1943–December 31, 1943.

227 *waving anything white*: Jim McManus describes this incident, including Ken's language, in his memoir, *My Journal*, on p. 19.

227 *torched the city's archives*: Morison, *SSA*, p. 311.

227 *food to fork over*: Norman Lewis, *Naples '44* (Cambridge, MA: Da Capo Press, 2005).

228 *"That makes the sixth time I saw it"*: Irvin Gebhart Diary, February 16, 1943.

229 *four boilers lit*: The ship's deck logs from Casablanca on had never reported the ship at flank speed on all four boilers until October 9, 1943. *Plunkett* was about to steam as fast as she ever had.

230 *evasive action against the Luftwaffe*: Jim Feltz described the wall of water this way in an interview March 17, 2017: "Everybody went back to look at it. I think we did about thirty-eight knots that night. About forty-two miles an hour. That's a big hunk of metal going through the water."

230 *"We couldn't open the door"*: Ken remembered this language in an audio interview recorded on October 20, 2017.

231 *whaleboat to investigate*: The action report Eddie Burke worked up after going out for the *Buck* reports that the whaleboat was dispatched from the ship at 7:50 p.m., or 1950.

231 *It never came*: The skipper of the U-boat that sunk *Buck*, Siegfried Koitschka, noted the black steam in a letter to Franklyn E. Dailey, Jr., which he referenced in *Joining the War at Sea*.

231 *"over the side by the explosion"*: Anderson's dialogue lifted exactly as stated from an action report filed October 10, 1943, by Commander G. L. Menocal of Destroyer Squadron 7.

232 *boilers had exploded*: One of *Buck*'s MM2s, L. R. Zuick, told Squadron Commander Menocal that he thought the "boiler exploded." Zuick's remarks were taken down verbatim for Menocal's October 10, 1943, report.

232 *hell on the viscera*: Effects of depth charge blast on men in the water from a May 1, 1943, article in the *British Medical Journal* entitled "Blast Injury to the Abdomen" by Denham Pinnock and Paul Wood.

233   *noses and buttocks*: McManus in his memoir, *My Journal*, notes the oil leaking from "every opening of their bodies" on p. 17.

233   *cut up bad*: Remarks from survivors quoted exactly from Squadron Commander G. L. Menocal's report on the "Search for Survivors of U.S.S. *Buck*."

234   *"All stop"*: Ken Brown on the moment when *Plunkett* shut down: "That's what we did. We took that chance to lose *Plunkett*, hoping the submarine having achieved the one ship would have left. We just sat there, a target for that submarine, had it elected to stay in the vicinity." Interview, May 27, 2017. Likewise, the ship's stopping unnerved Jim Feltz: "We sat idle with our searchlights on, and we were a dead target." Interview, April 29, 2018.

236   *Jack held him*: Remembering that death, Jack Simpson said in an interview on May 13, 2017: "I couldn't eat chicken noodle soup for years afterward."

238   *"All of that"*: Jack's visit to the chiefs' quarters recalled by Ken Brown in an interview at his house on October 21, 2017.

239   *they laughed and laughed*: McManus writes about the absurdity of the cotton and tape passed out after the *Buck*'s sinking in his memoir, *My Journal*, on p. 17.

239   *Palermo's catacombs*: Going to Mass and visit to church noted in Gebhart's journal.

239   *the destroyer* Edison: Gebhart notes the game and the score in his journal for December 8, 1943.

240   *midst of the game*: Reference to the *Edison*'s steward and the chair in center field in Franklyn E. Dailey, Jr.'s, *Joining the War at Sea*, p. 190.

240   *"like the old gang"*: Letter from John Gallagher to Sophie Tabayka, on December 7, 1943.

240   *"an office of my own"*: References to his thirty correspondents and quoted material come from John's six letters to Sophie Tabayka, the only letters from John that have survived the decades.

240   *"an expression of their gratitude"*: The letter was written by John A. Hoye, Lieutenant (jg) USNR; Edward J. Cummings, Lieutenant (jg) USN;

and David T. Hedges, Lieutenant (jg) USNR, and saved in Burke's service jacket.

241 *"You mean Oakley, gunner's mate third class"*: In McManus's memoir, he quotes Brown and Burke using the nomenclature used to describe a sailor's rating, GM2/c and GM3/c. I have spelled it out here for clarity.

242 *"Mark Clark was a butcher"*: Frank Gallagher, in a tape recording made the summer of 1998.

244 *"feel around fifty-seven"*: Letter from John Gallagher to Sophie Tabayka, on December 7, 1943.

244 *"very happy"*: Jim Feltz journal, December 25, 1943.

244 *wrote in gratitude*: Letter from John Gallagher to Sophie Tabayka, on December 25, 1943.

244 *Judy Garland in* Girl Crazy: Irvin Gebhart journal, December 28, 1943.

244 *"so is the crew"*: Russ Wright's doggerel was typed into the ship's deck logs after the 00-04 watch, January 1, 1944.

245 *"with your gunfire"*: Jim McManus, *My Journal*, p. 19.

247 *total complement of 285*: This accounting of men and officers comes from the December 31, 1943, muster rolls, noting the enlisted men, and the deck logs, which noted the officers.

247 *"Peace before '45"*: Russ Wright's doggerel was typed into the ship's deck logs after the 00-04 watch, January 1, 1944.

15: ANZIO

251 *"evil frame of mind"*: Atkinson, *The Day of Battle*, p. 356.

251 *fruit and wine*: Description of Pozzuoli on the eve of battle from Atkinson's *The Day of Battle*, pp. 351–352.

251 *Churchill's doing—"his baby"*: Morison, *SSA*, p. 325.

252 *first follow-up group*: Morison details the convoy on p. 395 of *SSA*.

252 *LST, was in this group*: Frank Gallagher said this in an interview in 1998: "I sailed with them that next day, too. We were on a LST, landing craft, and we sailed together—me on the LST in the same

convoy as the *Plunkett*. That's how we got up to Anzio." Frank always believed they sailed for Anzio the day after he met John on *Plunkett*. In fact, the red alert that bumped Frank off *Plunkett* was for Operation Webfoot, the dry run on Anzio.

253 *wake of that pattern*: In his journal entry for that day, Jim Feltz wrote that "cork and black stuff come to the surface."

253 *"scenery in a painting"*: Roscoe notes as much of the Anzio landings in *Destroyer Operations*, p. 339.

254 *"Red Anzio! Red Anzio!"*: Morison, *SSA*, p. 344.

254 *rebuffed the attack*: An *Our Navy* article, "Score One for the 'Charley P'" published February 1, 1945, notes the attack on *Mayo* and *Brooklyn*.

254 *"fun and shooting tomorrow"*: Burke's quote is lifted directly from an *Our Navy* article.

254 *certain parts of his job*: In a letter to Ken Brown in late 1992, Burke's daughter referenced this memory of her father at work on condolences to the people who'd lost one of their sons, and his crew on *Plunkett*, to the war: "I remember his anguish at writing letters to their families."

254 *some unpleasant business*: From *U.S. Navy Magazine*, "USS *Plunkett* Fights On," January 1945: "Just a few weeks earlier Commander Burke had had the task of telling Hollister that his two brothers, also in the Navy, had been killed in the Pacific."

254 *age of seventeen*: In a February 8, 1945, article in the *Minneapolis Star Tribune*, Howard Hollister said of his twin sons, "You couldn't keep them out of it after they read Lyle's letters."

255 *consolidated area at five knots*: *Plunkett*'s position noted in the ship's war diaries for January 24, 1944.

255 *doing a "splendid" job*: "Splendid" is the word used in *Plunkett*'s war diaries to describe *Davis*'s work.

255 *"see some action"*: Hot case kid's language from McManus's memoir, *My Journal*, p. 23.

256 *none of them could see*: Deck logs report anti-aircraft fire over the landing area at this time.

256 *when this is over*: John Gallagher wrote this line in a letter to Sophie Tabayka, on December 25, 1943.

259 *"I think I'll go down to the wardroom"*: Knaup's remarks noted in the *Our Navy* article "Score One for the 'Charley P'" published February 1, 1945.

260 *the bow than the beam*: The action report filed by the squadron commander, J. P. Clay, affirmed Burke's decision to turn toward the glide bombs: "Destroyers in the Mediterranean have been directed to turn toward glider bombs."

260 *"We've got dive bombers on our ass"*: Language on burners and dive bombers from Jim Feltz journal, January 24, 1944.

260 *stars were dark*: See Dailey's *Joining the War at Sea*, p. 180, for what speed and the wake of a ship do for enemy bomber pilots.

261 *four miles distant*: Relative position of *Gleaves* and *Niblack* at four miles noted in Clay's action report. Clay also notes that *Plunkett*'s surge to full steam would leave the ship "somewhat isolated."

261 *The ship usually lost*: Hornfischer, *Neptune's Inferno*, chapter 9: "Surface craft unless heavily protected by fighters, cannot stand up against shore-based aircraft."

261 *throw a man overboard*: McManus tells the story of the correspondent's remark on p. 66 of his memoir, *My Journal*. "The day of January 24, 1944, one of the war correspondents told the C. O. that every ship he had been on had been hit, ten minutes later we got hit. The old man was ready to throw that guy over the side." I'd hoped this correspondent's account of the battle might have been filed somewhere, but alas no such luck.

262 *scuttle the ship*: Jim Feltz noted on January 5, 2019, that the 20mm guns had been refitted with the new sights before Anzio.

262 *two hundred yards astern*: The action report states two hundred yards as the distance between *Plunkett* and the explosion of the glide bombs.

263 *giving them hell*: Language from Jim's journal, January 24, 1943: "We opened up with everything we had an [*sic*] I mean we gave em hell . . . all you could hear was a roar from the guns."

263 *crosscurrents of waves*: "Continuous concussion caves in your stomach"

is what one man said it felt like to be in proximity of the booming guns. (S. E. Smith, *The United States Navy in World War II*, p. 65.)

264   *made for a bad defense*: Burke wrote in the action report that "the silhouette of the ship must have been outlined by the continuous firing of the low-level planes."

264   *steady torrent of fire*: *Plunkett*'s action report affirms that the ship must have been outlined by its anti-aircraft fire.

264   *relayed the news: torpedo*: The action report notes that the torpedo was dispatched from a plane eight hundred yards distant, was spotted by the forward 20mm gun crews first, and occurred right after the explosion of the glide bombs.

264   *pilot in his cockpit*: Ken Brown, September 25, 2016: "I had a torpedo man, Robert Meade, who said one of the aircraft he had seen had made a drop of a torpedo, and he could see the pilot, and the pilot could see him."

265   *ship's hull but parallel*: Russ Wright typed up a recollection of what he'd experienced at Anzio, and passed it along to Ken Brown, in the wake of one of the ship's reunions.

265   *its torpedoes blew*: In his chapter on *Plunkett* in *Destroyers in Action*, Richard Shafter, notes that the first plane brought down by *Plunkett* was a casualty of both the destroyer's shell and its own torpedo.

265   *the ship's port bow*: Deck logs note time, 1750, of first plane down, as well as location of the plane's crash.

266   *their own problems*: Morison writes that fifteen fighter bombers attacked Anzio at twilight, forty-three more at dusk, and fifty-three after dark, in *SSA*, p. 345.

266   *"German motors in the sky"*: Ernie Pyle, April 19, 1944. *Ernie's War: The Best of Ernie Pyle's World War II Dispatches*, edited by David Nichols (New York: Random House, 1986).

267   *peel away trailing smoke*: The squadron commander, J. P. Clay, noted this in the action report: "The damaged plane was observed by the undersigned to have been hit by 20mm tracers." Jim Feltz in his journal wrote that "Gall. and Al. . . . both helped bring down a plane."

267 *change in German strategy*: In the *Our Navy* article: "Changes in tactics by the German pilots were noticeable; at Sicily and Salerno they dropped bombs at many ships during attacks but here [Anzio] they concentrated on single ships."

268 *P-38s out of Naples*: According to Russ Wright's written recollection, Burke did not order him to the chart room until after they'd dodged the torpedo.

268 *action had got underway*: Deck logs note the times of each of the two planes brought down by one of the ship's five-inch guns, as well as the plane's location relative to the ship.

269 *"Steadd-dy right rudder"*: Burke's quoted commands lifted directly from the *Our Navy* article "Score One for the 'Charley P.'"

269 *Turn it to the left*: Skunky Kline couldn't remember Burke's language in the wheelhouse during the battle, only the import of what was necessary. "I was on [the wheel] all the time we was engaged in combat," Skunky told me on the phone on October 18, 2016. "Turn it right, turn it left, he had me going in all directions, trying to dodge everything."

269 *Hector at Troy*: "War—I know it well, and the butchery of men / Well I know, shift to the left, shift to the right." *The Iliad*, Book 7, 275–276 (translated by Robert Fagles, London, Penguin Books, 1990).

270 *ship's port screw*: Jim Feltz described the succession of bombs in a phone call on April 10, 2016.

271 *ship was going down*: "rattled like dice in a cup" from the *Halyard*, December 15, 1944.

272 *"I'm going out!"*: After telling me about his experience at Anzio during our first talk on April 9, 2016, Jim probably told me this anecdote a half dozen times. He remembers what he called down into the hole variously, but usually as "I'm going out" or "I'm going aft," meaning to the rear of the ship.

272 *torture chamber out of hell*: Gebhart's escape from the engine room related by his two sons and grandson, who all told more or less the same version.

273   *installed in his skull*: In McManus's account, he characterized Geraghty's effort as "superhuman." Geraghty's daughter, Barbara, told me in a June 1, 2016, interview that her father's injuries were in his head, and that doctors later put a "plate in his head." She also noted that he "carried one of his shipmates out."

273   *deck blazing with fire*: Details of Zingler and Geraghty's escape also provided by daughter Cindy Zingler. Additional detail on the escape from the engine room comes from McManus's *My Journal*, p. 27.

274   *missing in action*: McManus notes in his memoir that Irving Diamond and Alfred Gelinas were two of the men on the 1.1-inch mount. Jim Feltz wrote in his journal of five more men who'd been on the 1.1. They are all now listed as missing in action.

274   *embrace of his harness*: Jim Feltz wrote this in his journal: "One 20mm aft had part of body still straped [*sic*] to the gun / ever time the ship would roll he would swing around. His legs were blown off and his body was full of shrapnel holes." The sight of this man was perhaps the most resonant of all the damage done. Russell Baxter, who came aboard *Plunkett* right after Anzio as a replacement, said that others told him that all that had been left of one gunner was just the torso.

275   *to be played later*: Details on Webber's predicament from details he shared with a newspaper reporter while recovering in a Charlestown, South Carolina, hospital. The family has retained the clipped article but not the name of the newspaper that published the story.

275   *the ship's second stack*: Jim Feltz's journal notes that the searchlight collapsed against the after stack.

275   *three shipmates in a heap*: Detail about location of wounds and broken bones from an email from Eddie's granddaughter, Christine Mott, December 5, 2018.

275   *"Well, this is the end"*: Ken Brown retained a written recollection by Jim Shipp, in which he wrote: "Everything went black. I remember saying to myself or in my subconscious, 'Well, this is the end.'"

276   *the range finder*: Ken Brown in an interview on May 12, 2016, noted that he "swung the guns around through 90 degrees of arc and settled

on a new target" immediately after the bomb hit, all the while alert to reports from his gun captains. He remembered hearing "Richy's" voice: "We're okay, boss."

277 *check our condition*: Russ Wright notes the captain's instruction as such in his report: "Capt. Burke told me to get as far aft as possible and see what our condition was." The *Our Navy* report "Score One for the 'Charley P'" confirms as much, and noted that Burke sent Oliver, Fitzpatrick, and Thomas to manage the repair crews.

277 *hole through his chest*: Russ Wright wrote this in a recollection of his time at Anzio: "When I rushed back out my talker was on the deck with a huge hole through his chest." This always puzzled Ken Brown, who couldn't imagine that such injuries were sustained as far forward as the bridge. He allowed that shrapnel might have traveled that far, but that talkers in the wheelhouse would not have been vulnerable. Ken also allowed that Russ told dramatic stories, and this might have been an instance of that. An accounting of casualties compiled on January 31, 1943, confirms that one yeoman, who might have served as a talker, went missing at Anzio. If he'd gone missing, Russ Wright would not have seen him.

278 *sixty gallons per minute*: Details on handy billy from the *Handbook for Damage Control*, developed by the U.S. Navy's Damage Control Training Center in Philadelphia and published in May 1945.

278 *on a suicide mission*: The *Halyard* reports that "an ensign plunged through amidship flames to check the safety setting" of the ship's TNT.

278 *that was the* Plunkett *hit*: It seems almost unbelievable that Frank actually saw the explosion. He always said he had. "I saw the ship hit," he said. "It didn't go down. It was burning, and they took off."

279 *an excellent target*: In the wake of the bomb blast, "an excellent target" is what Captain Clay called the ship in his action report.

279 *that had not happened*: The *Our Navy* article "Score One for the 'Charley P'" said it wasn't until three hours after the attack that they realized their magazines had not flooded.

280   *had plans to abandon ship*: McManus's memoir is the only source on this attempt to abandon ship. Though none of the other crew interviewed remembered the incident and allowed that the "clobbering" might be more a matter of stretched truth than what actually happened, there's no question that men would have been subject to hysteria on the imperiled ship in the midst of the action.

280   *before the fire kindled the TNT*: *Our Navy*, "Score One for the 'Charley P,'" is the source on Fitzpatrick's dousing of the depth charge.

281   *charges over the side*: Wright describes the status of the depth charges in his written recollection, and how they "literally threw them over the side." McManus wrote about this scene in his memoir, *My Journal*, and identifies the officer on the fantail as the torpedo officer. In his account of that night, Wright identifies himself as the officer in charge of the depth charges, so it must have been Wright that McManus encountered.

281   *fished him out*: Ken Brown was the source on Collingwood's trip overboard in an audio interview recorded on October 21, 2017.

281   *means to fight fire*: Over lunch one day long after the war, John Oliver reminded Ken Brown of Baechtold's actions. "He saved the ship," Oliver told Ken. That was how perilous the fire had been.

282   *front of the ship*: Jim Shipp's crawl from the wreckage and out onto the torpedo deck is described in his written recollection.

282   *expend during the war*: Deck logs note the amount of ammunition expended.

283   *I can't breathe*: Jim Shipp wrote this in a written recollection: "The compressed air cylinders in my life belt had ruptured from the concussion and the snaps did not come loose like they should have and the thing was squeezing me to the point that I could hardly breathe and one reason I couldn't stand. . . . [The Chief Radioman] asked who I was and I told him and asked if he could free me from the life belt. He released the belt, and picked me up and carried me to the crews mess."

283   *coming under control*: The fire would not be completely out for another

twelve minutes, but the deck logs report that it was "under control" at 1810.

285 *coup de grâce*: Captain Clay's action report underscores how critical the anti-aircraft fire was after the ship was hit: "The fact that the ship was able to and did continue fire for several minutes after being hit probably saved the ship inasmuch as the fire on board provided an excellent target to the enemy."

286 *a wayward sprite*: The *Halyard*, December 15, 1944, reported that the Luftwaffe dropped chandelier flares over the ship in the midst of the battle.

287 *their own flares*: The pilots were blinded by their own flares. Captain Clay writes that line exactly in his action report, assuming this was why they'd avoided a resumption of attack.

287 *changed course for Palermo*: Joseph Donahue on *Plunkett*'s escort that night, *Niblack*, wrote that they changed course for Palermo after seeing and hearing the attack on Naples (*Tin Cans and Other Ships*, p. 166). *Plunkett*'s deck logs note that this happened at 3 a.m.

288 *into a new bearing*: Jim Feltz, in a journal entry dated January 24, 1944, wrote about the man still strapped to gun no. 6: "Ever [*sic*] time the ship would roll he would swing around . . . his body was full of shrapnel holes." He wrote that "we were blown apart so bad you could find a hand or arm or foot lying all around where she was hit." Jim McManus wrote in his memoir, *My Journal*, that "there were bodies and body parts all over the place."

288 *It had to be Patten*: McManus writes this on p. 25 of his memoir: "They wanted me to identify a body. I looked at the body and said, 'How can I identify him? His head and left arm are gone.' They said check his ring finger, he has a Durfee High School ring on. It was a 1940 class ring. I said, 'It had to be Patten Signalman 3/C.'"

288 *seven of whom were now dead*: After the war, the one thing Dr. Knaup's children remembered that their father said about Anzio was that he'd have been dead if he'd stayed at his usual battle station. Interview with Marjorie Kaffenbarger, January 30, 2019.

288 *the downed searchlight*: Jim Feltz noted that when the picture of the searchlight was taken, Eddie Webber was still tangled at its base, unbeknownst to all of them.

289 *"I saw that guy's finger move"*: Quote is lifted exactly form McManus's memoir, *My Journal*. Jim Feltz said the picture of the searchlight wreckage was taken before Eddie Webber was found.

289 *clearing the way*: McManus singles out Dutch Heissler as one of the men who'd gone down into the after engine room to retrieve the bodies, on p. 26 of his memoir, *My Journal*.

290 *anything like this*: Jim said repeatedly in interviews that his mind shut down after Anzio, that something like amnesia had come over him, and there were certain things he wouldn't allow himself to remember.

290 *nostrils as a curse*: For all Jim decided he would not remember about that night, he did remember the smell: "Burnt human flesh, the smell stays with you forever. It just clings with you, it's sickening. It was in all the compartments [of the ship]. You never forget the smell." Interview, January 5, 2019.

290 *"no last vestige of dignity"*: *Ernie's War*, p. 322.

291 *each of them had died*: Jim Feltz first told me the story of Dutch's work on the fantail in an interview on March 28, 2017: "The crew was laid out on the deck at night, and they were all distorted and he was out there, straightening out their legs and everything. He was one of the guys who did that." When Jim told me this, he said that he had never once, not even through all of the reunions, ever talked about what Dutch had done on the fantail.

291 *what he did, "magnificent"*: Dr. Knaup acknowledged Heissler's role in an article that appeared in *Our Navy* on February 1, 1945.

292 *everywhere you looked, condoms*: The scattering of condoms noted by Ken in an interview on June 12, 2017.

292 *difference in the world*: Ken noted the chief's comment in a recorded audio interview, October 21, 2017.

292 *"severely damaged and ablaze"*: Letter from Secretary of the Navy James Forrestal to Kenneth B. Brown, June 16, 1944.

294 *redo the bandaging*: McManus writes about the bandaging on p. 27 of his memoir, *My Journal*.

296 *"it was a terrible scene"*: Interview with Patricia Morrone on January 9, 2019.

297 *"Those Germans can't kill me"*: John's words quoted exactly from Jim McManus's memoir, *My Journal*.

298 *coming out of him*: In his 1995 recollections, *The Ball*, Charlie Gallagher said he'd talked to a medic who treated John after the explosion. This was what he was told, that as fast as the blood was going in him, it was coming out of him.

299 *"Gallagher died at 0100"*: Gebhart's grandson transcribed Irvin's journal in the spring of 2016. These were the exact words written.

299 *"his back was pulverized"*: Time of John's death noted in Gebhart journal, and noted as well in McManus memoir, *My Journal*, p. 25.

16: AFTERMATH

302 *on the family piano had cracked*: Jim told me about the cracked glass in a phone interview on April 18, 2018.

304 *"He was killed"*: Bernice remembered this incident in conversation with the author on February 14, 2004.

306 *back to Oakton Avenue*: This accounting comes from a document in John Gallagher's service jacket in the National Archives.

307 *"If you don't believe me, try me"*: This is Burke's language as Jim remembered it during the several times he told me of the story of Burke's business collecting the booze.

307 *one night to fifty-two degrees*: Details on return trip in Jim Feltz journal.

307 *stored on the pier*: Reference to the new stuff for *Plunkett* in McManus's memoir, *My Journal*.

310 *"one for Bill"*: McManus wrote about his homecoming on pp. 30–31 of *My Journal*.

311 *"up off the floor"*: Ken told this story in an interview recorded on October 20, 2017.

312 *"everyone found out"*: Ken told me this anecdote when I visited his home on September 24, 2016.

312 *Some boxing*: In the same interview noted above, Ken describes Burke that morning as such: "Burke that morning when he got up wanted to box. It was a golden opportunity to pound me right to the floor. But I would have none of it."

313 *"Fighting Germans"*: Language lifted exactly from an interview with Jack Simpson on July 1, 2017.

314 *"against the smaller ship"*: This account of the *Morrison*'s fate in an account among Jack Simpson's papers.

316 *enlisted men, playing cards*: Jim McManus noted as much in his memoir, *My Journal*.

317 *"I would go to California"*: Interview with Bill Souza, May 21, 2016.

317 *"I am, too"*: John Ford related this story to Ken Brown, who told me in our talk on August 6, 2017.

318 *"leading the invasion with my cameras"*: *American Legion Magazine*, June 1964, p. 17.

318 *"beach as he wanted"*: McManus, *My Journal*, p. 34.

319 *"From the* Plunkett . . . *and waded ashore"*: *American Legion Magazine*, June 1964, p. 17.

320 *little regard to the facts*: "There's no question that Ford did not get ashore that day," says Ken Bowser, a New York–based director and Ford scholar. As quoted in *Sydney Morning Herald*, June 9, 2014.

321 *"Lousey Chow"*: Jim Feltz wrote about the homesickness and chow in his journal at Christmas 1944.

321 *"warship so distinguished"*: Accounting of ammunition and reference to invasions in a history of the ship compiled by its CO on June 19, 1945, and submitted to Commander Destroyers, Pacific Fleet.

323 *"Get in here, you Irish bastard"*: McManus tells this one touching anecdote, with language lifted exactly, on p. 115 of his memoir, *My Journal*.

324 *"Man, I was gone"*: Jim Feltz talked about leaving *Plunkett* in an interview on January 20, 2020.

324   *"Surprise, surprise"*: Jim detailed the circumstances of his homecoming in a phone interview on January 20, 2020.

327   *made to "artistic considerations"*: Letter from Richard Moore to Ken Brown, April 23, 1992.

328   *too much TV in his retirement*: Letter from Ken Brown to shipmates entitled "PLUNKETT at Anzio Lithograph: Final Report," January 21, 1997.

332   *"that's the last of the Hollister boys"*: *Minneapolis Star Tribune*, February 8, 1945, p. 1.

332   *"to be a family man"*: Interview with Gail Johnson, March 28, 2019.

334   *"I'm glad it's another daughter"*: Interview with Doris Warren on May 25, 2017.

334   *"three jobs all his life"*: Interview with Steve Gebhart on July 13, 2017.

336   *"letters to their families"*: Undated letter from Pat Gipple to Ken Brown, c. 1992.

340   *the goddamned trolley*: This language and the language below are lifted from an audio recording made with Frank during the summer of 1998.

346   *"straighten them out"*: The renowned cartoonist Bill Mauldin wrote about Truscott's dedication. What Mauldin wrote was recounted in *Bill Mauldin: A Life Up Front* by Todd DePastino (New York: W. W. Norton & Company, 2009), chapter 5.

ABOUT THE AUTHOR

JAMES SULLIVAN was born and raised in Quincy, Massachusetts. He graduated from Colby College and received an MFA from the Iowa Writers' Workshop, where he was a Teaching-Writing Fellow and was awarded a James Michener/Paul Engle Fellowship. He lives with his family outside Portland, Maine, a few miles from the birthplace of film director John Ford, who steamed into Omaha Beach on the destroyer USS *Plunkett*.